Studies in Bábí and Bahá'í History
Volume Three

IN IRAN

STUDIES IN BÁBÍ AND BAHÁ'Í HISTORY
VOLUME THREE

IN IRAN

EDITED BY
PETER SMITH, PH.D.

KALIMÁT PRESS
LOS ANGELES

First Edition

Manufactured in the United States of America

Library of Congress Cataloging-in-Publication Data
(Revised for vol. 3)

Studies in Bábí and Bahá'í history.

Includes bibliographies and indexes.
Contents: [1] [no title]—v. 2. From Iran east and west / edited by Juan R. Cole and Moojan Momen — v. 3. In Iran / edited by Peter Smith.
1. Baha'i Faith—History. 2. Babism—History.
I. Momen, Moojan. II. Smith, Peter.
BP330.S78 1982 297'.89 83-227
ISBN 0-933770-16-2 (v. 1)

CONTENTS

PREFACE

I

We all live at the end of the past. History always ends just a second ago. We live in the midst of historical change, even if we only experience it in the autobiographical terms of growing older. As human beings, it is natural for us to attempt to understand the past and the processes of change to which we are subject. The need to understand takes different forms, however.

Normally, and quite naturally, we all wish to see the past in terms that are subjectively important and meaningful to us. We see the past in terms of our experience of the present. We interpret historical actions in terms of archetypes of good and evil. We imbue the events of the past with mythical and legendary importance. All this is normal. What is strange is the approach of the academic historian. The historian attempts, deliberately and systematically, to demythologize the past, and attempts the impossible task of trying to understand historical events and actions in terms of the logics and contexts of the historical actors, rather than our own. He or she questions normally accepted patterns of meaning and throws popular interpretations of historical events and actions into doubt.

This disjunction between the common sense view of the past and the work of the academic historian assumes particular poignancy in the field of religious history. What the historian demythologizes, the believer may cherish as the basis for personal meaning or belief. In this event, there are, historically, two courses of action open to believers. They may reject the historian's demythologization out of hand, either denouncing or ignoring it. Alternatively, they may questioningly accept it and reflectively allow it to modify their own faith. Certainly, they should not forget that historians are inherently fallible interpreters of events. No competent historian claims to provide definitive and completely comprehensive accounts of the past. Again, believers need not fear that the historian's questioning of commonly accepted accounts of the past *of itself* need be destructive to faith. Religious faith may often be closely linked to accounts of the past, but it surely transcends them. Only if faith is rigid and unchanging does the historical enterprise pose a threat.

II

In writing about the history of the Bábí and Bahá'í religions, we are conscious of writing for two audiences: fellow academics and Bahá'ís. Doubtless, most of the initial readership of this book will be Bahá'ís. To them, we must assert—unambiguously—that the standards by which this book should be judged are those of modern academic historiography. As I have suggested in my opening remarks, there is a disjunction between everyday religious understandings of the past and the work of historical scholarship. This disjunction is only a problem to the individual believer if he or she lets it be so.

Let me also state that, whilst most of the contributors to this book are Bahá'ís, we are most certainly not presenting a "Bahá'í view" of Bábí and Bahá'í history. What is portrayed here is a series of separate views by the individual contributors. We are not advocating a collective position. Each essay is a contribution to the ongoing debates that surround our understanding of Bábí and Bahá'í history.

For those of us who are Bahá'ís, as for any other historians, the values which we hold will doubtless inform our work. Few historians imagine that history is "value-free." Believing Bahá'ís, just as believing democrats and believing Marxists, are unlikely to be able to set aside their values in their research, even if they should wish to do so. The holding of particular values, of course, should not determine the conclusions of research. Historians seek to evaluate evidence and deduce probabilities. Values enter in as part of the process of deduction—in regard to the assessment of human motivation, for example. But an honest regard for sources militates against the doctrinaire application of any belief system, be it that of liberalism, Marxism, or the Bahá'í Faith.

Again, outside of the most rigid examples of totalitarian thinking, the values of a particular belief system are never unambiguous or univocal. Individuals will subscribe to a common belief system in different ways. There is no single Bahá'í method or approach to history, any more than there is a single Catholic or Mormon method or approach. Shared values may lead to a certain unity of interests and even of purpose, but they do not imply any historiographic uniformity.

III

It is customary to link the Bábí and Bahá'í religions together. This is understandable. Most Bábís eventually became Bahá'ís, and there are many doctrinal continuities between the two movements. This linkage is also misleading, however. Just as the early Bábís were inclined to interpret Shaykhism as a preparation for their later religious beliefs as Bábís, so many Bahá'ís, down to the present day, have interpreted the Bábí movement in Bahá'í terms. Even independent scholars have followed suit, anachronistically attributing to the Bábís, for example, the Bahá'í belief in sexual equality. Again, by seeing the Bábís as proto-Bahá'ís, and therefore as non-Muslims, commentators on Iranian religious history have neglected the role of Babism in the development of nineteenth-century Iranian Shiism. This is unfortunate. If the Bábís are treated as being in some way separate from the mainstream of Iranian history, this seriously impedes our understanding of important aspects of its processes of change. Similarly, it is only when we recognize the essentially Shí'í concerns of the vast majority of the Bábís that their movement begins to make sense.

It is not just the Bábí movement that has been neglected. Despite extensive persecution, the Bahá'í community remains the largest non-Muslim minority in Iran. It represents a significant element in Iranian society. Undoubtedly, it has played a major role in the complex process of Iranian "modernization." Yet, in terms of Iranian studies, the Bahá'ís have received little serious attention. It is hardly sufficient to continue to rely on the works of such turn-of-the-century scholars as E. G. Browne.

IV

We trust that these essays will make a useful contribution not only to the development of Bábí and Bahá'í studies, but to the integration of such studies into the mainstream of work on Iranian religious history. The Bahá'í religion itself, of course, is no longer a predominantly Iranian phenomenon. Since the 1890s, it has experienced a gradual diffusion throughout the world. Today, out of a world-wide population of around four million Bahá'ís, only three hundred thousand or so reside in Iran. Even allowing for the extensive Iranian Bahá'í diaspora, it is unlikely that Iranians account for more than one in ten of the world's Bahá'ís. For the majority, Iran may be a sacred land infused with religious significance, the original social and religious context of their Faith, but culturally and intellectually they are strangers in that land.

Peter Smith
Bangkok
August 1986

ACKNOWLEDGEMENTS

I would like to acknowledge my gratitude to Kalimát Press, and particularly to Anthony A. Lee, for the hard labors which made the production of this book possible.

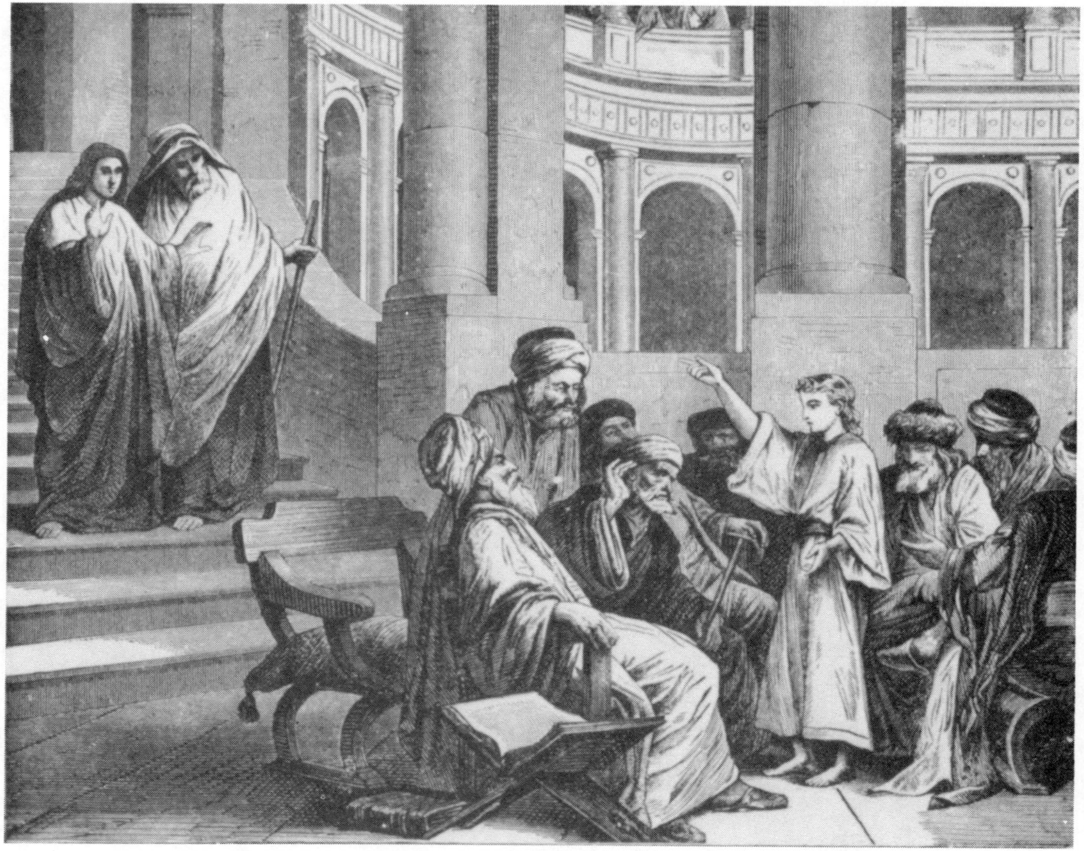

JESUS AS A CHILD IN THE TEMPLE
disputing with the doctors. Luke 2:46–47.

AN EPISODE IN THE CHILDHOOD OF THE BÁB

by Stephen Lambden

Few concrete facts are known about the childhood of Sayyid 'Alí Muḥammad, the Báb (1819–1850), the founder of the Bábí movement and the only son of the Shírází merchant Sayyid Muḥammad Riḍá (c. 1778?–c. 1828 [c. 1820?]) and Fáṭima Bagum (d. 1882).[1] It is clear though that he began his elementary studies as a boy of about five under the tutelage of a certain Shaykhí teacher variously known as Shaykh Zaynu'l-'Ábidín ('Ábid), Shaykh Mu'allim, Shaykh Anám, Shaykh Muḥammad, and Shaykhuná (d. c. 1846–7) in a school situated in the Bázár-i Murgh (poultry market) of Shiraz.[2]

Various stories exist in Bábí and Bahá'í literature about the school days of the Báb which allege his supernatural knowledge and extraordinary piety. They are reminiscent of the countless legendary anecdotes which came to be related of the childhood of Jesus in the apocryphal infancy Gospels and of hagiographic expressions of the miraculous youth of the Prophet Muḥammad and the Imams in Shí'í Muslim literature.[3] Pious devotees of those who have come to be seen as saints, prophets or messengers of God have often pictured the childhoods of the objects of their devotion as being attended by extraordinary phenomena and miraculous deeds, utilizing time-honored hagiographic motifs or legends. To some extent this kind of piety found oral and literary expression in nineteenth-century Bábí-Bahá'í circles. It is particularly noteworthy in connection with the stories of the Báb's first day at the school of Shaykh 'Ábid.[4]

ACCOUNTS OF THE BÁB'S FIRST DAY AT SCHOOL

In the Táríkh-i Jadíd.[5] The *Táríkh-i Jadíd* (New history) of Mírzá Ḥusayn Hamadání (d. c. 1881–2) exists in various recensions written in the early 1880s (roughly between 1296 A.H. and 1300 A.H.). Apart from Mírzá Ḥusayn Hamadání, whose original draft appears to have made considerable use of a version of the *Kitáb-i Nuqṭatu'l-Káf* (c. 1852), a number of writers, including Mírzá Abú'l-Faḍl Gulpáygání (d. 1914), Manakji Limji Hatari (the Zoroastrian agent in Iran, d. 1890), and Fáḍil-i Qá'iní (Nabíl-i Akbar, d. c. 1892), had a hand in the emergence of this variously titled work.[6] At least one recension of it, transcribed in June 1881 (Rajab 1298 A.H.) and referred to by E. G. Browne as the "London Codex" (British Museum [Library] ms., Or. 2942), contains the following version of the story of the Báb's first day at school attributed to Shaykh 'Ábid himself:[7]

> The first day that they brought him [the Báb] to me at the school, I wrote down the alphabet for him to learn, as is customary with children. After a while I went out on business. On my return, I heard, as I approached the room, someone reading the Ḳur'án in a sweet and plaintive voice. Filled with astonishment, I entered the room and enquired who had been reading the Ḳur'án. The other children answered <pointing to His Holiness [the Báb]> "He was." "Have you read the Ḳur'án?" I asked. He was silent. "It is best for you to read Persian books," said I, putting the *Ḥáḳḳu'l-Yaḳín* [of Muḥammad Báqir Majlisí] before him, "read from this." At whatever page I opened it, I saw that he could read it easily. "You have read Persian," said I; "Come, read some Arabic; that will be

better." So saying, I placed before him the *Sharḥ-i-amthila*. When I began to explain the meaning of the *Bismi'lláh* to the pupils in the customary manner, he asked, "Why does the word *Raḥmán* include both believers and infidels, while the word *Raḥím* applies only to believers?" I replied, "Wise men have a rule to the effect that <extension of form implies> extension of meaning, and *Raḥman* contains one letter more that *Raḥím*." He answered, "Either this rule is a mistake, or else that tradition which you refer to 'Alí is a lie." "What tradition?" I asked. "The tradition" replied he, "which declares that King of Holiness to have said: "The meanings of all the Sacred Books are in the Ḳur'án, and the meanings of the whole Ḳur'án are in the *Súratu'l-Fátiḥa*, and the meanings of the whole *Súratu'l-Fátiḥa* are in the *Bismi'lláh*, and the whole meaning of the *Bismi'lláh* is in the <initial letter> B, and the meaning of the B is in the point <under the B>, and the point is inexplicable.'" On hearing him reason thus subtilely I was speechless with amazement, and led him back to his home. His venerable grandmother came to the door. I said to her, "I cannot undertake the instruction of this young gentleman," and told her in full all that had passed. Addressing him, she said, "Will you not cease to speak after this fashion? What business have you with such matters? Go and learn your lessons." "Very well," he answered, and came and began to learn his lessons like the other boys. He even began with the alphabet, although I urged him not to do so.[8]

In the Táríkh-i Nabíl Zarandí. Mullá Muḥammad, a Bábí from 1848–9 (1265 A.H.) who became one of the leading disciples of Mírza Ḥusayn 'Alí, Bahá'u'lláh, and who was known as Nabíl-i Zarandí and Nabíl-i A'ẓam (1831–1892), completed his lengthy history of the Bábí and Bahá'í movements in about 1890 (1308 A.H.).[9] The first part of this history was edited and translated into English by the late Guardian of the Bahá'í Faith Shoghi Effendi Rabbani (1897–1957) under the title *The Dawn-Breakers: Nabíl's Narrative of the Early Days of the Bahá'í Revelation.*[10] The following episode, which obviously differs from the loosely parallel account in the London Codex of the *Táríkh-i*

Jadíd (see below), is again narrated on the authority of Shaykh 'Ábid:

"One day," he [Shaykh 'Ábid] related, "I asked the Báb to recite the opening words of the Qur'án: 'Bismi'lláhi'r-Raḥmáni'r-Raḥím.' He hesitated, pleading that unless He were told what these words signified, He would in no wise attempt to pronounce them. I pretended not to know their meaning. 'I know what these words signify,' observed my pupil; 'by your leave, I will explain them.' He spoke with such knowledge and fluency that I was struck with amazement. He expounded the meaning of 'Alláh,' of 'Raḥmán,' and 'Raḥím,' in terms such as I had neither read nor heard. The sweetness of His utterance still lingers in my memory. I felt impelled to take Him back to His uncle and to deliver into his hands the Trust he had committed to my care. I determined to tell him how unworthy I felt to teach so remarkable a child. I found His uncle alone in his office. 'I have brought Him back to you,' I said, 'and commit Him to your vigilant protection. He is not to be treated as a mere child, for in Him I can already discern evidences of that mysterious power which the Revelation of the Ṣáḥibu'z-Zamán [the Lord of the Age, one of the titles of the promised Qá'im] alone can reveal. It is incumbent upon you to surround Him with your most loving care. Keep Him in your house, for He, verily, stands in no need of teachers such as I.' Ḥájí Mírzá Siyyid 'Alí[[11]] sternly rebuked the Báb. 'Have You forgotten my instructions?' he said. 'Have I not already admonished You to follow the example of Your fellow-pupils, to observe silence, and to listen attentively to every word spoken by Your teacher?' Having obtained His promise to abide faithfully by his instructions, he bade the Báb return to His school. The soul of that child could not, however, be restrained by the stern admonitions of His uncle. No discipline could repress the flow of His intuitive knowledge. Day after day He continued to manifest such remarkable evidences of superhuman wisdom as I am powerless to recount." At last His uncle was induced to take Him away from the school of Shaykh 'Ábid, and to associate Him with himself in his own profession.[12]

In the Táríkh-i Amríy-i Shíráz. This narrative of the history of the Bábí and Bahá'í movements in Shiraz composed by Ḥájí Mírzá Ḥabíbu'lláh Afnán (c. 1875–1951), the son of Áqá Mírzá Áqá (a nephew of the Báb's wife) and the grandson of Áqá Mírzá Zaynu'l-'Ábidín (a paternal cousin of the father of the Báb) remains in manuscript.[13] It opens by providing valuable details about the Báb's parents and genealogy followed by a lengthy narrative attributed to Mullá Faṭḥu'lláh ibn Mullá Mand 'Alí—at the time of the Báb's childhood, an assistant of Shaykh 'Ábid known as the *khalíf* or *náẓim* (director) responsible for selecting suitable pupils (ms., p. 6)—which includes several interesting stories about the Báb's childhood allegedly communicated by the Báb's father to Shaykh 'Ábid. Since this narrative is likely to remain in manuscript for the immediate future, it may be useful to summarize parts of it:

The Narrative of Mullá Faṭḥu'lláh. One day early in the morning, Mullá Faṭḥu'lláh observed that Jináb-i Muḥammad Riḍá (the Báb's father) came to the *Qahway-i Awlíyá'* (the mosque-like structure which housed Shaykh 'Ábid's school [*maktab*]). A long-standing friend of Shaykh 'Ábid, the Báb's father sat next to him and explained that God, four years previously (in 1820–21), had bestowed a child on him whose characteristics caused him continual astonishment. When the Shaykh asked the reason for this astonishment, Muḥammad Riḍá expressed his inability to adequately communicate the nature of the Báb's uniqueness. Such wonders, he explained, surround his now five-year-old son that a lengthy volume would be required to fully express them. Having explained his plight, the Báb's father, anxious that his son begin schooling, illustrated with examples the remarkable nature of the Báb.

The Báb, he said, though a mere child, exhibits an amazing devotional preoccupation. He recites obligatory and other prayers during the night in a very touching manner. He is able to predict the sex of unborn children and is possessed of remarkable prophetic abilities. Though of tender age, he accurately predicted that five women and one child would be killed when disaster would strike the women's bath-house (*ḥamám*) of Mírzá Hádí in Shiraz. He has mysterious dreams indicative of his exalted status. On one occasion, he dreamed that he outweighed Imám Ja'far Ṣádiq (the sixth Sh̲í'í Imam) when placed opposite him on one of the (two) scales of a huge balance (*mízán*).

On account of his bewildering nature, Áqá Mírzá Sayyid Ḥasan (Ḥájí Mírzá Ḥasan 'Alí, a maternal uncle of the Báb) suggested that the Báb might have been injured (*maḍḍatí*, perhaps possessed) by fairies (*paríyán*) or malevolent spirits (*jinn*). His father consulted an astrologer-soothsayer (*munajjim*) named Áqá Muḥammad Ḥasan. Though no sign of disorienting supernatural influence was discerned by the latter, protective talismanic devices and prayers (*ta'widh wa ad'iyya*) were drawn up in the light of the Báb's date of birth. These he subsequently destroyed, making a cryptic statement to the effect that being a source of supernatural protection himself, he stood in no need of protective charms.

Despite, or in view of, the incredible characteristics of the Báb, Sh̲aykh̲ 'Ábid agreed to instruct him—both he and Mullá Fatḥu'lláh were astonished at what Muḥammad Riḍá had narrated. It was suggested he be brought to school at an appropriate hour on the coming Thursday morning (presumably in 1824-5 A.D. [1240 A.H.]). Then, as was the custom at the elementary school of Sh̲aykh̲ Ábid, the primer to be used by the Báb would be presented on a sweetmeat tray.

When the day came and the Báb was brought to school, he, in the light of the remarkable stories surrounding him, became the center of attention. Ḥají Mírzá Sayyid 'Alí (the maternal uncle and future guardian of the Báb) sat next to Sh̲aykh̲ 'Ábid when, following certain formalities, the shaykh asked the Báb to recite an Arabic verse:

> The shaykh, according to the custom, said [to the Báb], "Say: 'He is (*huwa*) the Opener (*al-faṭṭáḥ*), the All-Knowing (*al-'alím*).'" [Qur'án 34:25] His eminence [the Báb] was silent. The shaykh repeated himself. Still he remained silent. The shaykh persisted (*iṣrár karda*) [with his request]. [At length], he [the Báb] said, "Who is *huwa*? The shaykh replied, "*Huwa* signifies God. You are but a child! How is it that you ask the meaning of *huwa*? He [the Báb] said, "I, verily, am the Opener, the All-Knowing (*manam faṭṭáḥ al-'alím*)."

S͟hayk͟h 'Ábid was outraged at the Báb's stubbornness and his daring claim. He brandished a rod, as if to beat him, and sternly admonished him for his pretensions. At his school, the shaykh insisted, the Báb must busy himself with his elementary studies. To this end, the Báb's uncle, Ḥájí Mírzá Sayyid 'Alí, gave his remarkable nephew some kindly advice and went away.

Such, in outline, is the gist of Mullá Faṭḥu'lláh's narrative which draws, in large measure, on a reported conversation between the Báb's father and S͟hayk͟h 'Ábid.[14]

The Narrative of Áqá Muḥammad [*ibn*] *Ibráhím Ismá'íl Bayg.* Immediately after setting down the narrative of Mullá Faṭḥu'lláh concerning the Báb's reception at school, Mírzá Ḥabíbu'lláh records a story about the Báb's first day at school on the authority of Áqá Ibráhím, an older fellow pupil of the Báb. It has been paraphrased by Hasan Balyuzi:

> The Báb had taken a seat, with great courtesy, in between this boy [Áqá Muḥammad, then twelve years old] and another pupil [a certain Áqá Mírzá Muḥammad Riḍá, also twelve years old] who was also much older than Himself. His head was bowed over the primer put in front of Him, the first lines of which He had been taught to repeat. But he would not utter a word. When asked why He did not read aloud as other boys were doing He made no reply. Just then two boys, sitting near them, were heard to recite a couplet from Ḥáfiẓ, which runs thus:

From the pinnacles of the Throne they whistle down to thee;
How is it that in this snare thou now entrapped be?

"That is your answer," said the Báb, turning to Áqá Muḥammad-Ibráhím."[15]

This narrative is clearly meant to illustrate the Báb's exalted status and supernatural knowledge. As the couplet from Hafez indicates, his true abode is the heavenly world and not this narrow earthly sphere. Worth noting is the fact that as in the narratives quoted and summarized above, the Báb is pictured as being stubbornly silent when pressed to acquire knowledge through ordinary channels. His divinely bestowed knowledge renders normal study essentially unnecessary.

It will be obvious to the reader that the accounts of the Báb's arrival and first day at school cannot all be uncolored eyewitness accounts or strictly accurate historical narratives. The loosely parallel narratives of the *Táríkh-i Jadíd* and the *Táríkh-i Nabíl* cannot both be the exact records of the words, observations and actions of Shaykh 'Ábid. Neither can they be reconciled with the narratives of Mullá Faṭḥu'lláh and Áqá Muḥammad set down in the *Táríkh-i Amríy-i Shíráz*. The discrepancies indicate the fundamentally nonhistorical nature of these stories, while the theological points made by all of them are in harmony. The same is also suggested by the fact that the general setting, and certain details, of several of these stories of the Báb's first day at school are paralleled by legendary narratives about the childhood of Jesus as recorded in a wide range of Christian and Islamic literatures.

A comparative and traditio-historical study of the stories about the Báb's school days strongly suggests that they originated in Bábí-Bahá'í circles sometime before the 1880s, and that during a period of oral transmission several versions emerged that, in diverse ways, reflect much older legends about Jesus' first day at school. Before discussing the matter further, it will be convenient to give a few details about the Christian and Islamic accounts of Jesus' school days.

APOCRYPHAL ACCOUNTS OF JESUS' FIRST DAY AT SCHOOL

The canonical Gospels, as is well known, record little or nothing (in the case of Mark and John) of the childhood of Jesus. It is only in Luke 2:42ff. that we are told something of the precocious learning of the young Jesus.[16] By the time of the rise of Islam, however, a very large number of apocryphal stories about Jesus' childhood and youth were circulating in written form. One such apocryphal story which is widely attested is that of Jesus at school in Nazareth. It affords some remarkable parallels to the accounts of the Báb's first day at school. There are a very large number of versions of this story (which cannot possibly all be set down here). It must suffice to refer to one of the versions of the *Infancy Gospel of Thomas*, the many recensions of which (sixth century A.D.? and later, including Arabic versions) attempt to portray Jesus as an infant prodigy:[17]

> Now a certain teacher, Zacchaeus by name, who was standing there, heard in part Jesus saying these things to his father, and marvelled greatly that, being a child, he said such things. And after a few days he came near to Joseph and said to him: "You have a clever child, and he has understanding. Come, hand him over to me that he may learn letters, and I will teach him with the letters all knowledge, and to salute all the older people and honour them as grandfathers and fathers, and to love those of his own age. And he told him all the letters from Alpha and Omega clearly, with much questioning. But he looked at Zacchaeus the teacher and said to him: "How do you, who do not know the *Alpha* according to its nature, teach others the *Beta*." Then he began to question the teacher about the first letter, and he was unable to answer him. And in the hearing of many the child said to Zacchaeus: "Hear,

teacher, the arrangement of the first letter, and pay heed to this, how it has lines and a middle mark which goes through the pair of lines which you see, (how these lines) converge, rise, turn in the dance, three signs of the same kind, subject to and supporting one another, of equal proportions; here you have the lines of the *Alpha*." [The text here appears to be corrupt.]

Now when Zacchaeus the teacher heard so many such allegorical descriptions of the first letter being expounded, he was perplexed at such a reply and such great teaching and said to those who were present: "Woe is me. I am forced into a quandry, wretch that I am; I have brought shame to myself in drawing to myself this child. Take him away, therefore, I beseech you, brother Joseph. I cannot endure the severity of his look, I cannot make out his speech at all. This child is not earth-born; he can tame even fire. Perhaps he was begotten before the creation of the world. . . . I strove to get a disciple, and have found myself with a teacher. Therefore I ask you, brother Joseph, take him away to your house. He is something great, a god or an angel or what I should say I do not know."

And when Joseph saw the understanding of the child and his age, that he was growing to maturity, he resolved again that he would not remain ignorant of letters; and he took him and handed him over to another teacher. And the teacher said to Joseph: "First I will teach him Greek, and then Hebrew." For the teacher knew the child's knowledge and was afraid of him. Nevertheless he wrote the alphabet and practised it with him for a long time; but he gave no answer. And Jesus said to him: "If you are indeed a teacher, and if you know the letters well, tell me the meaning of the *Alpha*, and I will tell you that of the *Beta*." And the teacher was annoyed and struck him on the head. And the child was hurt and cursed him, and he immediately fainted and fell to the ground on his face. And the child returned to Joseph's house. But Joseph was grieved and commanded his mother: "Do not let him go outside the door, for all those who provoke him die."

And after some time yet another teacher, a good friend of Joseph, said to him: "Bring the child to me to the school. Perhaps I by persuasion can teach him the letters." And Joseph said to him:

"If you have the courage brother, take him with you." And he took him with fear and anxiety, but the child went gladly. And he went boldly into the school and found a book lying on the reading desk [Cf. Luke 4:16f.] and took it, but did not read the letters in it, but opened his mouth and spoke by the Holy Spirit and taught the law to those that stood by. And a large crowd assembled and stood there listening to him, wondering at the *grace* of his teaching and the readiness of his *words* [Cf. Luke 4:27], that although an infant he made such utterances. But when Joseph heard it, he was afraid and ran to the school, wondering whether this teacher also was without skill (maimed). But the teacher said to Joseph: "Know, brother, that I took the child as a disciple; but he is full of great grace and wisdom; and now, I beg you brother, take him to your house."

And when the child heard this, he at once smiled on him and said: "Since you have spoken well and have testified rightly, for your sake shall he also that was smitten be healed." And immediately the other teacher was healed. And Joseph took the child and went away to his house.[18]

Central to the many versions of the story of Jesus and the alphabet or of his first day at school is the so-called Alpha-Beta Logion which is found in the *Epistula Apostolorum* (4), attributed to the Marcosians by Irenaeus (Adv. Haer. I.xx.1) and contained in the *Infancy Gospel of Thomas* (Greek A + B + Syriac + Latin + Arabic, etc.) and the related *Gospel of Pseudo-Matthew* (Latin + Slavonic + Arabic + Ethiopic, etc.). Perhaps having originated among second-century Christian gnostics, the following are a few versions of it:[19]

Epist. Apost.: "[Before I say Alpha] First tell me what Beta is." (Greek text corrupt?)

Greek A [*Infancy Gosp. Thom.*]: "How do you, who do not know the Alpha according to its nature, teach others the Beta." (Also quoted above.)

Greek B [*Infancy Gosp. Thom.*] "Thou that knowest not the Alpha, how canst thou teach another the Beta?"
Arabic: "Explain to me Alaph, and then I shall say Beth."[20]

While Brian McNeil has argued that the source of the legend of Jesus and the alphabet is to be found in a proverb contained in the Story of *Aḥiḳar* (Syriac 8:36; Arabic 8:33; Armenian 8:23), Stephen Gero has speculated about a Christian developmental sequence:[21]

> A rather interesting, though admittedly very hypothetical, developmental sequence of the story of Jesus and the teacher emerges from this discussion. The original logion, in the first stage of oral transmission (1st–2nd century) developed a concise controversy apophthegm. The apophthegm was written down in the second century (*Epistula Apostolorum*, Marcosians, Irenaeus), but not thereby removed from oral circulation. In the next "tunnel period" of oral transmission, from the second to the sixth century, [during which the history of the transmission of the tradition is obscure] the narrative material was considerably expanded, but the saying itself was preserved unchanged. . . . The narrative was then fixed in writing in the sixth century, and did not thereafter undergo much further development. However, in this third stage of mainly *written* transmission, between the sixth and tenth centuries, the saying itself began to be expanded, and brought into conformity, by two successive additons, with a synoptic model. This final stage is represented by the Greek *Vorlage* of the Slavonic and Greek versions and by the Syrian prototype of the late Syriac versions.[22]

There are then many versions of the story of Jesus and the alphabet in Christian apocryphal and other literatures. As McNeil notes, however, they all agree in telling a story with the following features: "The master attempts to teach Jesus the alphabet. But, he cannot get beyond the first two letters, for Jesus demands that he explain the meaning of the letter Alpha. In most versions, he himself then expounds the mystic meaning of the alphabet."[23]

SOME EXAMPLES OF THE STORY OF JESUS AND THE ALPHABET IN ISLAMIC LITERATURES

Not only is the story of Jesus and the alphabet found in Christian sources, but it exists also in many different forms in Sunní and Shí'í Islamic literatures. It is doubtless these Muslim transformations of the Christian story that have contributed to both the form and the content of the stories of the Báb's first day at school. Only a few examples of the Islamic versions can be mentioned here:

> The son of 'Adí related on the authority of Abú Sa'íd al-Khadrí a tradition [from the Prophet Muḥammad] that when his mother handed over Jesus, son of Mary, to the school that one should teach him, the teacher said to him, "Write *Bismilláhi* (In the name of God)." Jesus said to him [the teacher], 'What is *Bismi* (in the name)?" The teacher replied, "I do not know." Then Jesus said, "[The letter] *Bá'* is *Bahá' Alláh* [the glory of God], and [the letter] *sín* is *Sanáhu* [His grandeur], and [the letter] *mím* is *Mulkuhu* [His Kingdom], and *Alláh* is the God of gods. And *al-Raḥmán* [the Merciful] means merciful in this world and the next; and *al-Raḥím* means Compassionate in the next world, . . . [etc.]"[24]

Here Jesus is represented as giving a profound explanation of the *basmalla* on his first day at school. The teacher does not know its deep meaning, so the child enlightens him. The Báb is pictured similarly in the *Táríkh-i Jadíd* and the *Táríkh-i Nabíl*.

Another example:

> Mary took Jesus to a teacher. The teacher asked, "What is your name?"

"Jesus," he said.
"Say the alphabet," said the teacher.
"What is the alphabet?" asked Jesus.
"I do not know," he replied.
Then said Jesus, "Get up from your place so I may sit there , and I shall teach you the explanation of the alphabet." The teacher got up, and Jesus sat down and said, "The alphabet begins with four letters, *alif, be, jim* and *dal*:

Alif: *Alláh*, "God";
Be: *Bahá' Alláh*, "God's splendour";
Jim: *Jalál Alláh*, "God's awesomeness";
Dal: *Dín Alláh*, "God's religion";
He: *Huwa Alláh*, "He is God";
Waw: *Waylat Alláh*, "God's woe";
Zayn: *Zabániyat al-káfirin*, "the myrmidons of infidels";
Ḥa: *Ḥiṭṭa li'l-kh//áti'ín*, "forgiveness for those in error";
Ṭa: *Shajarat Ṭúbá li'l-mu'minín*, "the Tuba tree for believers";
Ya: *Yad Alláh 'alá khalqihi ajam'ín*, "God's hand over all of his creation";
Kaf: *Kalám Alláh*, "God's Word";
Lam: *Liqá' Alláh*, "meeting God";
Mim: *Málik yawm al-dín*, "the king of the Day of Resurrection";
Nun: *Núr Alláh*, "God's light";
Sin: *Sunnat Alláh*, "God's path";
'Ayn: *'Ilm Alláh*, "God's knowledge";
Fa: *Fi'l Alláh*, "God's action";
Ṣad: *Ṣidq Alláh fí wa'dih*, "God's sincerity in His promise";
Qaf: *Qudrat Alláh*, "God's might";
Ra: *Rabúbiyyat Alláh*, "God's divinity";
Shin: *Mashí'at Alláh*, "God's will";
Te: *Ta'allá Alláh'ammá yashkurún*, "God is more exalted than that for which he is thanked."

The teacher said to him, "You have done very well, Jesus." He took him to his mother and said, "Your child did not need a teacher."[25]

This version of the story of Jesus' first day at school, translated from an Arabic recension of Muḥammad b. 'Abdu'lláh Kisá'í's *Qiṣaṣu'l-Anbiyyá'* (Tales of the prophets, thirteenth century A.D. and early translated into Persian), has Jesus assume the position of teacher and explain the significance of the twenty-two letters of the "Hebrew" alphabet. Jesus' bewildered tutor takes the learned child back to his mother, telling her that he is in no need of instruction. This is similar to the stories in which Shaykh 'Ábid takes the Báb back home to his grandmother (*Táríkh-i Jadíd*), or uncle (*Táríkh-i Nabíl*), his father being regarded as having passed away by this time in these two Bábí-Bahá'í versions.

In yet another version of the story of Jesus' first day at school (as a seven-month old baby), which is attributed to the fifth Shí'í Imam, Muḥammad b. 'Alí Báqir (c. 675–732), there are obvious parallels to the accounts of the Báb's first day at school found in the *Táríkh-i Jadíd* and the *Táríkh-i Nabíl*. Contained in the *Kitábu'l-Nubuwwat* of Muḥammad Báqir Majlisí's *Biḥáru'l-Anwár* (a massive compendium of Shí'í tradition and learning that was much read and quoted by well-educated Bábís and Bahá'ís at the time of the Báb and Bahá'u'lláh, who also quoted it), this story may well have inspired something of the form and content of the story of the Báb's first day at school:

> . . . Abí Ja'far said: "When Jesus son of Mary was born and but a day old he was as if a child of two months. So when he was seven months old his mother took him by the hand, brought him to the school (*al-kuttáb*), and entrusted him to the teacher (*al-mu'addib*). The teacher said to him, 'Say: *Bismi'lláh al-Raḥmán al-Raḥím*.' So Jesus said, 'Bismi'lláh al-Raḥmán al-Raḥím.' The teacher then said to him, 'Say: *abjad*.' Jesus lifted up his head and said, 'Do you know what *abjad* means?' [Outraged, the teacher] rose up with a thonged whip to strike him [Jesus]. He [Jesus] said, 'O teacher! Do not strike me if you know [the meaning of *abjad*]; otherwise ask

me so that I can expound [its meaning] for you.' He [the teacher] said, 'Expound for me!' Jesus said:

> 'The [letter] *alif* signifies the benefits of God (*álá' Alláh*); the *bá*, the delight of God (*baḥjat Alláh*); the *jím*, the beauty of God (*jamál Alláh*); and the *dál*, the religion (or judgement) of God (*dín Alláh*). In *hawwaz* [letters five through seven], the [letter] *há'* signifies the fear of hell (*hawl jahannam*), the *wáw*, "Woe unto the people of the Fire" (*wail li-ahl al-nár*), and the *zá'*, the moaning of [those in?] hell (*zafír jahannam*). *Ḥuṭṭí* [i.e., letters eight through ten] signifies that the sins (*khatáya*) of the penitents have been absolved. *Kaliman* [i.e., letters eleven through fourteen] signifies the speech of God (*kalám Alláh*): "There is no alteration for His words (*kalimátahu*)." *Sa'faṣ* [i.e., letters fifteen through eighteen] signifies "measure for measure and portion for portion (*ṣa' bi-ṣa' wa'l-jaza' bi'l-jaza'*)." *Qarishat* [i.e., letters nineteen through twenty-two] signifies "their collecting (*qarshuhum*) and their assembling (*ḥashruhum*)."

[Having heard Jesus' words] the teacher said [to Jesus' mother], 'O thou woman! Take your son by the hand [i.e., take him home]. He knoweth and standeth not in need of a teacher.'"[26]

It is of interest to note that the versions of the Christian apocryphal accounts of Jesus and the alphabet were early on elaborated and set in an imamological context by (proto-) Shí'í Muslim writers. The "proto-Ismailian" Persian treatise entitled *Ummu'l-Kitáb* (Mother of the book), which apparently reflects late-eighth-century Shí'í gnosis (in a Khaṭṭábí milieu)[27] and "abounds in precise Manichean reminiscences and features borrowed from the apocryphal books of the Bible,"[28] illustrates how the story was adapted by Ismaili esotericists. Commenting on the proto-Ismaili adaptation of the gnosis of antiquity, Henri Corbin has written:

> The book [*Ummu'l-Kitáb*] is presented in the form of an initiatory discussion between the fifth Imam, Muḥammad Báqir, and three of

his intimate disciples or "beings of light" (*róshanián*), as the Imam calls them. The prologue reports a story from the childhood of the holy Imam, when his teacher, 'Abdulláh Ṣabbáḥ, was preparing to teach him the arithmological powers and symbolic meanings of the letters— i.e., the *jafr*, or philosophic alphabet. . . . However, with the first letter, *alif*, their roles were reversed: the poor teacher, whose learning is outstripped, becomes the pupil, and the young Imam becomes his initiator. The story repeats the point by point one that is reported in the *Gospel of Thomas* and which is also known from the *Epistula Apostolorum*: the young Imam has purely and simply been substituted for Jesus . . ."[29]

PARALLELS WITH STORIES OF THE BÁB

Having set down some details of the Christian and Islamic versions of Jesus's early educational experiences, it will be convenient at this point to note a few of the detailed parallels with the stories of the Báb's first day at school:

1) As in certain Islamic versions of Jesus' first day at school, the Báb is asked to recite (or expound the meaning of) the *basmalla* (*Táríkh-i Jadíd* and *Táríkh-i Nabíl*);

2) As in certain Christian and Islamic accounts, several of the Bábí-Bahá'í narratives indicate that the Báb was stubbornly silent before displaying his supernatural knowledge to his bewildered teacher;

3) As in certain Christian versions and in some Islamic ones (for example, in the narrative attributed to Imám Ja'far Sádiq quoted above), the account of Mullá Faṭḥu'lláh in the *Táríkh-i Amriy-i Shíráz* has the teacher threaten his precocious pupil by brandishing a rod;

4) As in certain of the Christian and Islamic narratives, the Báb is said to have been taken home or sent away after displaying his divine knowledge, since he stood in no need of any teacher. Ultimately, however, he is sent back to school.

In connection with the last parallel, it should be noted that the various Bábí-Bahá'í accounts of the Báb's first day at school differ with respect to who took the Báb away and the place to which he was taken. The account in *Táríkh-i Jadíd* has it that Shaykh 'Ábid took the Báb home to his grandmother. That in the *Táríkh-i Nabíl* has Shaykh 'Ábid take him to the office of his uncle, Ḥájí Mírzá Sayyid 'Alí. The narrative of Mullá Faṭḥu'lláh in the *Táríkh-i Amriy-i Shíráz* records that Ḥájí Mírzá Sayyid 'Alí was present with the Báb during the first part of his first day at school and made sure that he commenced his education before going away. These discrepancies can be partly explained in the light of the confusion surrounding the date of the Báb's father's death and who thereafter took care of him.[30]

As already indicated, it would seem probable that several, if not all of the accounts of the Báb's first day at the school of Shaykh 'Ábid are, in large measure, hagiographic reworkings of elements contained in the Islamic versions of Jesus' first day at school.[31] While the Báb does appear to have been a remarkable youth, the details of the accounts of his first day at school are unlikely to be historically accurate. Though it is alleged that Shaykh 'Ábid "used to relate" (*Táríkh-i Jadíd*) or "related" (*Táríkh-i Nabíl*) such stories, it is unlikely that the accounts, in all their (sometimes) contradictory details, originated with him. The Báb's one-time teacher died around 1846–7, about thirty-five years before the *Táríkh-i Jadíd* was written and almost forty-five years before Nabíl completed his Bábí- Bahá'í history. The authors of neither work, it is very likely, had ever met Shaykh 'Ábid—Nabíl became a Bábí about two years after the shaykh passed away.

The narratives of the story of the Báb's first day at school are thus not direct eye-witness testimonies, but accounts attributed to an eye-witness (Shaykh 'Ábid) by others—no chain (*isnád*) for the transmission of the story is provided. Even if it is assumed that the narratives actually originated with Shaykh

'Ábid (and this is unlikely), they must have been orally circulated for between thirty-five and forty-five years before being written down, and so have been subject to embellishment. Shaykh 'Ábid, having apparently become a Bábí toward the end of his life, may have spoken about the remarkable behavior and erratic schooling of the Báb.[32] But it is almost certainly the case that whatever traditions about the Báb's early schooling that may have existed were, during a generation of oral circulation, embellished and linked with the unhistorical narrative of Jesus' first day at school contained in Christian and Islamic literatures. Just as proto-Ismailis adapted the Christian apocryphal account of Jesus and the alphabet to the fifth Imam, so did pious Bábís and Bahá'ís adapt the Islamic versions of the story to highlight the remarkable youth of the object of their adoration, the Báb.[33]

That certain details within the accounts of the Báb's first day at school are nonhistorical, or a pious reflection of the creative imagination of learned Iranian Bahá'ís who lived during the middle decades of the nineteenth century, should not be taken to indicate that these stories are meaningless fabrications.[34] Since they convey religious perspectives, they are no less meaningful than, for example, the ever-increasing number of New Testament (synoptic) pericopes which critical research now suggests are essentially unhistorical.

The legendary and mythic dimension of Bábí and Bahá'í historical narratives does not devalue these writings. The saintly characters from whom certain pericopes contained in such chronicles originated were, despite and because of their piety, given to myth-making and the creation of legend. The more or less precritical religious and ideological milieu within which nineteenth-century Bábí-Bahá'í narrators lived led them to creatively mix "what took place" with what, theologically speaking, "ought to have taken place." For many among the devout, legend and myth were important vehicles for the expression of meta-historical religious perspectives. It was their conviction that religious truth goes beyond what "actually took place." The primitive Bábí *kerygma* and the concrete facts of Bahá'í history were, in certain circles, adapted and embellished with legend and myth in order to infuse them with religious meaning, and thereby attract prospective converts to the Bábí and Bahá'í fold.

While it would be a gross exaggeration to suggest that Bábí-Bahá'í historical sources stand in need of a wholescale demythologization, the recognition that they contain legendary accounts and mythic elements and the appreciation of the function and meaning of these elements is important. The nonhistorical dimension within the sources cannot be ignored either by the scholar who desires to determine what happened or by the devotee seeking religious meaning.

Finally, I would like to make a few basic points of a general and methodological nature relating to the academic analysis of primary, nineteenth-century Bábí and Bahá'í historical sources. In studying these sources, it is important to develop an awareness of their frequent hagiographical, apologetical, or polemical orientations and an ability to recognize and understand the function of such levels of thought as meta-historical legend and myth. Failure to acknowledge or to understand such dimensions in the sources can result in an unconscious fundamentalism that will lead both to a distorted presentation of historical facts and an inability to divine the religious message conveyed in these sources.

Narratives, and other elements found in the sources, that are obviously nonhistorical or meta-historical to the knowledgeable student (who may nonetheless be alive to their religious meaning) may be mistakenly taken to be "concrete facts" of history by anyone who assumes a naively fundamentalist, or a narrowly historical, approach. It is thus important that the study of Bábí and Bahá'í doctrine—the universe of religious discourse—go hand in hand with any historical analysis. The pre-critical nature of a good many of the sources demands this methodological orientation.

Nonhistorical elements within Bábí and Bahá'í historical sources are frequently to be accounted for in the light of a desire on the part of the pious to demonstrate either a prophetological typology or some prophecy-fulfilment scheme. The early believers were eager to demonstrate that the lives of the Báb and Bahá'u'lláh mirrored and were as miraculous as those of such former major prophets as Muḥammad and Jesus.[35] In addition, they wished to demonstrate that Bábí-Bahá'í history is in conformity with all manner of eschatological prophecies.[36] While I am not suggesting that all the typological speculations and prophecy-fulfilment schemes that are spelled out in the sources have no concrete historical bases at all, it should be borne in mind that a consciousness of their theological function often enables the scholar to identify and explain a good many contradictions and proven errors.

It should be recognized, further, that certain narratives are the result of several decades of oral transmission, and that during this period even "eye-witness accounts" originally rooted in historical fact have been embellished with nonhistorical elements, censored (or partially altered) to conform to a developing Bábí-Bahá'í theology, or transmitted inaccurately.

The study of Bábí and Bahá'í history will be severely handicapped if a critical and comparative study of all available sources bearing on important episodes is not carried out. This is especially so inasmuch as certain historical chronicles have come to be accorded an almost canonical status within the modern Bahá'í community, while others of great importance have come to be ignored or viewed with considerable suspicion.[37] There are parallel accounts of major episodes in nineteenth-century Bábí and Bahá'í history that invite comparative and critical analysis. These numerous and often conflicting accounts exist in a plethora of Muslim, Bábí, Azalí, Bahá'í, and other sources that have, on the whole, never been carefully examined. Bahá'í historiography is in its infancy. It is hoped that this essay, if nothing else, will highlight the need for Bahá'í historians to acknowledge and appreciate the legendary and mythic elements within the rich legacy of their scriptural and historical tradition.[38]

NOTES

I would like to express my thanks to Mr. William Collins, Dr. Moojan Momen, Dr. Peter Smith, Dr. Denis MacEoin, and Mr. Abú'l-Qásim Afnán A'lá'í for valuable critical comments on various rough drafts of this essay.

1. Cf. Abbas Amanat, "The Early Years of the Babi Movement: Background and Development" (Ph.D. Thesis, Oxford University, 1981) p. 100f.

2. See Hasan Balyuzi, *The Báb: The Herald of the Day of Days* (Oxford: George Ronald, 1973) pp. 32ff, 230 note 4.

3. On legends surrounding the birth and childhood of the Imám Ḥusayn, see, for example, Mahmoud Ayoub, *Redemptive Suffering in Islam* (The Hague: Mouton Publishers, 1978) p. 69ff.

4. Other stories of the Báb's childhood also clearly utilize traditional motifs and legends. For example, the story that he exclaimed "The Kingdom is God's" (*al-mulk li'lláh*) at the moment of his birth (see, *Kitáb-i Nuqṭat al-Káf* [Leiden: Brill, 1910] p. 110f. and *Táríkh-i Jadíd* [Cambridge University Press, 1893] p. 262).

5. On the *Táríkh-i Jadíd*, see Denis MacEoin, "A Revised Survey of the Sources for Early Bábí Doctrine and History," Part II (Unpublished dissertation, 1977) p. 195ff.

6. MacEoin, "Revised Survey," pp. 205–206. Cf. Amanat, "Early Years," p. 427f.

7. See E. G. Browne, *Jadíd*, Introduction, p. xlix.

8. Browne, *Jadíd*, pp. 262–64.

9. Shoghi Effendi, *The Dawn-Breakers. Nabíl's Narrative of the Early Days of the Bahá'í Revelation* (Wilmette, Ill.: Bahá'í Publishing

Trust, 1932) Preface, p. xxxvii. Cf. MacEoin, "Revised Survey," p. 214ff.; Amanat, "Early Years," p. 429f.

10. *The Dawn-Breakers* is an edited English translation of the first part of Zarandí's history (up to 1852–3). The original text has not been published.

11. Ḥájí Mírzá Sayyid 'Alí was one of the maternal uncles of the Báb who looked after him following the death of his father. See Balyuzi, *The Báb*, p. 334f, 85ff.

12. Shoghi Effendi, *The Dawn-Breakers*, pp. 75–76.

13. Ḥájí Mírzá Habíbu'lláh Afnán was, like his father, a Bahá'í. He was originally named Muḥammad 'Alí. For some details of his life, see Muḥammad 'Alí Fayḍí, *Kitáb-i Khánidán-i Afnán* (Tehran, 132 *Badí'* [1975–6]) p. 230ff.; Balyuzi, *The Báb*, p. 32n.; idem., *Bahá'u'lláh: The King of Glory* (Oxford: George Ronald, 1980) pp. 430ff., 475; cf. Hussám Nuqabá'í, *Manábi'y-i Táríkh-i Amr-i Bahá'í* (Tehran, 133 *Badí'* [1976–7]) p. 64.

A manuscript of the *Táríkh-i Amriy-i Shíráz* exists in the Iran National Bahá'í Archives (Ms. no. 1027D) and a photocopy in the private library of the late Hasan Balyuzi (now the Afnan Library). I am extremely grateful to Dr. Moojan Momen for making a photocopy of Ḥájí Mírzá Habíbu'lláh's manuscript available to me.

14. See *Táríkh-i Amriy-i Shíráz* , pp. 5–14 (the narrative of Mullá Faṭḥu'lláh). This narrative puts into the Báb's father's mouth a cycle of infancy stories that probably originally circulated separately and orally.

At one point in the *Táríkh-i Jadíd* (London Codex), it is worth noting in connection with this cycle of stories, we read: ". . . as a boy he [the Báb] used to predict of pregnant women whether they would bring forth a male or a female infant, besides foretelling many chance occurences, such as earthquakes and the ruin of certain places, as they actually took place." (p. 265) Cf. also 'Abdu'l-Husayn Áyatí (Ávárih), *al-Kawákib al-Durríyya*, vol. I (n.p., n.d.) p. 33; Ḥájí Muḥammad Mu'ín al-Salṭana, *Táríkh-i Amr* (ms.) p. 28ff. Cf. Amanat, "Early Years," p. 124f.

15. See *Táríkh-i Amriy-i Shíráz* , pp. 14–15 (the narrative of Áqá Ibráhím) paraphrased by Balyuzi in *The Báb*, pp. 34–35. I have slightly altered Balyuzi's translation of the couplet from Hafez. Immediately

following the narrative of Áqá Ibráhím is an account of an episode in the childhood of the Báb designed to highlight his supernatural knowledge, the story of the "unresolved theological problem." (pp. 15–17, summarized by Balyuzi in *The Báb*, p. 35)

16. On the canonical Gospel accounts of Jesus' infancy, reference may be made to Raymond E. Brown, *The Birth of the Messiah* (London, 1977).

17. On the Infancy Gospel of Thomas and related Infancy Gospels, see Stephen Gero, "The Infancy Gospel of Thomas" in *Novum Testamentum* 13 (1971) pp. 46ff (and Bib.); E. Hennecke, *New Testament Apocrypha*, Vol. I (SCM Press, 1973) p. 388ff. (and Bib.).

18. *The Infancy Gospel* [*Story*] *of Thomas* 6:1ff.; 7:1ff.; 14:1ff.; 15:1ff.; *New Testament Apocrypha*, Vol. 1, p. 394ff (see fn. 17 above). Also, M. R. James, The Apocryphal New Testament (Oxford, 1926) p. 49ff. for an English translation of Greek Text A.

19. See S. Gero, "Thomas," p. 71f., for a more detailed list of versions of the Alpha-Beta Logion.

20. Translation from: Gk. A.—*New Testament Apocrypha*, Vol. I, p. 394; Gk. B.—James, *The Apocryphal New Testament*, p. 56; Epist. Apost. + Arabic—Gero, "Thomas," p. 71.

21. Brian NcNeil in "Jesus and the Alphabet" in *Journal of Theological Studies* (NS), Vol. 21 (1971) pp. 126–28, writes: "I suggest that the source of this legend is to be found in the Story of Aḥiḳar, in one of the proverbs which Aḥiḳar imparts to his nephew. This is now extant in three versions:

> a) Syriac viii.36. 'My son, they say to the wolf, "Why dost thou follow after the sheep?" He said to them, "The dust is exceedingly good for my eyes." . . . And they brought him into the schoolhouse [lit., "the house of the scribe"]: the master said to him, "Aleph, Beth"; the wolf said, "Kid, Lamb."'
> b) Arabic viii.33. 'O my boy! They made the wolf go to school that he might learn to read, and they said to him, "Say A, B." He said, "Lamb and goat in my belly."'
> c) Armenian viii.23. 'Son, they gave teaching to the wolf's cub, and said: "Say thou *ayb, ben, gim* [i.e., the first three letters of the Armenian alphabet]"; and he said, *ayts, bouts, garhn* [i.e., goat, kid, lamb].'"

(Citing texts and translations from F. C. Conybeare, J. Rendel Harris, and Agnes Smith Lewis, *The Story of Aḥiḳar* [Cambridge, 1913]).

22. Gero, "Thomas," pp. 72–73.

23. McNeil, "Jesus and the Alphabet," pp. 126–27.

24. Cited in J. Robson, *Christ in Islam* (London: John Murray, 1929) p. 92. The version of this tradition translated by Robson is closely parallel to that in al-Tha'labí's well-known *Qiṣaṣ al-Anbiyá'* (4th ed. [Cairo] 1382 A.H., p. 522).

25. Translation from W. M. Thackston, Jr., *The Tales of the Prophets of al-Kisa'i* (Boston, 1978) pp. 332–33.

26. Translated from Mullá Muḥammad Báqir Majlisí, *Biharu'l-Anwár* (Tehran: Dár al-kutub al-Islámiyya, n.d.) Vol.14, pp. 286–87. Note that in this version of the story of Jesus' first day at school Jesus is represented as explaining the *abjad* arrangement of the Arabic alphabet (eight meaningless words which act as a mnemonic device for remembering the numerical values of the letters) as if its first six "words" represent the 22 letters of the Hebrew alphabet. A similar version of Jesus' first day at school is referred to by E. Sell and D. S. Margoliouth in an article entitled "Christ in Mohammedan Literature" (in *A Dictionary of Christ and the Gospels*, Vol. II [Edinburgh, 1909])—again attributed to the 5th Shí'i Imám:

> Jesus was so intelligent that, when nine months old, his mother sent him to school. The master said the Bismillah—" In the name of God, the Merciful, the Compassionate"—which the child at once repeated after him. The Master then gave a number of words to be read, of which the first was *abjad*. Jesus wished to know why he should do this, upon which the master became angry and struck him. The child said: "If you know explain; if you do not, listen. In *abjad*, *a* stands for *Allah la ilah* ("there is no God but God"), *b* for *Bahjat Ullah* ("grace of God"), *j* for *Jalal Ullah* ("glory of God"), *d* for *Din Ullah* ("religion of God").

See also, for a more or less parallel version of this narrative, al-Tha'labí, *Qiṣaṣ al-Anbiyá'* (Cairo, 1382 A.H.) pp. 521–22.

27. So Corbin who notes that Abu'l-Khaṭṭáb was the 'too enthusiastic disciple of the Imam Ja'far al-Ṣádiq (d. c. 765)." (See *Cyclical Time and Ismaili Gnosis* [London, 1983] p. 154).

28. H. Corbin, Cyclical Time, p. 56, fn. 100.

29. Ibid., p. 168. The Persian treatise *Ummu' l-Kitáb* was edited by W. Ivanow in *Der Islam* XXIII.

30. Considerable confusion exists in Bábí-Bahá'í sources as to the exact date of the Báb's father's death. While, for example, Mírzá Abú'l-Faḍl Gulpáygání states in his *Táríkh-i Zuhúr* (c. 1900 ?, trans. in *The Bahai Proofs* [2nd. Ed., Chicago, 1914] pp. 31–113) that Sayyid Muḥammad Ridá ". . . died before his son [the Báb] . . . was weaned" (presumably before he was two years old, p. 35), Ḥájí Mírzá Habíbu'lláh explicitly writes (*Táríkh-i Amriy-i Shíráz*, p. 17) that he died when the Báb was nine years old (that is in 1828–9).

Amanat ("The Early Years," p. 102 + fn. 5) rejects the earlier dating of the Báb's father's death. Though he does not spell out his reasons, he is probably correct. This, it seems to me, in the light of a Muḥammad ("type")—Báb ("antitype") typology. Since the prophet Muḥammad's father, according to a multitude of Muslim sources (see for example, A. Guillaume, *The Life of Muḥammad: A Translation of Ibn Ishaq's Sirat Rasul Allah* [Oxford 1970] p. 69) died during his wife's pregnancy, the tendency would be to have the Báb's father die shortly after his wife's conception or giving birth.

It is probably in the light of such an underlying typology that the *Táríkh-i Jadíd* and *Táríkh-i Nabíl* presuppose (in the story of the Bab's first day at school) that Sayyid Muḥammad Ridá had died before the Báb entered Shaykh 'Ábid's school. That the Báb's father is not mentioned in the account of the first day at school in the narrative of Mullá Faṭhu'lláh (in the *Táríkh-i Amriy-i Shíráz* he fades from the scene), despite the fact that he is represented as having arranged for his schooling shortly before his entering Shaykh 'Ábid's school, may be rooted in a drawing on oral traditions that presuppose the early death of the Báb's father—not in harmony with the rest of his narrative, or indeed with Ḥájí Mírzá Habíbu'lláh's own statement that Sayyid Muḥammad Riḍá died when his son was nine years old, that is, about four years after he entered the school of Shaykh 'Ábid. Mullá Faṭhu'lláh's having Ḥájí Mírzá Sayyid 'Alí present at the time of the Báb's first day at school is in conformity with the widely attested fact that he (in particular) supervised the Báb's education *after* his father's death (cf. *Táríkh-i Nabíl*). If, of course, the Báb's father did die before the Báb's elementary education began—the "Muḥammad-Báb typology" reflecting historical fact or perhaps not being relevant—then the veracity of Mullá Faṭḥu'lláh's narrative is called into question; unless, and this is very unlikely, the Báb's father died a few days before the Báb went to school.

31. That elements derived from the Islamic accounts of Jesus' early school days were hagiographically reworked in Bábí-Bahá'í circles in order to fill out the doubtless reliable tradition that the Báb's early schooling was erratic and largely unsuccessful need not be taken to indicate a dishonest manipulation of written sources. In a missionary, promulgatory, or devotional context, the tendency to spontaneously embellish the story of the Báb by drawing on elements existing in the reservoir of prophetological legend would not, in a nineteenth century Bábí-Bahá'í context, have been something untoward or theologically illegitimate—especially in the light of the Bábí-Bahá'í conviction that major prophets of God are all essentially one.

32. Shaykh 'Ábid is said to have written a monograph or tract on the childhood of the Báb, presumably shortly before his death in c. 1846–7. (See Balyuzi, *The Báb*, p. 231, fn. 4; Amanat, "The Early Years," p. 104, fn. 4). It is apparently in the hands of Muslims not well-disposed toward the Bábí-Bahá'í movement. It would be rash, assuming this tract really does exist, to argue from silence that it must be the source of the diverse and contradictory accounts of the Báb's first day at school—some of the content of which could have been orally circulating. Unless Shaykh 'Ábid's alleged monograph surfaces, it would seem best to ignore the unlikely possibility that it contains an account of the Báb's first day at school parallel with the later written versions.

Even if this were proven to be the case it could be argued that Shaykh 'Ábid himself drew on and adapted the Christian-Islamic versions of Jesus' early schooling.

33. Other stories about the Báb's childhood seem to reflect a "Jesus-Báb typology." In, for example, the *Kashfu'l-Ghitá 'an Hiyálu'l-A'dá* (Ishqabad, n.d.), Mírzá Abú'l-Faḍl Gulpáygání (1844–1914) relates a story that he heard from Sayyid Jawád Karbalá'í (d. Kerman, c. 1882–3) to the effect that the Báb came late to school and, when asked by his teacher where he had been, stated that he had been (praying) in the house of his ancestor (*dar khánih-i jaddam*). (pp.

83–4. Cf. also, the similar story related on the authority of Ḥájí Sayyid Muḥammad Shírází, p. 84) It is not impossible that this narrative reflects the story of the young Jesus at the Jerusalem Temple (Luke 2:41–52)—as, for example, the Báb was understood to have been "in the house of his ancestor" so Jesus explained that he was in his "Father's [God's] house" (Luke 2:49). Cf. Amanat, "The Early Years," p. 126f.

34. An admittedly speculative suggestion would be that the circulation of the story of Jesus' first day at school in nineteenth century Bábí-Bahá'í circles owed something to the pious creativity of Sayyid Jawád Karbalá'í (on whom see, for example, 'Azízu'lláh Sulaymání (ed.), *Maṣabíḥy-i Hidáyat,* Vol. II [Tehran, n.d.] p. 471ff.). He had close links with the Báb's family, apparently induced Shaykh 'Ábid to view the Báb and Bábism with favor, and confided in Gulpáygání who had a hand in the writing of the *Táríkh-i Jadíd.*

35. Partly in view of the Bábí-Bahá'í doctrine of "return" (*raj'a*), such a typology also informs the accounts of the lives of leading Bábís and Bahá'ís. In the light, for example, of the fact that Mullá Muḥammad 'Alí Barfurushí, Quddús, was once seen as the "return of Jesus" (who figures in Muslim eschatology), he is said to have been born of a virgin (see *Kitáb-i Nuqṭat al-Káf* p. 199 and cf. *Táríkh-i Jadíd* [Appendix II] p. 366). Enemies of the Bábí-Bahá'í movements, it might also be noted here, take on the characteristics of traditional and eschatological opponents of Shí'í Islám. The Shaykh leader Karím Khán Kirmaní (1810–1870) is pictured in certain sources as being "one-eyed" or a latter-day manifestation of the Muslim Antichrist, the *Dajjál* (for some details, see my "Antichrist—Dajjal: Some Notes on the Christian and Islamic Antichrist traditions and their Bahá'í Interpretation" in *Bahá'í Studies Bulletin,* Vol. 1, No. 3 [December, 1982] pp. 3–43).

36. In Nabíl Zarandí's *Táríkh,* for example, it is asserted on the authority of Mullá Mírzá Muḥammad Furughí that in accordance with Islamic prophetic tradition (*hadíth*) Mullá Ḥusayn informed Quddús that exactly 313 Bábís had arrived at the shrine of Shaykh Tabarsí in Mázandarán (see *The Dawn-Breakers,* p. 256). Though it may have been the case that Mullá Ḥusayn arrived at this place with companions whose numbers eventually reached 313 (cf. E. G. Browne [ed.], *A Traveller's Narrative* [Cambridge University Press, 1891]

p. 37), the fact that estimates of the number of Bábís present during the Mazandaran upheaval (which lasted from mid-October 1848 to early May 1849) "differ widely" (For details see Momen, "The Social Basis of the Babi Upheavals in Iran (1848–53): A Preliminary Analysis" in *International Journal of Middle East Studies* 15 [1983] p. 161f.) suggests that the figure 313 is more meta-historical than concrete fact. The sources, furthermore, are confused as to at which point the number 313 was attained, if indeed, this figure is mentioned at all.

A study of the various accounts of the Báb's pilgrimage could provide further examples of the interplay between what "actually happened" and what, in the light of eschatological prophecies, "ought to have happened."

37. In modern Bahá'í circles the *Kitáb-i Nuqṭat al-Káf* (among other sources) has come, I think incorrectly, to be deemed an Azalí fabrication. While there are problems surrounding the origins and authorship of this work it does contain material which accurately reflects Bábí perspectives of the early 1850s. It is neither anti-Bahá'í, nor devoid of historical value. The part of the *Táríkh-i Nabíl* translated by Shoghi Effendi has, on the other hand, come to be invested with an exaggerated authority. Valuable and important though this work is, it is but one among other important Bahá'í *interpretations* (as far as the published part is concerned) of Bábí history. Its existence does not make reference to other, sometimes conflicting, sources meaningless, irrelevant, or "heretical."

That "parts of the manuscripts [of the *Táríkh-i Nabíl*] were reviewed and approved, some by Bahá'u'lláh, and others by 'Abdu'l-Bahá" (*The Dawn-Breakers*, p. xxxvii) need not be taken as proof that every detail within it is an infallible expression of concrete historical fact. It should be borne in mind that: We do not (apparently) know which "parts of the manuscripts" (note the plural, *manuscripts*) or which manuscript Bahá'u'lláh and 'Abdu'l-Bahá reviewed; that Bahá'u'lláh and 'Abdu'l-Bahá "reviewed" *parts* of the *manuscripts* of Nabíl's narrative should not be taken to signify that they were operating like modern Western reviewers who might be particularly concerned with empirical historical accuracy.

If a given narrative, such as that attributed to Shaykh 'Ábid, expressed a "spiritual truth," Bahá'u'lláh and 'Abdu'l-Bahá would very likely have regarded it as acceptable, whether or not it represented "historical fact" in all its details. In this respect, it is also worth bearing in mind that the writings of Bahá'u'lláh and 'Abdu'l-Bahá contain meta-historical materials. Prophet figures and holy men are primarily concerned with the promotion of spirituality, and not the furtherance of an academic historiography. Can one, indeed should one, imagine Jesus arguing with the scribes and pharisees about whether Old Testament pericopes come from the alleged "J," "E," "D," or "P," pentateuchal sources or whether Moses lived in the sixteenth or thirteenth century B.C.? This might be an exaggerated rhetorical question, but it is in this light that it is worth noting that 'Abdu'l-Bahá "reviewed" many of the writings of early Western Bahá'ís, praised them, and approved their publication despite the fact that a good many of them—as 'Abdu'l-Bahá was obviously well aware—contained ideas that were not in accordance with Bahá'í teachings. His generous doctrinal liberality, designed to encourage and foster unity, outweighed a rigid imposition of doctrinal orthodoxy in secondary matters. It is not then enough to assert that because Bahá'u'lláh and 'Abdu'l-Bahá "reviewed" parts of Nabíl's narrative that this work is alone worthy of scholarly attention, or that it constitutes an infallible touchstone for determining the *empirical* truth of divergent historical perspectives. In scholarly circles it is well known that Nabíl's narrative contains errors of a concrete nature.

The Bahá'í Faith is neither enhanced by nor dependent on an uncritical acceptance of narratives reported by Bahá'í historians. Bahá'ís are not obliged to view them as either canonical or infallible. Neither 'Abdu'l-Bahá nor Shoghi Effendi claimed infallibility when conveying historical data.

38. I should like to point out to the Bahá'í reader who may believe that an academic analysis of Bábí-Bahá'í historical sources is a "threat to faith" that such scholarly endeavors are not designed to destroy faith. Ultimately, they may actually promote a more balanced faith when findings are articulated by Bahá'í theologians. That certain narratives in well-known Bábí-Bahá'í sources can be shown to be essentially legendary or meta-historical does not mean that they become less meaningful for the Bahá'í believer. They may, in fact, become more meaningful, and less historically problematic. The modern

scholarly recognition that the Gospels are not exactly concrete historical narratives does not make them spiritually meaningless for the mature Christian believer.

In a devotional context, there is no reason why legendary Bábí-Bahá'í narratives should not be read and pondered. It would be unfortunate if a scholar should argue that his or her exposition of the nonhistorical nature of aspects of Bábí-Bahá'í history should necessitate the communal eradication of meaningful myth and legend. Also unfortunate would be the thoughtless condemnation of scholars who attempt to argue that cherished stories are legendary or contain nonhistorical elements.

BADÍ' (ÁQÁ BUZURG-I NÍSHÁPÚRÍ)
in chains and under torture after his arrest in Tehran.

THE BÁBÍ MOVEMENT: A RESOURCE MOBILIZATION PERSPECTIVE

by Peter Smith and Moojan Momen

It has become common to link the emergence and expansion of the Bábí movement to the wide-ranging social tensions and crises experienced by mid-nineteenth-century Iranians. We would not dissent from this view. We assert, however, that the nature of the linkage between the Bábís and the social tensions of the 1840s is as yet far from clear. Both the Bábí religion and the social structure of Iran in the 1840s remain underresearched, particularly in terms of the specific local situations and linkages which we believe are crucial to an understanding of the movement's development.

As research proceeds, we believe that it is essential that the theoretical as well as the substantive issues of explanation be made explicit. Such theoretical issues are always implicit in any historical explanation of a general nature, as with such assertions as that Babism represented an expression of class discontent (Ivanov), or proto-nationalistic sentiment (Avery, Ivanov, Keddie), regional antagonisms (Avery), political rebellion (Bayat), or social crisis (Smith).[1] Only when the theoretical assumptions underlying such theories are made explicit can they be adequately appraised.

In the present essay, we examine the Bábí movement in terms of a sociological resource mobilization perspective.[2] In so doing, we are not seeking to provide a "total" theoretical framework. Acceptance of one particular explanatory historical theory may lessen the importance attached to other theories, but it does not necessarily invalidate them.

What distinguishes the resource mobilization perspective from much of the other theoretical work on social and religious movements is that it is more concerned with means than with meaning. It assumes that participation in social movements is generally both normal and rational. It postulates that, given a commitment to expansion on the part of the movement's original membership, an effective system of organization, and a favorable social environment, the growth of any social movement is relatively unproblematic. The central (and more accessible) research questions from this perspective are concerned with the investigation of the practical means by which such organizations are constructed, rather than the putative reasons why human beings join them. Specifically, it is unnecessary to explain the recruitment of followers to a movement in terms of extraordinary motivations supposedly engendered by individual or social crises. Such crises may well enhance a movement's plausibility, but issues are defined, and may even be generated, by the movement's leadership. Recruitment need not be highly motivated. Meaningful social contact with the movement's partisans may of itself be sufficient to secure initial conversion. Thereafter, progressive resocialization assures the neophyte's continued commitment.

This is not to discount the importance of motivation.[3] Thus at a minimal level, we would assert that the content of a movement's ideology must be at least accessible and plausible to its potential recruits. More generally, we recognize the importance of ideal and material interests in motivating a movement's members. We would stress, however, that putative interests are often highly complex and need to be related in some detail to the actual contents and development of a particular movement. That recruitment to a movement flows along preexisting lines of social cleavage, for example, need not primarily indicate the articulation of specific class interests. It may, rather, reflect the pattern of social networks, here held to be of crucial importance in affecting recruitment.

Various component elements of the mobilization perspective may be identified. In the present discussion, we shall deal with the following: (1) the *social environment*, that is, the structural characteristics of Iranian society which defined and facilitated the emergence of Babism, the role of social control and opposition, and the interactive process by which the religion's political role came to be defined; (2) the *organization of resources* to secure the movement's objectives; (3) the *pattern of recruitment* to the movement; and (4) the form and content of *the movement's ideology* which defined and promoted its growth. We will then provide a general characterization of the social location and demographic importance of the early Bábís. Finally, we will offer a list of twenty-five propositions which we regard as basic elements for any future analysis of the social significance and context of the Bábí movement.

EMERGENCE AND DEVELOPMENT OF THE BÁBĪ MOVEMENT

Let us begin, however, with a brief account of the emergence and development of Shaykhism and Babism, thereby providing a base for our more theoretically grounded remarks.[4] In terms of the subsequent discussion, it is of particular note that the Bábí movement began as a sub-sect of the Shaykhí school, in the specific context of the succession crisis of 1844. As a religious movement, the early Bábí religion may be described as having passed through two very distinct phases of development: an initial "Islamic" phase (1844–48), and a later "radical"

IRAN

IN THE MID-NINETEENTH CENTURY

MAP 1

The international boundaries to the east of Iran were not defined or demarcated until the late 19th century. Iran's internal provincial boundaries were frequently changed.

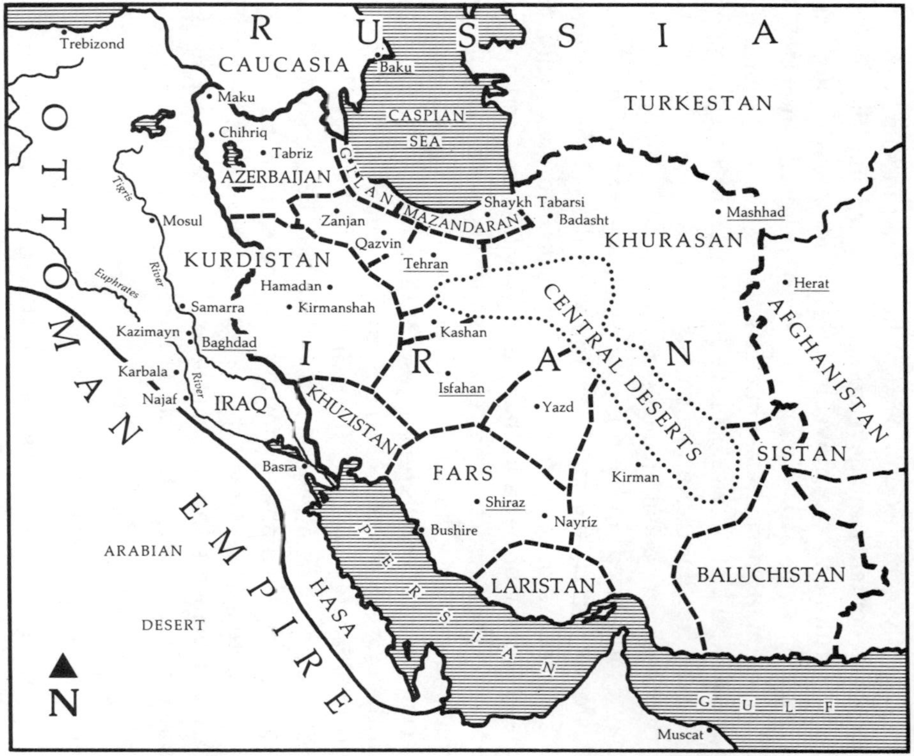

one (1848–53). We are not concerned, except incidentally, with developments after the collapse of Babism as an organized movement.

Shaykhism. Originating with the teachings of Shaykh Aḥmad al-Aḥsá'í (1753–1826), Shaykhism became a powerful expression of the tradition of theosophical Shí'í dissent.[5] Under the leadership of Shaykh Aḥmad's successor, Sayyid Káẓim Rashtí (c. 1795–1843/44), it developed into a well-organized movement within Ithná-'Asharí Shiism. Although clerically dominated, it gained a large popular following throughout Iran and the Shí'í areas of Iraq. At a time when the newly dominant Uṣúlí faction of the ulama was stressing the importance of orthodoxy and the authority of the *mujtahids*, Shaykhism represented an appealing continuation of speculative religious esotericism. It gained, thereby, the increasing enmity of Uṣúlí orthodoxy. Although careful to conceal their more heterodox teachings, the Shaykhí leaders also promulgated the doctrine that the spiritual guidance of Shí'ís depended on the existence in the world of a "true Shí'í" to function as intermediary between the Hidden Imám and the faithful. By implication, this was a function performed by the Shaykhí leaders. Again, some Shaykhís at least were evidently attracted by messianic expectation.

The succession crisis. When Sayyid Káẓim died, the Shaykhís were thrown into confusion. No successor had been designated, and a number of individuals contended for leadership. Chief among these came to be Ḥájí Karím Khán Kirmání (1809/10–1870/71) and Sayyid 'Alí Muḥammad Shírází, the Báb (1819–1850). There were also leadership contenders at Tabriz and Karbala. But these never succeeded in gaining more than localized support, although Sayyid Káẓim's son gained the allegiance of most of the Arab Shaykhís in Iraq, and the two leading S͟hayk͟hís in Tabriz came to dominate the Azeri-speaking S͟hayk͟hí communities of northwestern Iran.

In these latter cases, fragmentation of the movement simply proceeded along established lines of social division, but the division between the followers of Karím K͟hán and 'Alí Muḥammad was more complex.[6] In terms of leadership claims, both men continued the S͟hayk͟hí tradition of laying claim to unique and supernaturally derived authority. Karím K͟hán, a well-established cleric with considerable local political power in Kerman, phrased his claim in the elusive esotericisms of S͟hayk͟hí doctrine. 'Alí Muḥammad, a relatively unknown merchant, soon advanced a more radical claim which was generally understood as that of being the *báb* (gate), the direct intermediary between the Hidden Imám and the S͟hí'í faithful.[7] This was a claim which had messianic import and was of considerable potential interest to non-S͟hayk͟hís. Doctrinal differences between Karím K͟hání and Bábí Shaykhism readily followed from this difference in claims.

The Bábí movement. During the emergence of Babism as a subsect of Shaykhism, the movement remained strongly Islamic in its ethos. Advocating a strict adherence to Islamic law, the Báb appeared merely to accentuate the esoteric and millenarian motifs of traditional Shiism. This accentuation was radical enough in itself, but it did not breach the ideological confines of S͟hí'í Islam except in regard to the religious status implicit in the Báb's claim to authority. Thus, while in his early writings (1844–48) the Báb appeared only to claim that he was the agent of the Hidden Imám, several of his closest disciples and fiercest opponents perceived that a more direct claim to divine guidance was implicit in the general style and content of his work.[8]

Leading S͟hayk͟hí and Uṣúlí clerics began to condemn the movement as heretical. As opposition to the movement mounted, many of the Bábís themselves became more radical, advancing

I R A N

MAIN LINGUISTIC AND TRIBAL GROUPINGS

MAP 2

KEY:

- A. Arabs
- B. Bakhtiyaris
- G. Gilakis
- K. Kurds
- L. Lurs
- M. Mazandaranis
- Q. Qashqais

(Adapted from Halliday, Iran, Map 4)

or revealing clearly heterodox interpretations of their doctrines, and becoming more assertive in the prosecution and defense of their objectives. Some Bábís became militant, and several violent incidents occurred. The Báb himself was now imprisoned, and was increasingly alienated from the Qájár regime. In 1848, he announced his higher claims to authority, declaring himself to be the Hidden Imám and, even more radically, to be the bearer of a new divine revelation which totally abrogated Islam. Armed struggle and violent persecution followed (1848–53), during which the Bábí religion was effectively destroyed as an organized movement. The Báb (1850) and all of his leading lieutenants were killed.

RESOURCE MOBILIZATION: THE SOCIAL ENVIRONMENT

Social structure. The expansion of any social movement occurs within an existing social structure. Social networks, group interests, means of communication, and systems of social control all form part of the given environment. In the case of the Bábís, the relatively unintegrated nature of Iranian society was of crucial importance. Three times the size of France or California, divided by mountains and vast tracts of semi-desert, and possessed in the mid-nineteenth century of no modern means of communications, Iran was only nominally a unitary state. Centrifugal forces of localism and of ethnic and religious diversity necessarily limited Bábí expansion and led to considerable diversity of local situations. Under the circumstances, though the Bábís were largely confined to the peoples of Iran's Shí'í heartland, the construction of a new, more or less unified, national religious movement during the course of a few years was an impressive organizational achievement. The expansion of the movement reflected existing social divisions and was variously related to putative group interests. Existing networks of communication were efficiently utilized. But when the movement was proscribed, the Bábís' lack of communicative control rendered them powerless to defend their public image in the face of the increasingly hostile myth-making of their opponents.

Besides relative lack of societal integration, nineteenth-century Iran was structurally conducive to the emergence of what Neil Smelser has termed "value-oriented movements," that is, movements concerned not with reformist change, but with the radical transformation of basic social values and institutions.[9] The characteristics of such structural conduciveness included: (1) The close interconnections between the major social institutions, and between these institutions and the prevailing value system. A challenge to one part of the system thus readily became a challenge to all. Therefore, any major religious movement readily assumed political significance (as did Babism) regardless of its adherents' intentions. (2) The absence of means for most of the population to express their grievances, which inclined them to support movements which postulated total change. In such circumstances, economic and political demands were easily joined to programs of religious change. Although, in the case of the Bábís, the exact relationship between such factors may remain controversial, their presence occasions no surprise.

Social control and opposition. Social movements are most likely to emerge when existing holders of power either encourage their emergence or are unable to apply effective social controls.[10] Effective action can prevent a movement from developing into a significant threat to the established order, albeit that the costs of such action can be high. In the case of the Bábí movement, no overall effective action was applied to prevent the movement's emergence and initial expansion. Divided among themselves, neither clerical nor secular authorities made any decisive move until the Bábís were well established. As a result, the costs of extirpation were correspondingly greater.

In the case of the religious authorities, the Shí'í ulama were weakly structured to oppose any perceived heresy. In the absence of a unified national hierarchy, individual clerical leaders made their own variant responses to the new movement. Even in a single locality the response was often diverse. Only when a cleric combined his antagonism with a secure local dominance —as did Karím Khán in Kerman—was Bábí expansion halted.[11] Elsewhere, the diversity of response worked in the Bábís' favor. Even in the face of official condemnations for unbelief, the continued sympathy or tolerance of some local clerics prevented effective persecution. In Qazvin, the power of the vehemently anti-Shaykhí and anti-Bábí *mujtahid*, Ḥájí Mullá Muḥammad Taqí Baraghání, was not sufficient to prevent the growth of an active (though semi-secret) Bábí cell.

As for the secular authorities, their initial response was similarly diverse and ineffective. When the Bábí missionaries were cautious in their work and provoked no public disorder, local governors were generally content to let them be. The underlying relationship between secular and religious authorities was often antagonistic in any case. Even if a particular official perceived the heterodox nature of Bábí teaching, he might well relish the prospect of clerical discomforture. Again, the patrician politics of local elites might give the Bábís powerful friends as well as important opponents, such that local opposition was ineffective (as in Shiraz).[12]

Although severe opposition can crush a movement, opposition may also be useful to a movement in increasing the commitment of its members and in attracting the attention of the wider public.[13] Even when opposition leads to members being killed, as long as the human and organizational resources of the movement are not overwhelmed, such opposition is liable to facilitate movement growth. Such, certainly, was the case with the Bábís.

Emerging in a religious culture which glorified heroic martyrdom, the Bábís encountered a mounting force of ill-coordinated opposition. Distinctions between the pious faithful and the ungodly were thus reinforced, giving rise to a fervor of resistance which was to terrify their opponents at the conflicts of Tabarsi, Zanjan, and Nayriz. Only when these lengthy struggles were concluded, and an extensive and bloody suppression of the movement instituted, was that fervor finally overwhelmed.

Political interaction. The interaction between a movement and its wider environment plays a crucial role in its development.[14] In the process, a movement's objectives and modes of action are rarely unchanged. Thus, while any major millenarian movement in a premodern society bears an implicit or explicit political dimension, the actual expression of that political charge is not predetermined. Of note, however, is Smelser's observation that harsh but ineffective repression of a movement engenders revolutionary action.[15] The Báb's challenge to the existing social order was itself interactive with the response of his potential supporters and opponents. Successive rebuttals, at first by the non-Bábí Shaykhís, then by other clerical leaders, and finally by the government, shaped the nature of the continuing Bábí challenge. Whatever the exact planning behind the summons to gather in Karbala in 1845—which at least some Bábís took to be a call to arms, the Báb at that point still accorded the Qájár regime at least nominal legitimacy and sought to convert its chiefs to his cause.[16] The positive intervention of the governor of Isfahan on his behalf (1846–47) marked the zenith of such hopes. Only after his exile to Azerbaijan were these hopes dashed and the court declared to be the object of divine wrath and chastisement.

The growth of Bábí radicalism and militancy was similarly interactive.[17] From the beginning, some Bábí missionaries (such as Mullá Ṣádiq in Shiraz and Ṭáhirih in Karbala) were prepared to be quite provocative in the public presentation of their cause. As clerical opposition hardened and the incidence of persecution increased, many Bábís became increasingly intransigent and radical in their attitudes. Some went further. In several towns Bábís began to carry weapons openly and in Qazvin they began to manufacture swords.[18] In this deteriorating situation, even quite trivial incidents could provoke violent confrontations. Once such incidents had occurred, the escalation and extension of violence became ever more likely. As such escalation took place, government intervention against the Bábís became virtually inevitable. In the resultant armed struggles, the process of polarization was completed: the Bábís despatched their ungodly opponents "to hell," while the government leaders readily and increasingly saw all Bábís as active insurrectionaries.

The wider purpose of these conflicts remains a matter of controversy. However, whether or not they formed part of a carefully prepared insurrectionary conspiracy—a view which the present authors would seriously question, the conflicts should be viewed against the background of established patterns of religious and urban violence in nineteenth-century Iran. Most Iranian towns were divided into a number of rival and religiously defined district factions, each with its own patrician patrons and local associations. Intercommunal fighting was common. Large-scale conversions to the Bábí religion reflected these divisions. Again, leading ulama were linked to the factions by their patronage of groups of toughs (*lúṭís*). With the increasing assertion of clerical power, interclerical disputes were thus readily prosecuted by resort to street fighting and the physical intimidation of opponents. The persecution of Bábís and their own resort to violence were not abnormal in this regard.[19] What was abnormal was the length and intensity of the resultant conflicts. The religious interests of the rival parties were crucial here. Fervent in their commitment to their cause, the Bábís confronted an increasingly assertive clergy whose leaders perceived Babism as a dangerous heresy fundamentally inimical to their own interests.

As to the actual outbreaks of violence, particular local factors were also evidently crucial. Thus, despite the widespread expansion of the movement, both violent confrontations (Qazvin, Mashhad) and major conflicts (Barfurush-Tabarsi, Yazd, Nayriz, and Zanjan) were limited to a number of particular towns and Bábí groups. Whatever the motivation of the Bábís in these particular incidents, the local situations appear to have been characterized by an unusual degree of tension. In Mashhad and Yazd, Bábí violence took place against a background of wider civil unrest; in Qazvin and Barfurush powerful and militant anti-Bábí clerics confronted uncompromising groups of Bábís; and in Zanjan and Nayriz the conversion of leading religious notables led to large-scale Bábí conversions and conditions of local political instability. Where these factors did not develop, there were no Bábí upheavals.

RESOURCE MOBILIZATION: BÁBÍ ORGANIZATION

As organizations, successful social movements must achieve certain goals: motivate, integrate, and direct their memberships; and maintain their existence.[20] In the case of the Bábí movement, these various objectives were closely interlinked, particularly as the full messianic import of the movement became apparent. Shí'ís believe that the anticipated return of the Hidden Imám will revolutionize the whole world and usher in the Day of Resurrection. The Bábís believed themselves to be the elect who had recognized the Imám (or initially his agent) and were thus charged with the recreation of the world. Their existence as a community was itself an integral part of the process of transformation.

Overall Strategy. Given these revolutionary expectations and objectives, the question of overall strategy naturally comes to the fore. The Bábís wanted to establish a theocracy, initially in Iran and ultimately in the whole world. How was this to be accomplished? The traditional Islamic expectation was that the Imám, returned as Mahdi, would wage holy war against the ungodly. This view was initially reiterated by the Báb. Thus, in his early writings, the faithful were summoned to prepare for the forthcoming "day of slaughter" when they would slay the unbelievers and thus purify the earth for the Promised One.[21] Does this mean that the Bábís were consciously and preparedly insurrectionary in intent, as Bayat, for example, has recently argued?[22]

As yet we remain unconvinced. In terms of formal doctrine, the Báb's initial endorsement of the concept of holy war (*jihád*) was not a call to his followers to straightaway engage in such a struggle. Moreover, as the Báb retained for himself the exclusive right to call such a holy war, none of his followers could legitimately have called one on his behalf. Later, after 1848, Bábí doctrine changed. In the most systematic of his later works, the Persian Bayán, the Báb made only passing reference to holy war. He also stated that no one should be slain for unbelief.

Again, although the Báb's attitude toward the state became more hostile after his imprisonment, he evidently retained hopes that its chief officers would voluntarily convert to his cause: an objective that was unlikely to have been aided by mounting an insurrection. Even in the case of the armed struggles which occurred between 1848 and 1853, we would emphasize the importance of local (and national) political interaction. Whatever strategic considerations were involved, these conflicts were also (and perhaps predominantly) tactical responses to particular situations.[23]

We may be wrong, of course. The early years of Bábí expansion may have masked the conspiratorial planning of an insurrection, but we are not aware of any conclusive evidence which might prove such a hypothesis. Our understanding of human action and religious enthusiasm inclines us more to emphasize the interactive processes of development and the unintended consequences of action. Indeed, if the Bábís had made a plan of insurrection, then, given their degree of organization, we would expect it to have led to a far more coherent and coordinated campaign of action than in fact was the case.

If, as we maintain, the Bábís were not consciously and preparedly insurrectionary, then what was their overall strategy? Indeed, did they have one? For the present, we reserve judgment. Certainly, the Bábí leaders were faced with strategic choices. But these were concerned with immediate tasks and were usually linked to the general problem of ensuring the movement's continued survival.

Survival and adaptation. For the leaders of a social movement to accomplish their objectives, it is generally necessary for them to ensure the movement's survival. A key factor in that survival is the relationship which develops between the movement and the wider society. Only when this relationship is relatively stable and peaceful can the thought of external threats to survival be ignored and the movement's membership concentrate on the accomplishment of established goals.[24] Conversely, when the relationship between the movement and its environment is turbulent and uncertain, survival is liable to become the central concern for movement leaders. The primary strategic task becomes the concern with learning to adapt to change. Those movements whose leaders choose to ignore this task, or who are unaware of the implications of environmental interaction, are unlikely to survive. In those cases where actual conflict with the authorities has occurred, non-survival may take the form of physical extirpation.

The relationship between the Bábís and the wider Iranian society was evidently unstable and eventually conflictual. Although the movement was finally destroyed by the authorities, most of its leaders seem to have been aware of the implications of environmental interaction and to have taken pains to ensure the movement's survival. That they were unsuccessful in this objective is an indication of the difficulty of successfully managing such interaction. Certainly, in organizational terms the Bábís were flexible and responsive to change.[25] Their leaders and missionaries were not bureaucratic functionaries tied to static goals and methods, but rather charismatic leaders who creatively responded to a variety of contexts and local situations. Likewise, their followers were unlikely to have been involved in the movement on a purely instrumental basis. Participation was necessarily its own reward, and high levels of commitment were soon engendered.

Given this organizational flexibility, questions of strategic choice and tactical management are central. Robert Lauer has suggested that movements are differentiated in terms of three strategic choices, and by the degree of consensus and persistence with which these choices are pursued.[26] Without leadership agreement as to strategy, a movement in an unstable environment is liable to pass through a series of variant ideological and strategic phases. Given the organizational flexibility of Babism, and its later loss of communicative cohesion, this is precisely what occurred.

FIGURE 1: Stategic Choices for Social Movements

Type	*Primary target for change*	*Use of force*	*Who is expected to implement change*
(i) Educative	Individuals	Nonviolent	Society
(ii) Small group	Individuals	Nonviolent	Movement
(iii) Bargaining	Social structure	Nonviolent	Society
(iv) Separatist	Social structure	Nonviolent	Movement
(v) Disruptive	Social structure	Coercive/violent	Society
(vi) Revolutionary	Social structure	Coercive/violent	Movement

Figure 1: Robert Lauer's typology of strategic choices faced by leaders of social movements. R. H. Lauer, *Social Movements and Social Change*, p. 93.

The framework of strategic choices outlined by Lauer is shown in Figure 1. Given the Bábís' intention to establish the theocratic kingdom of the Mahdi, their predominant target for change consistantly remained that of the social structure rather than the individual. Individual change was subsumed under broader societal objectives. In Lauer's terms, the "educative" and "small group" options were not relevant possibilities, and the strategic choices were those concerning the use or non-use of violence, and of the location of responsibility for affecting change (that is, whether the society as a whole or the movement itself was expected to play the primary role). Consequently, the movement's development may be described in terms of its leaders' changing responses to these two strategic choices. Although it is difficult to reconstruct the exact changes involved, under the pressure of events, Bábí strategy appears to have changed from social bargaining, to social disruption, and then (for a minority) to revolution.

Initially Bábí leaders eschewed the actual use of force (though not the concept of its use) and were in clear expectation of the eventual support of the wider society for the establishment of a Bábí theocracy. Their strategy was one of "bargaining." When society proved unsupportive and Bábís were attacked, a reconsideration of strategic choices became vital. Tensions then developed within the movement over the choice of strategy, the ideological division between Bábí "conservatives" and "radicals" mirroring the strategic one. In the changing circumstances of the time, the conservative option (the continuance of nonviolence and the expectation that society would arise to implement the desired change) proved increasingly untenable, however. More radical strategies soon came to the fore.

The expectation of societal support was apparently stronger than the commitment to nonviolence. The "separatist" choice of nonviolent sectarian communitarianism seems never to have been considered. Still perhaps hoping for a widespread uprising in their favor (or perhaps divine intervention), the Bábí leaders were drawn into disruptive action involving relatively limited use of violence. Tabarsi became a spiritual *pronunciamentio* for the cause of the Mahdi. When this failed, and all hope of support was lost, effective strategic coordination of the movement came to an end. In the absence of such coordination, tactical responses to local situations tended to determine events. Some of the remaining Bábí leaders (Ṣubḥ-i Azal, Shaykh 'Alí Turshízí, and Sulaymán Khán) unsuccessfully gave their support to revolutionary terrorism.[27] Thereafter, the movement was destroyed.

As the wider social environment became more hostile, tactical management became more constrained. This had several aspects. At the outset of the expansion of their movement, the Bábí leaders were often able to act with relatively little risk to their persons. Opposition was ill-coordinated, and the nature of the Bábí cause and even the name of the Báb were unknown. Confrontations with clergy had the advantage of surprise, and, if not physically restrained, a Bábí missionary might well attract considerable interest in his master's teachings. Later, opposition became more resolute and better coordinated. The risks of Bábí membership, let alone of public declarations of faith, became considerable. Concealment, secrecy, and covert proslytism became necessary for all but those Bábís who were able to physically defend themselves.

Conflict management also became more difficult. During the early phase of the movement, potentially conflictual situations could be avoided. Bábí missionaries encountering opposition could move on. Indeed, the Báb himself may well have determined to avoid appearing at Karbala in 1845, after hearing of the scale of the hostility which his emissaries had generated amongst the orthodox ulama.[28] Later, as Bábí communities were established and hostility towards the Bábís hardened, such avoidance became increasingly difficult to accomplish. Even if some Bábís had not themselves become more militant, the potential for conflict had greatly increased.

Primary goals. For the early years of Bábí expansion, the manifest goals of the movement were to win public support and gain adherents. To mobilize public support, the Bábís needed to gain visibility and legitimacy. Visibility was relatively easy to gain. Even the initial declaration that the *báb* of the Imám had appeared was sufficient to attract widespread public attention. This was furthered by an extensive missionary campaign, and the dispatch of letters from the Báb to various religious and political leaders. A series of proclamatory events was also planned. These included the Báb's public declaration of his mission during his pilgrimage to Mecca, the gathering together of believers in Karbala to await the Imám (January 1845), and the changing of the call to prayer to include the name of 'Alí Muḥammad. The public challenges (*mubáhalát*) made by several Bábí disciples to leading ulama also served this purpose, as did the resultant denunciations and attacks which were meted out to them.[29]

Legitimacy was far more difficult to attain. The Bábís might win public attention, but they were relatively powerless to shape the public definition of their movement. Apart from informal contacts and group associations, communicative control of public opinion was dominated by the ulama. Those Bábí converts who were prominent clerics were able to exert influence, but in general the ulama closed ranks against the Bábís and denounced them savagely from their pulpits. With the initiation of bloody confrontation and persecution, the Bábís became practically powerless to combat the malicious representation of their motives and morals. In context, heroic stuggle and martyrdom remained the only means for the Bábís to demonstrate the truth of their cause.

Again, unlike the various clerical contenders for the leadership of Shaykhism, the Báb had no established religious position on which to base his claim to authority. Similarly, though some of his first disciples were well-respected students of Sayyid Káẓim, none of them were sufficiently influential to secure the ready allegiance of others for their new master. Even Mullá Ḥusayn Bushrú'í (1814–1849), the first and initially the most influential of the disciples, lacked the formal authority to possess a following. Only with the later conversion of a few of the leading ulama were the advantages of established position brought to the aid of the new movement. These advantages were by then localized in nature and tangential to the overall development of legitimacy claims promulgated by the Bábí leaders.

The Bábí leaders were restricted in their attempt to legitimate their movement. In terms of the possible bases of legitimacy, the Báb's claims were largely and necessarily charismatic in nature.[30] Shaykh Aḥmad and Sayyid Káẓim had exercised their authority both on the basis of their traditional roles as religious scholars and jurisconsults and on their charismatic claims to privileged visionary access to the sacred knowledge of the Imáms.[31] Lacking any established religious position or clerical training, the Báb's claim to authority was justified almost solely on charismatic grounds. Ultimately, as he himself made clear, legitimation of his authority rested in the believer's response to the sacred power manifested in his person and his writings. Traditional or rational proofs were not regarded as sufficient validations of his claims.[32] Such a stance undoubtedly made public legitimation of the movement more difficult. But for believers the implications were revolutionary, enhancing commitment and facilitating the acceptance of radical changes in the movement's claims and ethos during its later development.

To gain adherents to a movement requires the establishment of some sort of organization. The Báb addressed written (and unsuccessful) appeals for support to various religious and political leaders (including the shah), but the main means of promulgating his claim was the missionary apparatus established by himself and his first eighteen disciples, the Letters of the Living (*ḥurúf al-ḥayy*)

It is of note that, in contrast to the clerical contenders for the leadership of the Shaykhís, the Báb and his disciples had few of the advantages of established position. They had limited access to existing networks of higher clerical contacts and patronage relationships. They had no circles of disciples or students to mobilize. They had no local political power base to employ. They did, however, have access to the existing network of mosques and local Shaykhí communities; they were able to utilize the commercial network of the Báb's merchant uncles as a means of communication; and they presumably had access to sufficient funds to further their immediate purposes.[33] Thus, while the Báb was on pilgrimage, or later under house arrest, or otherwise restricted in his movements, his disciples dispersed throughout the greater part of Iran, and also to Iraq and India.[34] Moving from town to town as itinerant propagandists, they embarked on an intensive missionary campaign. Acting as the movement's primary agents of diffusion, they established a network of Bábí groups throughout the country. They secured and recorded conversions, disseminated the Báb's writings, and in some instances engaged in public confrontations with leading ulama. If and when they became more or less settled, they provided leadership for the local Bábí groups.

No system of formal organization was adopted for the emergent network of Bábí groups. The Báb would appear to have intended that his followers should be grouped into units of nineteen (the numerical equivalent of the word *wáḥid* [unity]).[35] The first "unity" was to consist of himself and the eighteen Letters of the Living. Thereafter, successive groups of converts were to be formed into unities, and the unities further grouped into units of 361 (19x19), called *kullu shay'* ("all things," a term with the numerical equivalence of 361). Beyond the first, or perhaps the second *wáḥid,* this cell-like structure in fact never appears to have come into being. Perhaps the missionary enterprise was itself so time-consuming and turbulent that the task of organization proved more difficult than expected. In any event, no uniform organizational system emerged. Where any of the Letters of the Living resided they provided a focus for leadership, but elsewhere the local communities were led, if they were led at all, by individuals of established social standing. Usually these were Bábí clerics, but merchants, landowners, officials, and courtiers might also act as informal leaders. In his later writings the Báb also introduced a complex hierarchical system of spiritual ranks consisting of various sequences of Mirrors (*maráyá*).[36] Although several individuals were thus designated, no practical organizational system appears to have emerged.

Commitment. All voluntary organizations face the problem of precariousness. Lacking the means of coercion, they depend for their existence on the continuing support of their members. To this end an organization will generally develop distinctive "commitment mechanisms" to maintain its membership's motivation.[37] In the case of the Bábís such mechanisms appear to have been mostly informal in nature. No conversion experience was necessarily demanded. There was no ceremonial initiation or requirement of public testimony of belief. Distinctive patterns of behavior appear to have been voluntarily undertaken, rather than socially enforced. And, in general, no vicinal or social segregation was demanded. Nevertheless, high levels of commitment were maintained, as evidenced both by the willingness of so many Bábís to die for their faith, and, more indirectly, by Bahá'u'lláh's later reanimation of the movement after its seeming total collapse under the pressure of persecution.

In the first instance, commitment appears to have been generated primarily by the movement's ideology. For devout Shí'ís, recognition of the Imám (or his agent) was at the very center of religious meaning. To become one of the elect who had attained such recognition in the age of the Mahdi must, of itself, have constituted a powerful experience of commitment. The ideological distinction between believer and unbeliever doubtless reinforced this experience.

Beyond such ideological factors, there were initially no uniform commitment mechanisms. The Báb called on his followers to perform various supererogatory acts of piety—additional prayers and fasts, abstinence from smoking, and the employment of distinctive rituals—but without social enforcement the observance of such acts remained voluntary.[38] Where such acts were observed, however, they were associated with very high levels of commitment. The group of zealots surrounding Ṭáhirih in Karbala at one stage even refused to eat from the (non-Bábí) bazaar, as they regarded it as ritually impure.[39] Again, where conversion was closely linked to all-inclusive social networks—as in the Bábí strongholds of Zanjan and Nayriz—levels of commitment became very high. Here, "being a Bábí" became an inherent part of normal daily life and not a voluntary commitment to be renewed or abandoned at will. Given the uneven operation of such mechanisms, it is scarcely surprising that very different levels of commitment existed within the movement. Indeed, in Karbala at least, such differences contributed to an acrimonious division within the local Bábí community.[40] Elsewhere, it is likely that groups of Bábís simply varied in their commitment and ethos. Recruitment was to a particular local Bábí group and should not be thought of as having been uniform in its implications.[41]

The pattern of commitment mechanisms changed as the Bábí movement became more radical. Ideological ties with traditional Islamic expectations were broken as the movement's leaders asserted the reality of a new divine revelation. Social ties with non-Bábís were strained as the movement's relationship with clerical and political authorities rapidly deteriorated. Those Bábís who found the newly emerging ideological and social context unacceptable presumably lost commitment or defected. Those who remained were necessarily highly committed. The charismatic legitimation of Bábí authority aided the acceptance of change. The constraints of traditional legitimation were disregarded. Psychologically, the sense of a separate identity is likely to have been enhanced. The abandonment of Islamic law (the *sharí'a*) and participation in conflict with unbelievers would have constituted definite bridge-burning acts. The experience of persecution underlined Bábí separateness and stimulated communal identity and action. In the large and close-knit Bábí communities, social pressures to conform or depart may be assumed to have increased. Heroic martyrdom provided a powerful validation of Bábí claims in Shí'í terms. Eventually, external definition by non-Bábís reinforced the sense of separate identity and in some cases may have made even defection difficult to accomplish.

Integration and control. Given that recruitment to a social movement is to a particular local group, the leaders of any larger movement face problems of integration and control if they wish to preserve the movement's unity. Of course, in certain cases, segmentation can be highly effective. As Gerlach and Hine have argued, a movement which is strongly experiential in emphasis (Pentecostalism, for example) may spread far more rapidly without centralized organization. A sense of "conceptual community" provides the basis for continuing interaction between a diversity of local groups.[42] A movement which is based on a more restricted sense of charismatic authority lacks this option. Thus in the case of Babism, the initial focal point for belief was the doctrine that the agent of the Imám had appeared and was summoning all people to his cause. A unified movement was clearly desirable.

The problems of integrating and controlling the Bábí movement were immense, however. Effective communications were of great importance. The mercantile network established by the Báb's uncles initially played an important role in this regard. With agents and offices in various parts of Iran and the Gulf, the Báb's family and their business partners could be utilized to forward correspondence between the Báb and his chief disciples. For example, when Mullá Husayn reached Khurasan in 1844, he was able to send a report to the Báb in Shiraz, via business associates of the Báb's uncle in Tabas and the family's office in Yazd.[43]

This was probably not an ideal system. During the Báb's lifetime most of his family remained unbelievers and would presumably have been unwilling to devote too many of their resources to Bábí activities. Again, the system was geared to the needs of wholesale trade, rather than to religious proselytization. Thus as the size of the Báb's following grew, a new system of communication evolved based on itinerant Bábí couriers. Working eventually on a full-time basis, individuals such as Mullá Ádí Ghuzal (Sayyáḥ, the "Traveler") made their way between the Báb and the various Bábí groups, disseminating the writings of the Báb and bringing back reports and messages to him. Amanuenses in attendance on the Báb helped deal with this growing correspondence. Elsewhere believers worked as copyists to distribute more copies of the Báb's writings. The steady stream of Bábís from all parts of Iran who journeyed to visit the Báb augmented this communication. Even when the Báb was imprisoned in remote fortresses in Azerbaijan (Maku and Chihriq), this system continued to function with considerable efficiency. Only with extensive persecution was it disrupted, and even so later Bábí and Bahá'í couriers, working under the direction of Bahá'u'lláh, apparently found it relatively easy to revive.

Efficient communications by themselves were not sufficient to ensure the continued integration of the Bábí movement. As the primary agents for the religion's expansion, the role of the leading disciples were crucial. If they had asserted their own independence from the Báb, the movement could have rapidly fragmented. Their continued loyalty to their master ensured its unity. In formal terms, their authority derived from him. As the movement developed, however, the nature of this authority changed (albeit in ways that are not entirely clear). Although all of the Letters of the Living were accorded a special status, initially it was only Mullá Ḥusayn—the *bábu'l-báb*—who was generally regarded as possessing any unusual authority within the movement, functioning effectively as the Báb's deputy.[44] The intense relationships which existed between Ṭáhirih and her devotees in Karbala, and between Ḥujjat Zanjání and his followers, appear to have been localized and exceptional. Only after the movement had entered its second and more radical phase did this situation change. Sequestered in the remote northwest, the Báb now revealed his full claims. Whether or not in a strictly parallel development, three of the disciples —Mullá Ḥusayn, Ṭáhirih, and Mullá Muḥammad 'Alí Bárfurúshí (Quddús)—now came to be accorded quasi-theophanic status. The three disciples shared something of the Báb's charismatic authority: the two men at least symbolically reenacted various of the prophecies relating to the coming of the Mahdi in the place of their imprisoned leader.

This changing relationship between the Báb and his chief disciples was rapidly brought to an end by the violent deaths of all four. Deprived of its original charismatic focus, the movement rapidly fragmented. Individual claims to charismatic authority proliferated, and in some respects the Bábís began to resemble the segmented conceptual community described by Gerlach and Hine. Only later, with the reintroduction of a centralized organisation and the general acceptance of a single charismatic leader in the person of Bahá'u'lláh did Babism again become a unified movement.

RESOURCE MOBILIZATION: RECRUITMENT AND CONVERSION

According to the resource mobilization perspective, the most salient characteristic in the recruitment of the membership of most social movements is prior social interaction.[45] Contact with a movement is normally assumed to follow from significant interaction with its existing members. Recruitment thus tends to follow preexisting and positively valued social relationships, whether these be based on ties of kinship, patronage, or vicinal proximity. Conversion occurs as a process of progressive resocialization, the stereotype of sudden and dramatic personal transformation being untypical.[46]

The extent to which this model is applicable to the Bábí movement is difficult to evaluate. Certainly there were a number of individual Bábís who appear to have undergone sudden transformatory conversions, whether as a result of visions, encounters with the Báb, or perusals of his writings. It may well be of course that these conversions were concentrated amongst the religious *virtuosi* who comprised the movement's leadership.[47] On the other hand, that few such accounts are recorded for rank and file Bábís may simply reflect the sparseness of available historical sources. It is also possible, however, that normal processes of compression and emphasis during oral transmission have transformed some of these conversion accounts into idealized patterns.[48]

Apart from the dramatic conversions of a number of prominent Bábís, the evidence—though scanty—lends support to the use of the mobilization model.

Thus, in the first instance, diffusion of the movement was strongly concentrated within the existing network of the Shaykhí communities. (See Table 1, below.) Gathered together in Shiraz during the Báb's initial declaration of his mission, the Letters of the Living then dispersed to various parts of Iran, Iraq and India.[49] The initial expansion of the movement resulted

TABLE 1: Previous Religious Identities of Prominent Bábís by Date of Conversion

Conversion before 1264 A.H. (1848 A.D.)		
	- Shaykhís	75
	- not identified as Shaykhís	70
	Total	145
Conversion in 1264 or after		
	- Shaykhís	2
	- not identified as Shaykhís	38
	Total	40
Date of conversion not known		104
	Total	289

SOURCE: Mázandarání, *Ẓuhúru'l-Ḥaqq*, vol. 3

from the missionary conversions gained by these disciples. Whether or not the Báb had instructed them to concentrate their energies on the Shaykhí communities, their initial contacts were largely confined to their fellow sectaries. Several of them —notably Mullá Ḥusayn—had already attained some prominence as disciples of Sayyid Káẓim and were doubtless able to address their coreligionists with authority, as well as on the basis of sectarian fraternity. Others were sent to their home areas, where they presumably utilized their own existing social networks as a means of diffusing the Báb's message. In some instances, entire local communities of Shaykhís were converted.[50] In Kerman, by contrast, Karím Khán's authority within the local Shaykhí community effectively prevented the Bábí missionaries from gaining access to the social networks which were most susceptible to their message.

Conversions also occurred following contact with the Báb himself. Thus individual Shaykhís who had been particularly impressed by the young merchant when they had met him in Karbala in 1841–42, (that is, prior to his putting forward any claim), were later amongst the most devoted of his followers.[51]

Again, at least eighteen Bábís dated their conversions to their experience of the Báb's public appearance in the Vakíl Mosque in Shiraz in 1845—supposedly made to recant his claim.[52]

As the Báb's disciples went about their mission, news of the Báb's claim soon began to spread before them. Despite the initial concealment of the Báb's name, the messianic import of his claim attracted attention well beyond the Shaykhí community. In several instances, individuals set out for Shiraz or some other Bábí missionary center to investigate the matter for themselves. Some were sent as delegates on behalf of others. When such delegates converted, new social networks were opened to Bábí expansion, and further conversions readily followed. Thus when Shaykh Salmán of Hindijan returned to his home town from Shiraz, he succeeded in converting some seventy families of the Afshár tribe.[53] Again, Mullá Muḥammad Furúghí's conversion was important in the expansion of Babism to the Turbat-Haydari area of Khurasan.[54]

The opening of new social networks was even more effective when leading ulama were involved. Sayyid Yaḥyá Darábí Vaḥíd abandoned his associations with the court in order to become an itinerant Bábí propagandist, thereafter converting many of those who regarded him or his father as their spiritual guides. His existing networks of contacts in both Yazd and Nayriz, where he had houses, were especially important in this regard. Again, the conversion of Shaykh Muḥammad 'Alí, Ḥujjat Zanjání, was followed by the mass conversion of those of the inhabitants of Zanjan who regarded him as their religious leader.[55]

In the case of Nayriz and Zanjan, the role of preexisting social networks in determining conversion patterns depended on more than just relationships of religious patronage and guidance. It was common in mid-nineteenth-century Iran for even quite small towns to be divided into a number of mutually antagonistic urban districts (*maḥallihs*), each with its own intense communalism and linkages to the web of partrician politics.[56]

The conversion of a religious notable, such as Ḥujjat or Vaḥíd, or Ḥájí Shaykh 'Abdu'l-'Alí—the Imám Jum'ih of the Chinár-Súkhtih quarter of Nayriz, thus favored the conversion of the entire local community to which they were related. Correspondingly, success in one urban district disfavored success in rival districts. Within each town, these districts often coalesced into two competing and largely endogamous urban factions defined in terms of religious labels. Bábí expansion was inevitably moulded by these divisions, especially where Shaykhism had become a factional identifier, as in Barfurush and Qazvin where all or part of the Shaykhí faction simply converted to the Bábí faith.[57] Even where Shaykhism was not a factional label, support for the Báb was influenced by community divisions. In Shiraz, support came predominantly from within the Ni'matí faction, whilst those within the Ḥaydarí faction tended to be opposed.[58]

Associational and class networks were also important as channels of Bábí expansion. Prominent here were the linkages between the members of the ulama. Although the most important formal linkages were between the various leading ulama, and between each of these individuals and their own students and the clients of their patronage, the whole body of the ulama represented an informal grouping with considerable intercommunicative potential. Though largely confined to the lower or middle ranks of the ulama, the Bábí missionaries were well able to realize this communicative potential. Identified as clerics by their distinctive dress and their literacy, with ready access to the network of mosques and colleges, the learned Bábís, like other members of the ulama, were able to disseminate new ideas and form new social relationships with their fellows with relative ease. Thus, even at a personal level, the Bábí challenge could be directed with particular immediacy to the one social group which was most able to further or retard the movement's progress.

The other associational networks which were important were those of the bazaar. The wholesale merchants (*tujjár*) were the key figures here. Educated, resourceful, and with a reputation for piety, the merchants enjoyed close association with the upper- and middle-ranking ulama. The two groups were also often related by intermarriage and business associations. The Bábí ulama were thus able to gain an audience among the merchants. Again, the merchants themselves by dint of their occupation, had wide-ranging national linkages with their fellow merchants, and local contacts with the craftsmen, shopkeepers, and petty traders who like them worked in the bazaar. Artisanal and petit bourgeois elements were thus also accessible to the Bábí preachers, and in Isfahan at least, the guilded craftsmen (*aṣnáf*) of the bazaar became a major network by which the movement spread.[59]

Rural linkages in Bábí expansion are less clear. Iranian peasants were socially interlinked in a variety of ways, but as yet we have only been able to identify patronage relationships as an evident channel of Bábí diffusion. This one factor may well account for the highly uneven expansion of Babism into the rural areas, but more research into the role of working and marketing relationships is needed.

Kinship linkages as a basis for conversion also need to be researched.

RESOURCE MOBILIZATION: BÁBÍ IDEOLOGY

Mobilization theory emphasizes the effect and form, rather than the specific content, of the beliefs and doctrines propounded by a particular movement. This approach to content reflects the belief that official ideology is not a good guide to the reasons why individuals join particular movements. Mobilization theory deemphasizes the importance of motivation. It indicates that movement members are often found to hold a diversity of beliefs, to be variously motivated, and to hold beliefs which are highly discrepant from those of their leaders.[60] Thus, as a mobilizing factor, the significance of movement ideology is held to lie in its adaptability and in its provision of conceptual certitude.[61]

Certitude—which enhances commitment—is provided by an all-embracing meaning system which eludes falsification. Such, certainly, the Bábí movement appears to have had, though the intricacies of its validation strategies have yet to be studied. Adaptability facilitates the coexistence of a common rhetoric (to symbolize the movement's unity) with the diversity of ordinary members' beliefs. If a set of beliefs is structured too tightly the movement is exposed to the danger of schism.[62] Again, though the diversity of Bábí popular belief has yet to be properly evaluated, it is clear that beneath the unitary symbol of belief in the Báb, there existed a great array of beliefs by which Bábís expressed simultaneously the appeals of messianism, esoteric rationalism, pietism, legalistic reformism, and popular thaumaturgy. The very diversity of those who embraced the movement provides an adequate testimony to the adaptability of its appeal. Adaptability can also find expression in a "split-level" ideology.[63] In the case of Babism, this found formal recognition in a distinct hierarchical structure of belief. The esoteric truths accepted by the Bábí elite were only gradually revealed to the rank and file.

If a movement lacks a distinctive ideology of its own it is unlikely to preserve its unity and independent existence. Unity requires that there be a clear locus of ideological authority beyond the individual adherent. Independence requires that there be a distinction between adherents and nonadherents. Among Bábís, the primary locus of authority was provided by the person of the Báb. However diverse the interpretations of Bábí doctrine, and in whatever manner the Báb's claims may have been understood by his adherents, he himself stood at the center of their system of meaning. He was the measure by which truth was to be distinguished from falsehood. Those Bábís who relied on alternative sources of authority found continued commitment to his cause difficult to sustain. After the Báb had been executed, there was no longer a point of unity and the movement rapidly fragmented.

As to the distinction between believers and unbelievers this again centered on belief in the Báb. During the movement's Islamic phase, those who rejected the Báb were thought to have ceased to be Muslims and were thus ritually impure. They were assigned to hell. In practice, however, this belief (and many others) was generally concealed by the provisons of the Shí'í doctrine of pious dissimulation (*taqiyya*). The Bábís might know themselves to be the true elect, but to outward seeming they at first appeared to be Shaykhí sectaries, distinguished as much by their pietistic legalism as by the radical nature of their religious beliefs. As Gerlach and Hine have argued, in a hostile environment, ideological ambiguity can play a crucial role in a movement's survival and successful propagation.[64]

As against the more utilitarian statements of mobilization theory, we would contend that the content of ideology—at least at a general level—is of considerable significance. Religious innovation occurs within a preexisting context of traditional belief. For adherents to be gained, a new religious movement must at least possess ideological plausibility. Its doctrines must possess an elementary accessibility to its potential membership. In this area the Báb was eminently successful. Though heterodox in the eyes of the custodians of religious orthodoxy, the Bábís articulated many of the traditional concerns of popular Shiism and Shí'í dissent. The adaptability and ambiguity of its ideology augmented its appeal. To Shaykhís and others in this tradition of dissent, Babism reinterpreted the concerns of esoteric Shiism with its ideas of true knowledge, perfect men, and prophetic evolution. To all Shí'ís, it reasserted the traditions of messianic expectation, pietistic devotionalism, and charismatic leadership. Its adherents came to witness to its truth with the blood of martyrdom, consciously reenacting the traditions of Karbala. In an age which readily accepted the miraculous, those who sought miracles from its grace found what they sought.

There is a clear continuity between many of the central teachings of Shaykhism and those of Babism, especially during the period of its early development. 'Alí Muḥammad S͟hírází may not have been a distinguished cleric, nonetheless he forcefully reasserted the S͟hayk͟hí concern with charismatic leadership. Like the S͟hayk͟hí masters, he laid claim to supernaturally derived authority, differing from them only in the unambiguous uniqueness and openness of his claim. Like them, he offered veracious knowledge from the Imáms of guidance and the unveiling of the inner meaning of scriptural truth. Again like them, but more explicitly, he challenged the newly established scholastic orthodoxy of the Uṣúlí school. As part of the continuing tradition of dissent, he asserted the potency of divinely inspired knowledge.

In terms of motifs, he continued the powerful polar and esoteric concerns of Shaykhism, thereby appealing directly to the now leaderless S͟hayk͟hís.[65] When compared with the other claimants to S͟hayk͟hí leadership, he gave more radical, and probably more popular, emphasis to these motifs. As a noncleric, his claim to supernaturally derived knowledge represented a far more radical critique of the legalistic scholasticism of the Uṣúlís. Unlike S͟hayk͟h Aḥmad and Sayyid Ká︢im, a distinctly anticlerical element entered his teachings. Unlike Karím K͟hán, he asserted that access to religious truth did not require an elaborate array of acquired knowledge. It required only the spiritual perception of the true believer.

Such concerns had a general appeal beyond the S͟hayk͟hí circle. The quest for charismatic authority was common to both official and popular nineteenth-century Iranian religiosity.[66] Esotericism remained a potent theme in S͟hí'í life. At a time when the Uṣúlí establishment sought to regularize and control these motifs, the Bábís vigorously reasserted them. Similarly, Babism gave powerful expression to Shí'í millenarianism, giving it a further linkage to the popular religiosity of the time. Though mahdist anticipation remained normative in official Shiism, it presented a potentially unstable enthusiasm which the ulama preferred to control. In announcing his mission in the prophetic year 1260 A.H. (1844)—a full millennium after the concealment of the Hidden Imám—the Báb directly addressed the popular millenarian speculation of the time.[67] Moreover, as actual mahdist expectation and enthusiasm were apparently mounting at this time—perhaps particularly after the Ottoman sack of the holy city of Karbala in 1843—the Bábí missionaries were able to directly address and interpret popular sentiment in their own terms, and to considerable effect.[68] Indeed, it is notable that pre-Bábí Shaykhism itself appears to have been affected by adventist speculation, and a definite tension between the proponents and opponents of adventism seems to have emerged. Whether or not the Bábís were correct in later attributing adventist themes to the oral teachings of the Shaykhí masters, it is clear that a number of Shaykhís had become adventists prior to 1844, and that these individuals were among those who became Bábís. Correspondingly, those Shaykhís who had been opposed to adventist expectation were amongst the Báb's chief opponents.[69]

One further motif in early Bábí teachings which may be assumed to have contributed to the movement's initial appeal was that of "pietistic legalism."[70] Despite the novelty of his claims and his ultimate abrogation of Islamic law, the Báb at first advocated a strict observance of the law. His followers were initially distinguished more by their fervent devotionalism than by any obvious deviation from the accepted codes of Islamic practice. Only with the radicalization of the movement did this situation change, and the Bábís' heterodoxy become fully revealed.

As the radical nature of Bábí doctrine became more evident,

those who found its innovations reprehensible abandoned the movement, or rose up in opposition. The Báb's failure to appear in Karbala in 1845, the radical nature of the validation of his authority, the esoteric interpretation of the messianic tradition, the Báb's later claims to be a new divine messenger, and the abrogation of the Islamic holy law all broke conceptual norms. This placed strains on the process of recruitment and engendered defections from the movement. Some of these strains were lessened, however, by the gradual progression in the Báb's claims. According to the Báb's own account, his later and more extreme claims were initially concealed as a matter of deliberate policy so that "men might not be disturbed by a new book and a new Cause."[71] Certainly, this was the sociological effect of this progressive revelation. When the Báb's more radical claims became widely known, the Bábís were already integrated into the movement. If the Báb's higher claims had been known from the start, it is unlikely that he would have been able to gain so ready an audience, or his disciples gain so many recruits.

At the same time, however, radicalization gave even greater emphasis to the polar and millenarian motifs. Appearing now as a theophany, the Báb gave potent expression to ideas of extreme charismatic legitimacy which, while far removed from orthodoxy, were not unknown in popular religious culture. More specifically, as opposition mounted, the Bábís perceived the antagonistic arrays of Shí'í apocalypticism come into being: the hosts of the Mahdi confronted the forces of Antichrist. By the Bábí doctrine of "return" (*raj'a*), the cosmic roles of the fourteen Very Pure (Muḥammad, Fáṭima, and the Imáms) were reenacted in the persons of the Letters of Living, while Karím Khán and Ḥájí Mírzá Áqásí enacted the roles of their opponents —Dajjál and the hideous Sufyání.[72] Specific acts, such as the march of Mullá Ḥusayn and his companions out of Khurasan bearing a black standard, made literal appeal to messianic prophecy.[73]

Appeal was now also made to the S͟hí'í motif of pious martyrdom. The powerful symbolism of blood sacrificed in the struggle against the enemies of true religion was readily evoked. The Bábís saw themselves as being like the Imám Ḥusayn and his followers, cut down at the battle of Karbala in 680 by the Umayyads. Shaykh Tabarsi was Karbala reenacted. The Qájárs had become latter day Umayyads seeking to extinguish God's religion. This symbolism won sympathizers, even among the armies of the "latter-day Umayyads."[74]

THE SOCIAL LOCATION OF THE BÁBÍ COMMUNITY

The social location and demographic significance of the Bábís are central factors in any consideration of the religion's wider importance as a social movement. As yet, our knowledge of this basic data remains incomplete—a lacuna with serious implications for higher level theories of the reasons for the emergence and expansion of the movement.

Bábí numbers. The demographic significance of Babism is particularly difficult to discern.[75] Estimates for the total size and composition of the Iranian population in the mid-nineteenth century vary widely and there are no detailed records of the total number of Bábís. Both the Báb and the Russian and British Ministers in Tehran refer to a total of one hundred thousand Bábís. If this were the figure, then the Bábís represented a significant element in the contemporary Iranian population, perhaps between 1.7 and 2.2 percent of the total. Good organization and a particular concentration of adherents in the towns would have made this number of Bábís a formidable force in Iranian society.

But were there one hundred thousand Bábís? The figure of one *lak͟h* (100,000) is clearly a rounded figure, and may well simply have been a synonym for "a large number." It is only too easy to attribute a false facticity to figures employed without modern statistical intent or exactitude. It may well be that there were markedly fewer Bábís than one hundred thousand. Some sources refer to fifty thousand, but again this may well have no real statistical base. Certainly, given the considerable disincentives of membership and the very limited period in which the Bábí missionaries were able to actively recruit members, a lower figure for membership seems highly probable. A lower number would also be commensurate with a recent reevaluation of the number of Bábí martyrs which reduces the commonly-cited figure of twenty thousand to approximately two or three thousand.[76]

Whatever the total number of Bábís, it is clear that at least in certain localities they attained a considerable importance. Indeed, it may well be that what distinguished Zanjan and Nayriz, the two towns in which there was sustained conflict between the Bábís and their opponents, was the unusually high concentration of the Bábís in those localities. Thus in Zanjan, an important town on the Tabriz to Tehran route, the Bábís may have represented some fifteen percent of the local population (perhaps 3,000 out of some 20,000). In Nayriz, the figure was even higher, Bábís representing perhaps 43 percent of the population (1,500 out of about 3,500).[77] Elsewhere the local concentrations of Bábís undoubtedly varied quite considerably. Baghdad, for example, may have had about 70 believers during the period of Ṭáhirih's residence, and Karbala perhaps the same. In Tehran, by contrast, there were about 2,000 Bábís.[78]

Social location. Nineteenth-century Iran was neither a unified nor homogeneous society. Bábí expansion was thus inevitably constrained by the existing patterns of religious, social and geographical division. While we are not yet able to provide a precise description of Bábí expansion in terms of these patterns, we feel that some of the main characteristics are now more or less clear.

Besides impressionistic evidence, we employ two quantitative analyses. The first of these, which has already been presented elsewhere, is an analysis of the identified Bábí participants at the Shaykh Tabarsi conflict (Table 2; N = 365 out of c. 540).[79] The second which is presented here for the first time is an analysis of the biographical information of prominent Bábís provided in the third volume of Fáḍil Mázandarání's *Ẓuhúru'l-Ḥaqq*, one of the standard Bahá'í accounts of the period (Tables 1, 2, 3, and 4; N = 282). Individuals merely listed by Mázandarání are assumed not to have been prominent and are excluded from the analysis. We assume that in general those Bábís whom Mázandarání describes in any detail constituted part of what we might term the "leadership cadre" of the movement.

Religious background. Most nineteenth-century Iranians were Shí'í Muslims and the overwhelming majority of Bábís were drawn from this grouping. Of the non-Muslim religious minorities—perhaps 3 percent of the population—no Assyrian or Armenian Christians were converted, but there is record of one Zoroastrian convert and several Jews.[80] Of the non-Shí'í Muslims, no Sunnís appear to have been converted, but a few converts were drawn from amongst the Ahlu'l-Ḥaqq ('Alíyu'lláhís).[81] Of the Shí'í converts, most were initially Shaykhís. But as the movement expanded, adherents were drawn from all schools of Shiism. Few members of Sufi orders converted, but those that did included a Ni'matu'lláhí leader (*murshid*). A few wandering ascetics (Qalandar dervishes) also came to be associated with the movement.

It is of note that of the prominent Bábís mentioned by Mázandarání at least a quarter were Shaykhís (Table 1). Indeed, of those known to have converted during the early "Islamic" phase of Bábí development (that is, prior to 1264 A.H. [1848 A.D.]), at least half had been Shaykhís. As the former religious identity of many of the individuals mentioned is unknown, it is highly likely that both these figures represent underestimates for the

Table 2: Occupational Background of Selected Bábís

	BÁBÍS AT TABARSI[1]		PROMINENT BÁBÍS[2]	
	no.	%	no.	%
Ulama	136	37.3	144	49.8
Major	(14)	3.8	(19)	6.6
Minor	(122)	33.4	(125)	43.3
Landowners	12	3.3	4	1.4
High government officials and and notables			19	6.6
Minor officials and government employees	0	–	7	2.7
Wholesale merchants (*tujjár*)	5	1.4	34	11.8
Retail merchants (guild members)	9	2.5	9	3.1
Craftsmen and other skilled urban workers	39	10.7	20	6.9
Unskilled urban labourers	6	1.6	0	–
Peasants	6	1.6	15	5.2
Tribespeople	0	–	6	2.1
Occupational unknown	152	41.6	31	10.7
Urban	(61)	16.7		
Rural	(73)	20.0		
Origin unknown	(18)	4.9		
	365	100.0	289	100.0

(The Tabarsi figures 12 / 3.3 are bracketed together for Landowners and High government officials and notables.)

SOURCE: (a) Momen, "The Social Basis of the Bábí Upheavals in Iran," p. 162; (b) Calculated from Mázandarání, *Ẓuhúru'l-Ḥaqq*, vol. 3.

NOTES: As missing values ("occupation unknown") have not been excluded from the percentage figures, the other figures represent minimum values.

1. Figures refer to identified Bábí participants at Shaykh Tabarsi, i.e., 365 individuals out of a total of c. 540.

2. For definition of "prominent Bábís" see text.

proportion of S͟hayk͟hís. For example, it seems probable that most of those converted by Mullá Ḥusayn during his first missionary journey were S͟hayk͟hís, but only a minority are explicitly identified as such.

Ethnicity and nomadism. Perhaps one-third or more of the mid-nineteenth-century Iranian population belonged to nomadic or semi-nomadic tribes.[82] Linguistic and religious divisions reinforced their separation from the settled S͟hí'í population. Elements of some of these tribes did become sedentary, however, and were drawn into settled society. Although we know of no nomads who became Bábís, members of more settled tribal groups did convert.[83] Prominent among these were some seventy families of the Afs͟hárs of Hindijan (Fars), but a number of Kurds were also converted.[84] Of prominent Bábís (Tables 2 and 3), five were identified solely as tribesmen, and another two (a military officer and a landowner; and the son of a courtier) were of tribal background. These individuals included three Afs͟hárs (one a tribal leader), a Jalílú Kurd (a tribal leader), and a Turkaman.

Among the settled population, ethnic divisions do not seem to have been a significant barrier to Bábí expansion. Although most Bábís were drawn from the majority Persian (*fársí*-speaking) population, the movement spread readily amongst both Azerbaijani Turks and Mazandaranis. Lack of success amongst Gilakis and Iranian Arabs is likely to have been due solely to a lack of effective proselytism in those areas. Arabs in Iraq were converted without any problem.

Class divisions. Nineteenth-century Iranian class divisions may be described in terms of three socio-economic formations: pastoral nomadism, peasant agriculture, and petty-commodity production and trade.[85] Government officials and ulama represented distinctive non-class groups. Bábí expansion was unevenly distributed within these various classes and groupings,

TABLE 3: Prominent Bábís by Occupation and Geographical Origin

	A	B	C	D	E	F	G	H	I	J	K	Total
1. Khurasan (incl. Qa'in & Simnan)	6	32	0	3	0	2	2	0	0	0	3	48
2. Mazandaran	2	8	1	5	0	0	0	1	0	0	6	23
3. Azerbaijan	2	22	0	6	3	2	2	3	0	0	6	46
4. Qazvin & Khamsih	2	10	0	0	4	17	0	9	1	3	1	47
5. Tehran & Qum	2	5	0	3	0	0	0	0	0	0	1	11
6. Kashan & Mahallat	1	8	0	0	0	9	0	2	0	0	7	27
7. Isfahan	1	14	1	1	0	0	3	1	0	0	3	24
8. Fars	1	13	1	1	0	3	2	2	12	2	2	39
9. Yazd & Kerman	2	8	1	0	0	1	0	2	0	0	0	14
10. Kermanshah & Hamadan	0	1	0	0	0	0	0	0	0	0	2	3
11. Iraq	0	4	0	0	0	0	0	0	2	1	0	7
Total	19	125	4	19	7	34	9	20	15	6	31	289
Percentage (excl. column K)	7	48	2	7	3	13	3	8	6	2		99

A - *Major Ulama*: *mujtahids, Imám-Jum'ihs* and any ulama who had a following
B - *Minor Ulama*: all other ulama and *ṭulláb* (religious students)
C - *Landowners & Employers*: landowners and landowning farmers
D - *Notables & High Govt. Officials*: governors, court officials, army officers of rank of *sartíp* and above, high government officials
E - *Minor Govt. Officials*: Secretaries, couriers, soldiers, *kadkhudás*
F - *Wholesale Merchants (tujjár)*
G - *Retail Merchants*: Guilded retail merchants, petty commodity producers
H - *Skilled Urban Workers*: guilded craftsmen (*aṣnáf*) and other service workers
I - *Peasants*
J - *Tribal elements*
K - *Occupation unknown*

SOURCE: Mázandarání, *Ẓuhúru'l-Ḥaqq*, vol. 3.

the most obvious restriction being its confinement to the settled population.

Within the settled population it seems possible that, as between the urban and rural sectors, the overall distribution of Bábís did not differ significantly from that of the population as a whole.[86] That is, most or at least a significant minority, of Bábís may have come from the same rural and small town background which constituted the social milieu of perhaps two-thirds of the settled population of Iran. Even among prominent Bábís, some 37 percent were of this background (Table 4).

It should be noted, however, that while Bábí expansion in the urban sector was well distributed throughout the towns of the Shí'í heartland, rural expansion was highly localized. Most rural areas were never effectively proselytized. In terms of its

TABLE 4: Rural/Urban Origins of Prominent Iranian Bábís

	No.	%
Large Towns (pop. over 22,000)	114	40
Medium-sized Towns (7,000–22,000)	65	23
Small Towns (2,000–7,000)	37	13
Villages	66	23
Total	282	99

SOURCES: Mázandarání, *Ẓuhúru'l-Ḥaqq*, vol. 3. The list of towns given by Thompson in *Parliamentary Papers*, vol. 69 for 1867–68, pp. 507–15 (reprinted by C. Issawi, *Economic History of Iran*, p. 28) has been used for the large and medium-sized towns. For the small towns and villages, we have used information from the *Gazetteer of Persia*. It should be realised that this information is very imprecise and it is impossible to determine the size at that time of certain large villages such as Bushru'iyyih which has been classified here under villages, but may well have had more than two thousand inhabitants.

NOTE: The seven Iraqis included in Tables 1, 2 and 3 have been excluded from this table, hence the difference in totals.

social impact, Babism was predominantly an urban movement, but with a significant rural constituency.

We must assume that the Bábís of rural origin were mostly peasants. Unfortunately we are not yet able to say if they came from any particular stratum within the peasantry, either in terms of wealth or degree of independence. Given the distribution of power and education in Qájár Iran, it is scarcely surprising that only 5 percent of the prominent Bábís were peasants (Tables 2 and 3). These were mostly fruit-growers from Nayriz. The Bábí religion may have succeeded in gaining a significant peasant following, but it was not (except in certain localized instances) a peasant movement. Bábí peasant conversions might follow that of respected religious leaders (as at Nayriz), but it also followed that of the peasants' own landlords (as in Mazandaran).

Within Qájár society, land ownership and the political office which such ownership could support provided the most stable basis for power. This tiny minority of notables was significantly represented within the Bábí movement, constituting at least 8 percent of the prominent adherents (Tables 2 and 3). Again, we are not able to specify the location of these individuals in detail. But it is of note that most do not appear to have been politically influential, though several moved in court circles, including Mírzá Riḍá K͟hán Turkaman, Riḍá Qulí K͟hán Afs͟hár, and Mírzá Ḥusayn 'Alí Núrí, Bahá'u'lláh. The only exception to this observation was Manúc͟hihr K͟hán Mu'tamidu'd-Dawlih, the governor of Isfahan. Several of the (numerous) Qájár princesses are also said to have been converted, as well as a number of petty officials and government employees.[87]

Apart from landowners and government officials, the other elite groups in Qájár society were the wholesale merchants (*tujjár*) and the higher ulama. Both groups were well represented among the more prominent Bábís, constituting respectively at least 12 percent and 7 percent of this grouping. Their total numbers were necessarily limited, however.

The merchants dominated the economic life of the bazaar. It was here that much of the strongest support for the Bábí movement was gained, perhaps particularly from the craftsmen and petty-traders who belonged to the various guilds. These groups between them contributed some 29 individuals (10 percent) to the group of prominent Bábís. The extent of Bábí representation amongst the unskilled workers and urban peasants who comprised the invisible majority of the urban population is unknown. None became prominent in the movement, but it is possible that a large proportion of the Bábís in Zanjan came from these groups. It is notable that, from the beginning, Ḥujjat Zanjání appears to have developed a strong relationship with his poorer followers. When the conflict began, it was these who followed him with greatest constancy, while some of his richer followers defected to the Muslim side.[88]

The ulama did not constitute a unitary social class as such, but rather a distinctive series of groupings with varying economic interests. Although the lesser ulama—especially theological students—dominated the Bábí leadership (43 percent or more), a significant number of the prominent Bábís (7 percent) were drawn from the higher ulama. Ulama were also the largest single group identified at the fortress of Shaykh Tabarsi (136 out of 537).

Most prominent Bábís were men, and it is probably that the majority of the Bábí rank-and-file were also men. Full "familialization" of the movement probably only developed after its transformation into the Bahá'í religion.[89] Nevertheless, 11 women were included in the category of prominent Bábís. Given the extreme subordination of women in Iranian society of the time, this is remarkable. Whatever the symbolic significance of Ṭáhirih's role as a Bábí leader for Iranian women of her own day, the very fact of her prominence as one of the four leading Bábís represents one of the most distinctive features of Babism as an Islamic religious movement.

Geographical extent. The geographical expansion of Babism reflected the extent of missionary activity and the social composition of the movement.[90] Bábí missionaries concentrated their attention on the S͟hí'í shrine cities of Iraq and the S͟hí'í heartland of Iran. Areas with non-S͟hí'í minorities (which also tended to be areas dominated by minority tribes) received little or no attention. As a result there were no Bábís in Baluchistan, the Gulf littoral, or most parts of the Western mountains. Other areas, such as S͟hí'í Arabistan (Khuzistan), Sistan, and Gilan were neglected for no apparent reason (other than perhaps their peripheral location). The sustained opposition of Karím K͟hán in Kerman prevented effective expansion there, but otherwise all the major cities and provinces of Iran were reached. We have insufficient data to make any definite remarks about the overall distribution of the movement. We note that, reflecting the population distribution of the time, most of the prominent Bábís at least were northerners. This observation contradicts the hypothesis that the Bábí movement reflected southern discontent.[91]

ADDENDUM: TWENTY FIVE PROPOSITIONS

In considering Babism as a social movement, we have resisted the temptation to present high-level hypotheses as to origins and development. We will doubtless succumb to this temptation elsewhere. But for the present we have sought to establish some of the basic questions concerning *how* the movement developed, rather than address the more intractable issues of *why* it developed.

This is not to devalue these wider questions. We recognize their importance. As a contribution to this work of theoretical analysis we present twenty-five propositions regarding the religious, political and social significance of the Bábí religion. We regard these propositions as basic elements in the construction of higher level theories. We have and will write in support of these propositions elsewhere. Some are supported in the present article. This propositional form lends itself to ready falsification by those who would disagree with us.

A. Religious Factors

1. The Bábí movement was a phenomenon within Shiism. It made no significant impact beyond the confines of Shiism.
2. The movement carried a strong religious charge. It gave expression to a number of powerfully evocative Shí'í motifs. Its leaders spoke to the religious concerns of the day and presented (some) Bábí beliefs in a manner that was accessible to religiously inclined contemporaries.

3. More controversial beliefs were initially concealed from both non-Bábís and from the Bábí rank-and-file.
4. At a time of increasing emphasis on orthodoxy (as defined by the higher ranking ulama), the movement gave voice to elements of the popular and dissenting religious traditions.
5. The movement's leaders initially called for a religious reformation and condemned clerical corruption.
6. Local variation in appeal was probably great.
7. The movement provided a comprehensive system of meaning and could ultimately provide an alternative sense of identity to Shiism. Initially, however, most Bábís probably saw themselves as true Shí'ís rather than as members of a separate religion.
8. There is little evidence for a contemporary crisis of meaning in Iran. Other than the possible effects of repeated military defeat at the hands of the infidel Russians, there had been no traumatic challenges to the indigenous Shí'í religious tradition. The intellectual impact of the West was as yet extremely limited.

B. Political Factors

1. The Bábís were explicitly political in their demands. The Báb's claim to Mahdihood challenged the legitimacy of all existing institutions. Their attempt to establish a theocracy entailed the displacement or cooption of the existing regime.
2. The government perceived the Bábís as insurrectionaries and suppressed the movement accordingly.
3. Although there were individual Bábís who were insurrectionary, it has not yet been established that the Bábís, as a community, were consciously and preparedly insurrectionary. If they were, then their attempt was poorly coordinated for such a well-organized movement.

4. Both Bábí radicalism and militancy and the outbreak of violence are best seen as part of a developing and interactive process.
5. Local factors were crucial. Where large Bábí communities developed, they were inevitably drawn into the complex web of communal politics.
6. Prepolitical discontent does not appear to have been a significant factor. Nonreligious forms of political protest (such as insurrection) were readily available.
7. Anti-Qájár sentiment does not appear to have become a factor until the Bábís had become alienated from the state.
8. There is no convincing evidence to support the thesis that Babism was proto-nationalist in its appeal.

C. Socio-economic Factors

1. Differential recruitment to the Bábí movement proceeded along social networks and along class lines. A wide cross-section of urban social groups was included, and in certain areas village groups were well represented. No effective contact was made with the nomadic tribes.
2. The thesis that Babism represented a form of bourgeois reformism is not well supported. Bábí laws favoring merchant interests were a late addition and do not appear to have contributed to the religion's appeal.
3. "Modernistic" social reform was not a central part of Bábí teaching, albeit that there was some amelioration in the social laws regarding women.
4. The popular radicalism of the later Bábís may be seen as reflecting eschatologically heightened, but traditional Islamic, ideas of charity, equity, and the struggle against injustice.
5. The movement may have reflected opposition to the economic and political powers of the higher ulama.

6. Divisions among Bábís between "radicals" and "conservatives" proceeded on class lines. The more affluent laity and the more established clerics were generally the more conservative.
7. Babism expanded throughout the Shí'í heartland of Iran. It was not an expression of regional sentiment.
8. Mid-nineteenth-century Iran was experiencing a profound and multi-faceted economic crisis, but in what manner this may have been linked to the emergence of the movement remains unclear.
9. The Bábís were not anti-European. The Báb commended the adoption of various aspects of European life and manners.

NOTES

1. Avery, *Modern Iran*, pp. 52–58; Bayat, *Mysticism and Dissent*, pp. 87–131; Ivanov, *Babidski Vostanii i Irane*; Keddie, "Religion and Irreligion in Early Iranian Nationalism", pp. 267–71; idem, *Roots of Revolution*, p. 49; Smith, "Millenarianism in the Babi and Baha'i Religions".

2. For an introduction to the resource mobilization perspective see McCarthy and Zald, "Resource Mobilization in Social Movements," and Zald and McCarthy, *Dynamics of Social Movements*. See also the slightly variant approaches of Beckford, *Religious Organization*, and Gerlach and Hine, *People, Power, Change*.

3. For the distinction between the utilitarian and motivational approaches to resource mobilization see Fireman and Gamson, "Utilitarian Logic," and Perrow, "The Sixties Observed."

4. The best recent accounts of the development of Babism are provided by the as yet unpublished doctoral dissertations by Amanat, "The Early Years of the Babi Movement," and MacEoin, "From Shaykhism to Babism." See also the more general account by Smith, *Babi and Baha'i Religions*, and idem, "A Sociological Study of the Babi and Baha'i Religions."

5. For an account of the "tradition of dissent," see Bayat, *Mysticism and Dissent*. For accounts of the general S̲h̲í'í context see Algar, *Religion and State in Iran*, and Momen, *Introduction to Shí'í Islam*.

6. See MacEoin, "Early S̲h̲ayk̲h̲í Reactions to the Báb"; and idem, "From Shaykhism to Babism," pp. 126–55.

7. On the term "*báb*" in S̲h̲í'í usage, see Momen, *Introduction to Shi'i Islam*, pp. 162–64. For its Bábí usage, see Amanat, "Early Years," p. 173. At least some S̲h̲ayk̲h̲ís appear to have applied the term to S̲h̲ayk̲h̲ Aḥmad and Sayyid Káẓim (see, for example, the treatise by

al-Qatíl ibn al-Karbalá'í, cited in Mázandarání, *Ẓuhúru'l-Ḥaqq*, vol. 3, pp. 512–32 *passim*).

8. See Momen, "The Trial of Mullá 'Alí Basṭámí."

9. Smelser, *Theory of Collective Behaviour*, pp. 313–81.

10. Ibid., pp. 364–79.

11. Crucially, Karím Khán was also able to control the local Shaykhí congregation and thus deny the Bábí missionaries access to its local network. By contrast, antagonistic non-Shaykhí clerics, such as Muḥammad Taqí Baraghání in Qazvin, were not able to exercise such primary control.

12. Amanat, "Early Years," p. 280.

13. Gerlach and Hine, *People, Power, Change*, pp. 183–97.

14. On the interactive nature of social movement development, see Lauer, "Social Movements," and Oberschall, "Protracted Conflict."

15. Smelser, *Theory of Collective Behaviour*, p. 367.

16. See MacEoin, "The Babi Concept of Holy War", pp. 104–6.

17. See also Smith, *Babi and Baha'i Religions*.

18. MacEoin, "The Babi Concept of Holy War." p. 112.

19. See further Smith, "Sociological Study," pp. 269–72. On the general role of the *lúṭís* see Floor, "The Lúṭís." On their role in Karbala in the 1830s and 1840s, see Cole and Momen, "Mafia, Mob and Shi'ism."

20. On organizational needs, see Burrell and Morgan, *Sociological Paradigms and Organizational Analysis*, pp. 167–81.

21. MacEoin, "The Babi Concept of Holy War," pp. 102–3.

22. Bayat, *Mysticism and Dissent*, pp. 93–94, 118–25.

23. Smith, "Millenarianism," pp. 243–48; idem, "Sociological Study," pp. 157–67.

24. On the appropriate responses to stable and unstable environments see Burrell and Morgan, *Sociological Paradigms*, pp. 171–79.

25. On the relevant desiderata, see ibid.

26. Lauer, *Social Movements and Social Change*, pp. 92–96.

27. On this group see Balyuzi, *Bahá'u'lláh*, pp. 74, 90; Browne, *Traveller's Narrative*, vol. 2, p. 323.

28. Momen, "The Trial of Mullá 'Alí Basṭámí," p. 140. We are grateful to Mr. R. Mehrabkhani for drawing to our attention an important passage in the Báb's writings that refers to this episode. In this

passage, the Báb states that he had ordered the ulama to gather at Karbala in order to await his return in order that the "Hidden Covenant" of God be publicly revealed. But that, having heard in Mecca of the rejection by the ulama of his message, he decided not to go that way in order to avoid sedition and so that no one would be harmed. (See Mehrabkhani "Some Notes on Fundamental Principles" in *Bahá'í Studies Bulletin*, p. 40.)

29. On *mubáhalih* challenges, see MacEoin, "The Babi Concept of Holy War," pp. 109–10.

30. We are following here Weber's distinction between traditional, rational-legal, and charismatic bases of legitimacy. See Weber, *Economy and Society*, pp. 212–45.

31. On the range of "charismatic options" in nineteenth-century Iranian Shiism, see MacEoin, "Changes in Charismatic Authority."

32. On the Báb's validation of his claims, see Smith, "Sociological Study," pp. 125–28; idem, *Babi and Baha'i Religions*.

33. The financial basis of Babism has not yet been researched.

34. On Shaykh Sa'íd Hindí, the disciple who was delegated to proceed to India, see Nabíl, *Dawn-Breakers*, pp. 588–89. There is as yet no further information as to this man's activities.

35. Nabíl, *Dawn-Breakers*, p. 123. See MacEoin, "Hierarchy, Authority and Eschatology," pp. 119–122. (This volume.)

36. MacEoin, ibid.

37. On commitment mechanisms, see Kanter, *Commitment and Community*. See also Gerlach and Hine, *People, Power, Change*, pp. 99–158.

38. MacEoin, "Ritual and Semi-ritual Observances," pp. 4–7.

39. MacEoin, "From Shaykhism to Babism," pp. 205–6.

40. Ibid., pp. 203–5.

41. On the local nature of recruitment see Lofland and Jamison, "Social Movement Locals."

42. Gerlach and Hine, *People, Power, Change*, pp. 33–78.

43. Nabíl, *Dawn-Breakers*, p. 126.

44. The general role and status of the leading disciples are described in Smith, "Sociological Study," pp. 130–33, 155–57; idem, *Babi and Baha'i Religions*.

45. See for example Gerlach and Hine, *People, Power, Change*,

pp. 79–97; and Snow et al., "Social Networks and Social Movements."

46. Lofland and Skonovd, "Conversion Motifs."

47. See for example the accounts given by Nabíl in *Dawn-Breakers* for the Letters of the Living (pp. 52–71), Ḥujjat (pp. 178–79), and Vaḥíd (pp. 171–76).

48. For example compare the several accounts of Mullá Ḥusayn's conversion all purporting to derive from him: see Browne, *Taríkh-i-Jadíd,* pp. 33–39; Muhammad, "Some New Notes on Babism," pp. 447–49; Nabíl, *Dawn-Breakers,* pp. 52–68.

49. For a description of the Báb's possible instructions to his disciples see Momen, "The Trial of Mullá 'Alí Basṭámí," p. 115.

50. MacEoin, "From Shaykhism to Babism." p. 187.

51. See for example statements regarding the conversions of Mullá Aḥmad Mu'allim, Ḥájí Muḥammad Iṣfahání, Mírzá Muḥammad 'Alí Nahrí, and Mullá Zaynu'l-'Ábidín Sháhmírzádí (Mázandarání, *Ẓuhúru'l-Ḥaqq,* vol. 3, pp. 158, 101, 97, 200 respectively). See also those of Mullá Muḥammad Ṣádiq Muqaddas (Nabíl, *Dawn-Breakers,* p. 100), Ḥájí Rasúl Qazvíní (Samandar, *Taríkh,* pp. 16–17), and Sayyid Javád Karbalá'í (Balyuzi, *The Báb,* pp. 37–38). Karbalá'í had known the Báb since childhood.

52. Personal communication of material to be presented in a forthcoming book by Abú'l-Qásim Afnán.

53. Mázandarání, *Ẓuhúru'l-Ḥaqq,* vol. 3, p. 301.

54. Ibid., p. 155n.

55. On Vaḥíd and Ḥujjat see Browne, *Taríkh-i-Jadíd,* pp. 111–15, 135–41, 349–51; idem, "Personal Reminiscences," pp. 770–80; and Nabíl, *Dawn-Breakers,* pp. 171–79, 465–68, 475–81, 529–34.

56. For a recent account of these communal factions see Mirajafari, "The Haydarí-Ni'matí Conflicts in Iran."

57. Amanat, "Early Years," pp. 87–88, 303–305; Mázandarání, *Ẓuhúru'l-Ḥaqq,* vol. 3, pp. 406–7.

58. Amanat, "Early Years," p. 278–83.

59. Of the 53 Isfahanis identified as being amongst the participants of Shaykh Tabarsi, 19 are known to have been *aṣnáf*. These constituted almost half the *aṣnáf* at Ṭabarsí. (Momen, "Social Basis," p. 162).

60. Marx and Wood, "Theory and Research in Collective Behaviour," pp. 382–84.

61. Gerlach and Hine, *People, Power, Change*, pp. 159–82.

62. Borhek and Curtis, *A Sociology of Belief*, pp. 111–21; Snow and Machalek, "Second Thoughts on the Presumed Fragility of Unconventional Beliefs," pp. 31–35.

63. Gerlach and Hine, *People, Power, Change*, pp. 165–66.

64. Ibid., 169–71.

65. On these and other S͟hí'í and Bábí motifs, see Smith, "Motif Research"; idem, "Sociological Study," pp. 96–102, 117–35, 169–83.

66. On the appeal of charismatic authority, see MacEoin, "Changes in Charismatic Authority." On the popular religiosity of the time, see Amanat, "Early Years," pp. 56–99.

67. Amanat, ibid., pp. 75–79. On S͟hí'í mahdist speculation in India in this period see Cole, "Imami Shi'ism," pp. 348–49.

68. On the sack of Karbala see Cole and Momen, "Mafia, Mob and Shi'ism in Iraq."

69. Prominent S͟hayk͟hí adventists included Mullá Yúsuf Ardibílí and Ḥájí Asadu'lláh Saysání. Their opponents included the S͟hayk͟hí leaders Karím K͟hán, S͟hayk͟h Ḥasan Gawhar and Mullá Muḥammad Mamaqání. See Mázandarání, *Ẓuhúru'l-Ḥaqq*, vol. 3, pp. 44–46, 49–50.

70. Smith, "Sociological Study," pp. 118–19.

71. MacEoin, "Early S͟hayk͟hí Reactions," p. 18.

72. See Smith, "Sociological Study," pp. 172–74; idem, *Babi and Baha'i Religions*.

73. Nabíl, *Dawn-Breakers*, pp. 324–25.

74. Mázandarání, *Ẓuhúru'l-Ḥaqq*, vol. 3, p. 42.

75. See Smith, "A Note on Babi and Baha'i Numbers in Iran."

76. MacEoin, "A Note on the Number of Babi and Baha'i Martyrs in Iran."

77. The estimates for the number of Bábís are taken from Momen, "Social Basis," pp. 166–70. The population estimate for Zanjan (1867) is taken from Issawi (ed.), *The Economic History of Iran*, p. 28. That for Nayriz (1871) is taken from Lovett, "Surveys on the Road from Shiraz to Bam."

78. On numbers in Baghdad see Mázandarání, *Ẓuhúru'l-Ḥaqq*,

vol. 3, p. 317. On those in Tehran see Momen, *Babi and Baha'i Religions*, p. 6. By the 1860s some 6 percent of the population of Tehran may have been Bábís (i.e., c. 5,000 out of 80,000, Gobineau, *Religions et Philosophies* p. 272).

79. Momen, "Social Basis." See also Smith, "Sociological Study," pp. 238–45.

80. On the one Zoroastrian, see Mázandarání, *Ẓuhúru'l-Ḥaqq*, vol. 3, p. 395n. There were six Jewish converts in Turbat-i Haydari in about 1850 and a number of Jewish converts in Baghdad. There may also have been some Christian converts in Baghdad. The whole question will be dealt with in more detail in a forthcoming Ph.D. thesis by Stephen Lambden at the University of Newcastle, England.

81. Ahlu'l-Ḥaqq converts included Muḥammad Beg Chapárchí, the Báb's escort from Isfahan to Tabriz (Browne, *Nuqṭatu'l-Káf*, p. 124; idem, *Taríkh-i-Jadíd*, p. 217), and three residents of Qazvin, one a Kurdish tribal leader (Mázandarání, *Ẓuhúru'l-Ḥaqq*, vol. 3, pp. 385).

82. There are a wide range of variant estimates. See Momen, "Social Basis," p. 174; and Smith, "Sociological Study," p. 233.

83. This modifies an earlier research statement by Momen, "Social Basis," pp. 166, 173.

84. Mázandarání, *Ẓuhúru'l-Ḥaqq*, vol. 3, pp. 301, 386.

85. For a more detailed account of these divisions see Smith, "Sociological Study." pp. 231–37.

86. Momen, "Social Basis," pp. 173–75.

87. On the Qájár princesses, see Ávárih, *Kawákibu'd-Durriyyih*, vol. 1, pp. 114, 117–8.

88. Browne, "Personal Reminiscences of the Bábí Insurrection at Zanjan"; Momen, "Social Basis," p. 170.

89. Smith, *Babi and Baha'i Religions*.

90. For a more detailed discussion see Smith, "Sociological Study," pp. 245–50.

91. Avery, *Modern Iran*, p. 53.

BIBLIOGRAPHY

Algar, Hamid, *Religion and State in Iran, 1785–1906: The Role of the Ulama in the Qajar Period*. Berkeley and Los Angeles: University of California Press, 1969.

Amanat, Abbas. "The Early Years of the Babi Movement: Background and Development." D. Phil. dissertation, University of Oxford, 1981.

Ávárih, 'Abdu'l-Ḥusayn. *al-Kawákibu'd-Durriyyih*. 2 vols. Cairo: Matba'a Sa'áda, 1342(1924).

Avery, Peter W.. *Modern Iran*. London: Benn, 1965.

Baghdádí, Muṣṭafá. *Risála Amriyya*. Cairo: Matba'a Sa'áda, 1919.

Balyuzi, Hasan M. *The Báb: the Herald of the Day of Days*. Oxford: George Ronald, 1973.

______ . *Bahá'u'lláh: The King of Glory*. Oxford: George Ronald, 1980.

Bayat, Mangol. *Mysticism and Dissent: Socioreligious Thought in Qajar Iran*. Syracuse, N. Y.: Syracuse University Press, 1982.

Beckford, James A., *Religious Organization: A Trend Report and Bibliography*. *Current Sociology*, 21 (1973), No. 2.

Browne, Edward G. (ed. and trans.) *The Táríkh-i-Jadíd or New History of Mírzá 'Alí Muḥammad the Báb*. Cambridge: Cambridge University Press, 1893.

______ . (ed.) *Kitáb-i-Nuqṭatu'l-Káf*. E. J. W. Gibb Memorial Series, Vol. 15. Leyden: E. J. Brill and London: Luzac, 1910.

______ . (trans.) "Personal Reminiscences of the Bábí Insurrecton at Zanjan in 1850", *Journal of the Royal Asiatic Society*, 29 (1897) pp. 761–827.

______ . (ed. and trans.) *A Traveller's Narrative Written to Illustrate the Episode of the Báb*. 2 vols. Cambridge University Press, 1891.

Borhek, James T. and Curtis, Richard F. *A Sociology of Belief*. New York: John Wiley, 1975.

Burrell, Gibson and Morgan, Gareth. *Sociological Paradigms and Organisational Analysis: Elements of the Sociology of Corporate Life*. London: Heinemann, 1979.

Cole, Juan R. "Imami Shi'ism from Iran to North India, 1722–1856: State, Society and Clerical Ideology in Awadh." Ph.D. dissertation, University of California, Los Angeles, 1984.

Cole, Juan R. and Momen Moojan, "Mafia, Mob and Shi'ism in Iraq: The Rebellion of Ottoman Karbala, 1824–43," *Past and Present*, No. 112 (August 1986) pp. 112–43.

Fireman, Bruce and Gamson, William A. "Utilitarian Logic in the Mobilization Perspective". In *The Dynamics of Social Movements*, ed. M. N. Zald and J. D. McCarthy (Cambridge, Mass.: Winthrop, 1979) pp. 8–44.

Floor, W. M. "The *Lúṭís*: A Social Phenomena in Qájár Persia". *Die Welt des Islams* (n.s.), 13 (1971) pp. 103–20.

Gazetteer of Persia. 4 vols., prepared by the General Staff, Headquarters. Simla, India: Government Press, 1910.

Gerlach, Luther P. and Hine, V. H. *People, Power, Change: Movements of Social Transformation*. Indianapolis, Ind.: Bobbs-Merrill, 1970.

Gobineau, Joseph Arthur, Comte de. *Religions et philosophies dans l'asie centrale*. 10th ed. Paris: Gallimard, 1957 (1st published 1865).

Halliday, Fred. *Iran: Dictatorship and Development*. Harmondsworth: Penguin Books, 1979.

Issawi, Charles (ed.). *The Economic History of Iran. 1800–1914*. Chicago and London: University of Chicago Press, 1971.

Ivanov, M. S. *Babidski Vostanii i Irane, 1848–1852*. Moscow: Trudy Instituta Vostok-vedeniya, 1939.

Kanter, Rosabeth Moss. *Commitment and Community: Communes and Utopias in Sociological Perspective*. Cambridge, Mass.: Harvard University Press, 1972.

Keddie, Nikki R. *Roots of Revolution*, (with a section by Yann Richard). New Haven and London: Yale University Press, 1981.

______ . "Religion and Irreligion in Early Iranian Nationalism," *Comparative Studies in Society and History*, 4 (1962) pp. 265–295.

Lauer, Robert H., "Social Movements: An Interactionist Analysis." *Sociological Quarterly* 13 (1972) 315–28.

______ . (ed.) *Social Movements and Social Change*. Carbondale and Edwardsville, Ill.: Southern Illinois University Press, 1976.

Lofland, John and Jamison, Michael. "Social Movement Locals: Modal Member Structures." *Sociological Analysis* 45 (1984) pp. 115–29.

Lofland, John and Skonovd, Norman, "Conversion Motifs." *Journal for the Scientific Study of Religion* 20 (1981) pp. 373–85.

Lovett, Beresford. "Surveys on the Road from Shiraz to Bam," *Journal of the Royal Geographical Society*, 42 (1872) pp. 202–12.

McCarthy, John D. and Zald, M. N. "Resource Mobilization and Social Movements: A Partial Theory." *American Journal of Sociology* 82 (1977) pp. 1212–39.

MacEoin, Denis. "A Note on the Numbers of Babi and Baha'i Martyrs in Iran". *Bahá'í Studies Bulletin*, vol. 2, no. 2 (1983) pp. 84–88.

______. "Changes in Charismatic Authority in Qajar Shi'ism". In *Qajar Iran: Political, Social and Cultural Change, 1800–1925*, ed. E. Bosworth and C. Hillenbrand, pp. 148–76. Edinburgh University Press, 1984.

______. "Early Shaykhí Reactions to the Báb and His Claims". In *Studies in Babi and Baha'i History, Vol. 1*, ed. M. Momen, pp. 1–47. Los Angeles: Kalimát Press, 1982.

______. "From Shaykhism to Babism: A Study in Charismatic Renewal in Shí'í Islam". Ph.D. dissertation. University of Cambridge, 1979.

______. "Hierarchy, Authority and Eschatology in Early Bábí Thought." This volume.

______. "Ritual and Semi-ritual Observances in Babism and Baha'-ism". Revision of a paper presented at the fourth Baha'i Studies Seminar, University of Lancaster, 12–13 April 1980.

______. "The Babi Concept of Holy War". *Religion*, 12 (1982), pp. 92–129.

Marx, Gary T. and Wood, J. L., "Strands of Theory and Research in Collective Behavior". *Annual Review of Sociology* 1 (1975): 363–428.

Mázandaránı́, Fáḍil, *Kitáb-i Ẓuhúru'l-Ḥaqq*, vol. 3. Tehran, n.d., n.p.

Meer Hasan Ali, Mrs. *Observations on the Musulmans of India*. Reprinted Karachi: Oxford University Press, 1974.

Mehrabkhani, Ruhullah. "Some Notes on Fundamental Principles: Western Scholarship and the Religion of the Báb." *Bahá'í Studies Bulletin*, vol. 2, no. 4 (1984) pp. 22–43.

Mirjafari, Hossein. "The Ḥaydarí-Ni'matí Conflicts in Iran." Trans. and adapted J. R. Parry. *Iranian Studies*, 12 (1979) pp. 135–62.

Momen, Moojan. *The Bábí and Bahá'í Religions, 1844–1944; Some Contemporary Western Accounts*. Oxford: George Ronald, 1981.

______. *An Introduction to Shi'i Islam: The History and Doctrines of Twelver Shi'ism*. Oxford: George Ronald, and New Haven and London: Yale University Press, 1985.

______. "Early Relations Between Christian Missionaries and the Bábí and Bahá'í Communities," *Studies in Bábí and Bábí History*,

Vol. 1, ed. M. Momen (Los Angeles: Kalimát Press, 1982), pp. 48–82.

______. "The Social Basis of the Bábí Upheavals in Iran (1848–53): A Preliminary Analysis", *International Journal of Middle East Studies,* Vol. 15 (1983) pp. 157–183.

______. "The Trial of Mullá 'Alí Basṭámí: A Combined Sunní-Shí'í Fatwá Against the Báb", *Iran,* Vol. 20 (1982) pp. 113–143.

Muhammad, Khan Bahadur Agha Mirza. "Some New Notes on Babism," *Journal of the Royal Asiatic Society* (1927) pp. 442–70.

Nabíl (Muḥammad Zarandí). *The Dawn-Breakers: Nabíl's Narrative of the Early Days of the Bahá'í Revelation.* Trans. and ed. Shoghi Effendi. Wilmette, Ill.: Bahá'í Publishing Trust, 1932.

Oberschall, Anthony. "Protracted Conflict." In *The Dynamics of Social Movements,* ed. M. N. Zald and J. D. McCarthy, pp. 45–70. Cambridge, Mass.: Winthrop, 1979.

Perrow, Charles, "The Sixties Observed." In *The Dynamics of Social Movements,* ed. M. N. Zald and J. D. McCarthy, pp. 192–211. Cambridge Mass.: Winthrop, 1979.

Samandar, Shaykh Káẓim. *Táríkh-i Samandar.* Tehran: Mu'assisih-i Millí Maṭbú'át-i Amrí, 131 *Badí'* (1974).

Smelser, Neil J. *Theory of Collective Behaviour.* London: Routledge and Kegan Paul, 1962.

Smith, Peter. "A Note on Babi and Baha'i Numbers in Iran." *Iranian Studies.* 17 (1984) pp. 295–301.

______. "A Sociological Study of the Babi and Baha'i Religions." Ph.D. dissertation, University of Lancaster, 1982.

______. "Millenarianism in the Babi and Baha'i Religions." In *Millennialism and Charisma,* ed. R. Wallis, pp. 231–83. Belfast: The Queen's University, 1982.

______. "Motif Research: Peter Berger and the Baha'i Faith." *Religion,* 8 (1978) pp. 210–34.

______. *The Babi and Baha'i Religions: From Messianic Shi'ism to a World Religion.* Cambridge University Press, 1986.

Snow, David A. and Machalek, Richard. "Second Thoughts on the Presumed Fragility of Unconventional Beliefs." In *Of Gods and Men,* ed. E. Barker, pp. 25–44. Macon, Ga.: Mercer University Press, 1983.

Snow, David A., Zurcher, Louis A., and Ekland-Olson, Sheldon. "Social Networks and Social Movements: A Microstructural Approach to Differential Recruitment". *American Sociological Review* 45 (1980) pp. 87–801.

Weber, Max. *Economy and Society: An Outline of Interpretive Sociology*, 2 vols. ed. G. Roth and C. Wittich. Berkeley and Los Angeles: University of California Press, 1978.

Zald, Mayer N. and McCarthy, J. D. (eds.) *The Dynamics of Social Movements: Resource Mobilization, Social Control, and Tactics.* Cambridge, Mass.: Winthrop, 1979.

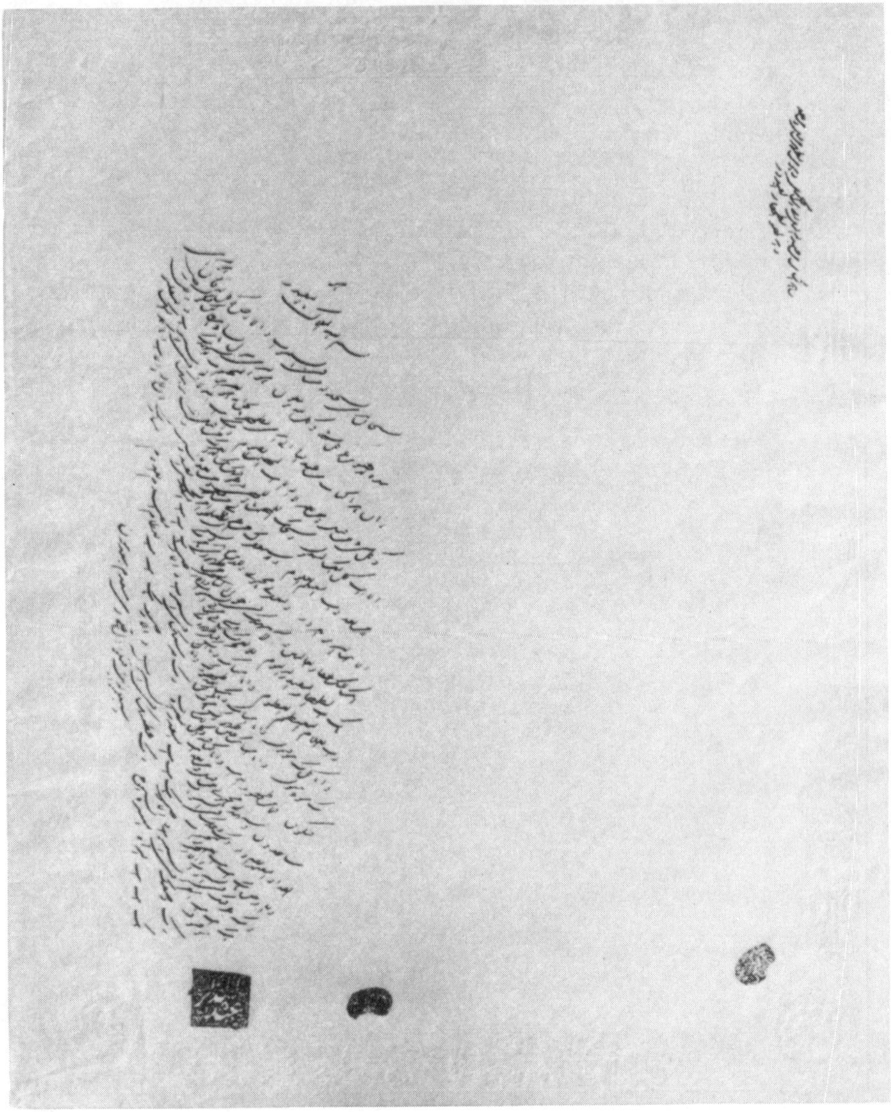

A TABLET OF THE BÁB
to "him whom God shall manifest."

HIERARCHY, AUTHORITY AND ESCHATOLOGY IN EARLY BÁBÍ THOUGHT

by Denis MacEoin

In recent years, the history of the early development of the Bábí movement has undergone extensive and often trenchant rewriting at the hands of several scholars, including the present writer.[1] There is still much work to be done, but there can be no doubt that a great deal of light has already been shed on areas not long ago regarded as impossibly dark. Problems have been usefully identified in topics long considered settled beyond any need for discussion. We now possess clear pictures, for example, of the main features in the transition from Shaykhism to early Babism, of the Báb's early career and claims, of the progress of the Bábí uprisings after 1848, or of the writing and dissemination of the Bábí scriptural canon. Advances have been made not only in the realm of factual data, which has been greatly expanded by numerous discoveries, but, more importantly, in the field of interpretative historiography, with the fresh analysis of both familiar and unfamiliar material.

There can be little doubt, however, that one period of Bábí history continues to stand out as unrelievedly obscure, namely the years between the execution of the Báb in 1850, and the emergence of distinct Bahá'í and Azalí factions within the Bábí exile community in Edirne about 1866, and subsequently in Iran. This period has for a long time been all but passed over by historians as a time of confusion, anarchy, and deep doctrinal division within Babism for which virtually no documentary evidence exists that might enable us to reconstruct its essential details. Between 1848 and 1852, the Bábí community of Iran had suffered serious losses in the course of clashes between adherents of the sect and the population at large. Between two and three thousand Bábís[2] died violently in this period, including the Báb himself and all but a handful of the intellectual leadership of the movement. After the abortive attempt on Náṣiru'l-Dín Sh͟áh's life in August 1852, the survivors (a small number in terms of active affiliation with the movement) either recanted, went underground, practised dissimulation (*taqiyya*), or chose to go into exile outside Iran.

The effects of this rapid disintegration of an already little-organized community (if community it can be called) were, from the point of view of the later historian, quite devastating. Numerous documents, particularly letters, were lost, destroyed, or stolen.[3] Among the most serious casualties were undoubtedly works by the leading figures of the Bábí hierarchy who perished in the uprisings at Sh͟ayk͟h Ṭabarsí, Nayríz, and Zanján. To make matters worse, fear of discovery led the Bábís of this period to adopt a deliberately enigmatic and idiosyncratic style that now requires considerable effort and ingenuity to decipher, with the result that many materials that have survived the tribulations of those years may often present as many obfuscations as they do glimmers of light.

And yet this is without question a period of the most extreme importance, both as a postscript to the short-lived experiment of primitive Babism and as a preamble to the later reconstructions of the movement in its Azalí and Bahá'í versions. Unfortunately, it is precisely the emergence of Azalí and Bahá'í Babism that renders the task of the historian unusually arduous and confronts him with serious problems of research and interpretation. Both parties to the later dispute looked back to the earlier period, particularly the years immediately following the death of the Báb and the transfer of the headquarters of the sect to Baghdad, with visions much clouded by the demands of contemporary polemic or ex-post facto justification of current theological positions and concepts of authority. The polarization of Azalís and Bahá'ís resulted in the rapid displacement of any serious alternative definitions of Bábí orthodoxy. And, since we possess very few manuscript materials from the intermediate period, we are forced to rely almost exclusively on documents reflecting, usually quite strongly, the sectarian biases of the two opposing groups. It is, quite frankly, often impossible for the historian to choose between one or the other version of the same events. Very little corroboratory evidence is ever produced by either side, and there are almost no independent sources to which one may have recourse.

Nevertheless, it seems to me that the main outline of events and, to a lesser extent, doctrines may be reconstructed without serious prejudice to either side of the dispute. If we are willing to ignore such questions as "who was right?" or "who was wrong?," we can, I think, state what happened during this period and, as far as is possible, suggest why.

Before the main features of this period can be studied, however, there is a pressing need for a survey of certain doctrinal issues from the early years of the movement. It is the aim of this paper to provide such a survey, both for its own interest and as preparation for a future study of the later period.

EARLY THEOPHANIC AND QUASI-THEOPHANIC CLAIMS TO AUTHORITY

It will be useful to begin our investigations with a brief examination of the nature of religious claims in the early period and a survey of the later theories of the Báb that can be shown to have influenced the tone and direction of subsequent speculations. Doctrinally speaking, Babism is a notoriously difficult movement to define. There were important shifts in belief and practice within the space of very few years, coupled with significant differences in the doctrines promulgated by various sections of the Bábí leadership, not to mention the innumerable obscurities and vaguenesses of even the most reliable texts. I have discussed in detail elsewhere[4] the early claims of Sayyid 'Alí Muḥammad, the Báb himself and will not return to that question here. Suffice to say that there is ample evidence that for several years he regarded himself and was regarded by his followers as the *báb*, or representative on earth of the hidden Twelfth Imám, whose appearance in 1845 was imminently expected by all the first Bábís. Exactly how his claims developed after that is not entirely clear. Even at the earliest period, there is evidence that the Báb claimed for himself and his writings a level of inspirational authority well above that normally associated with the role of *bábu'l-imám*. This is not to suggest that he entertained notions of a more exalted status for himself at this point, merely that the function of *bábiyya* (or *niyába*) as he understood and expressed it involved the ability to reveal inspired verses and to possess innate knowledge. As I have indicated elsewhere,[5] it was the Báb's status as a source of pure knowledge more than anything else that attracted followers to him at this time.

A Bahá'í writer, Sayyid Mahdí Dahají, basing his remarks somewhat loosely on an important passage of the *Dalá'il-i sab'a* (seven proofs), has put forward the idea that, in the first year, Sayyid 'Alí Muḥammad referred to himself as "the gate of God" (*bábu'lláh*), in the second year as "the remembrance" (*dhikr*), in the third as "the proof" (*ḥujja*), in the fourth as "another name," and in the fifth as the Qá'im in person.[6] Although based on the Báb's own application of part of a tradition of the Imám 'Alí (*ḥadíth Kumayl*) to each of the first five years of his career, such a picture of a gradual "unfoldment" of the Báb's claims is, however, based largely on polemical considerations.[7] The simultaneous use of terms such as *báb*, *dhikr*, and *ḥujja* is well attested from the earliest period,[8] and there is no evidence of major changes in emphasis (apart from a period of dissimulation [*taqiyya*] in 1845, when he renounced all claims) during the first five years of the Báb's career.

The Báb himself refers more than once to the radical shift that took place at the end of this period. In several passages of the *Kitáb-i panj sha'n* (Book of five proofs), he states that he revealed himself (or God revealed him) in the station of "gatehood" (*bábiyya*) (*fi 'l-abwáb; bi-ismi abwábiyyatika*, sic) for four years, whereupon he appeared as the promised Qá'im (*bi-ismi qá'imiyyatika; bi-ismi 'l-maqṣúdiyya al-maw'údiyya*).[9] We possess no exact date for the initial proclamation of *qá'imiyya* by the Báb, but there is sufficient evidence to place this event (which was marked by the issue of a letter sent to Mullá Shaykh 'Alí Turshízí, 'Aẓím)[10] in the later part of the Báb's confinement in the fortress of Máků, that is in the early months of 1848.[11] In the Persian *Bayán*, the Báb states that when the return of all that had been created in the Qur'án and the beginning of the creation of all things in the Bayán occurred, his dwelling-place was Mákú (*arḍ-i ism-i básiṭ*).[12] The Báb's claim to be the Qá'im was not, however, restricted to the adoption of the simple messianic role outlined for the Twelfth Imám in Shí'í prophetic literature, but also involved the assumption of theophanic status coupled with prophetic office as the inaugurator of a new religious dispensation abrogatory of Islam.[13]

In developing the elaborate theory of theophanies and religious cycles around which all of his later thinking revolves, the Báb made use of a series of metaphysical concepts common to the main Shí'í sects. But while many of his ideas and the forms in which they are cast find important and sometimes detailed parallels in Ismá'ílí and Ḥurúfí thought in particular, it is not, I think, necessary to look for direct influences from these sources. The main themes and terms are all to be found in Twelver Shí'í literature, including, of course, the works of Shaykh Aḥmad ibn Zayn al-Dín al-Aḥsá'í. The root of the Báb's doctrine lies in the belief that the divine or eternal essence (*dhát-i iláhí, dhát-i azal*) is wholly unknowable and inaccessible to human beings,[14] but since the purpose of the creation is for men to know and love God,[15] it is necessary for the creator to reveal himself to them in a form appropriate to their condition: "in every dispensation, he makes himself known through his own creation."[16] Although the Báb employs the conventional Islamic terminology of prophet and messenger (*nabí; rasúl* [frequently]; *payghámbar*),[17] and adopts a schema of regularly-spaced prophetic revelations (among which those of Moses, David, Jesus, and Muḥammad stand out),[18] he is less concerned with the role of the prophets as divinely-inspired legislators (*shári'ún*) than with their function as theophanic representations of the divinity on earth.

The Báb's doctrine of theophanies is expressed chiefly through the Arabic root *ẓhr* (to become visible, manifest), which appears in a number of related technical terms.[19] *Ẓuhúr* (manifestation) is the self-revelation of God to his creation and also the period during which he is thus manifest. It is contrasted with *buṭún* (concealment), the state of God's invisibility to men and the period between one prophet and the next, during which he is hidden to men. *Maẓhar* is the term most often used to describe the place of this revelation, the created being in whom the Divinity manifests himself to other created beings. This *maẓhar* is in one sense the locus in which God himself is manifested to men: "the hidden reality of the divine unity (*ghaybu' l-tawḥíd*) is only affirmed through that which is revealed in the outward aspect (*ẓáhir*) of the messenger";[20] "know that in each *ẓuhúr*, he has been and is the representative (*qá'im maqám*) of the eternal and hidden essence (*dhát-i ghayb-ı azal*)";[21] "bear witness that God, may his praise be glorified, makes himself known to his creation in the place of manifestation (*maẓhar*) of his own self, for whenever men have recognized God, their Lord, their recognition of him has only been attained through what their prophet caused them to know."[22] In the Persian Bayán, the appearance of the Báb (as the *nuqṭa*, Point) is thus equated with the revelation of God himself: "the self-revelation of God (*ẓuhúru'lláh*), which is the self-revelation of the Point of the Bayán;[23] 'the seat of the Point, who is the place of manifestation of Lordship."[24]

It is emphasized by the Báb, however, that the divine essence as such is not manifested directly to men.[25] What appears in the manifestations (*maẓáhir*) is the Primal Will (*al-mashí'a al-awwaliyya*), itself created by God *ex nihilo*: "That command (i.e., the place of manifestation) is not the eternal and hidden essence, but is a Will that was created through and for himself out of nothing.[26] In the Persian Bayán, the Báb writes that "there has never been nor will there ever be either revelation or concealment for the eternal Essence in himself, nor can any other thing either manifest or conceal him. . . . Instead, he created the Primal Will in the same way that he created all things by himself, creating it likewise by himself and all things (other than it) by it, and he related it to himself in its exaltation and sublimity. . . . From the beginning that has no begining to the end that has no end, there has ever been but a single Will which has shone forth in every age in a manifestation (*ẓuhúr*)."[27]

Although the Primal Will is single, it appears in each age in a different person, whose physical form is variously expressed as its "throne" (*'arsh*),[28] "seat" (*kursí*),[29] "temple" (*haykal*),[30] "mirror" (*mir'át* [the Will being described as the sun appearing in it]),[31] or simple place of manifestation (*maẓhar*).[32] The Will itself in its manifest form is referred to by a variety of titles, including the Tree of Reality (*shajaratu'l-ḥaqíqa*),[33] or, most commonly, Primal Point (*nuqṭay-i úlá*).[36] It is from this Point that all things have been originated[37] and all the prophets and revealed books sent down.[38]

As in the case of the Imáms in Shí'í Islam, the exact status of the manifestation (*maẓhar*) is often blurred. Just as the Imáms are referred to as God's "outward form amidst his creation" (*ẓáhiruhu fí khalqihi*),[39] so the Báb speaks of the *maẓhar* as the "throne of God's revelation" (*'arsh ẓuhúri'lláh*),[40] the "representative of the divine essence,"[41] or the "locus of the manifestation of his self' (*maẓhar nafsihi*).[42] In the same way that knowledge of the Imáms is knowledge of God[43] (the latter being impossible without the former) the *maẓáhir* are, for the Báb, the only means whereby men may know their creator.[44] God has made the manifestation "the mirror of his self. . . , in which nothing is seen but God."[45]

The human locus of God's appearance is, therefore, an essentially ambivalent creature. Outwardly, he is merely a mortal man: "what your eyes behold of the outward form of the thrones is but a handful of clay. . . . If you did not look at what is (manifested) in them, there would be nothing (to see) but earth in its own place."[46] Inwardly, however, these beings are divine: "Do not behold the thrones in respect of what they are in themselves, for I have shown you that they originate as a drop of sperm and return as a handful of clay. Instead, look within them, inasmuch as God has manifested himself (*tajallá*) to them and through them."[47] Expressed differently, "the inward aspect (*báṭin*) of the prophets is the words 'no god is there but God,' while their outward aspect (*ẓáhir*) is the mention of their own selves in each *ẓuhúr* through what is manifested from them."[48] It is because of this difference that the statements of the prophets differ one from the other, itself the main cause of religious disunity.[49] Otherwise, they are all one,[50] being compared frequently to a single sun that appears on different days or in different mirrors.[51] The number of these places of manifestation is incalculable,[52] nor can they be said to have any beginning or end.[53]

This much is, I think, relatively straightforward. But the Báb's doctrine is, in fact, rather more complex than this and involves several important elements that were to influence markedly the development of the religion after his death. The existence of a problem can already be seen in the Shí'í doctrine of the Imáms. Not only are the Imáms regarded as identical one with another,[54] they are also identical in essence with the major prophet figures of the past: "I," says 'Alí in one tradition, "am Adam, I am Noah, I am Abraham, I am Moses, I am Jesus, I am Muḥammad; I move through the forms as I wish—whoso has seen me has seen them, and whoso has seen them has seen me."[55] I do not wish to enter here into a discussion of what became a subtle problem for later Shí'í doctrine, namely the relationship between Imám and prophet,[56] merely to draw attention to an apparent dichotomy between the status of the Imáms as successors of the prophet Muḥammad and their identification with the prophets of the past. This dichotomy is to some extent resolved through the doctrine of *ḥujjiyya*, whereby it is maintained that there must always be on earth a proof (*ḥujja*) from God to men, be it a prophet or Imám.[57]

Nevertheless something of a problem remains, for it is, on the one hand, an established Shí'í doctrine that the pleroma of Muḥammad and the twelve Imáms was created before and is superior to all other beings, including earlier prophets, who were indeed created after them from the residue of their light[58] and who can only approach God through them.[59] They are often described in terms that make them responsible for the inspiration and instruction of even the major prophets of the past: "The Commander of the Faithful said to Salmán and Abú Dharr: 'I am al-Khiḍr, the teacher of Moses: I am the teacher of David and Solomon,'"[60] or in terms that place them in a relationship to former prophets comparable to that of God: "He ('Alí) said: 'I am the one who carried Noah in the Ark at the command of my Lord; I am the one who brought Jonah out of the belly of the fish by the permission of my Lord; I am the one who caused Moses the son of 'Imrán to pass (over the Red Sea) at the command of my Lord; I am the one who brought Abraham from the fire by the permission of my Lord. . . .'"[61] On the other hand, they are identified, not only with these prophets, but also with their successors: "Whoso wishes to behold Adam and Seth, behold I am Adam and Seth; whoso wishes to behold Noah and his son Shem, behold I am Noah and Shem; whoso wishes to behold Abraham and Ishmael, behold I am Abraham and Ishmael; whoso wishes to behold Moses and Joshua, behold I am Moses and Joshua; whoso wishes to behold Jesus and Simon, behold I am Jesus and Simon.'"[62] To turn this equation around, Seth, Shem, Ishmael, Joshua, and Simon are (in this instance) the Twelfth Imám, who is, in turn, the teacher of the prophets and a locus of the Primal Will.

Now this problem, like any other of its kind, can be and has been solved by the ingenuity of theologians, but I do not wish to enter into an account of that here. What is of interest in terms of the present paper is that the paradoxes involved in these concepts retained their basic dynamism throughout the early Bábí period and became critical causes of uncertainty in the Baghdad years. To begin with, there were the numerous tensions implicit in the varying statements of the Báb, not only with respect to his changing status—from "a servant" chosen to be the gate and representative of the hidden Imám, to the Qá'im, to the place of manifestation of the divinity and the promulgator of a new *sharí'a* after that of Islam, but also with respect to each one of these roles in its different modes and emphases. Secondly, the Báb sought to endow his immediate followers, primarily the eighteen "Letters of the Living" (*ḥurúfu'l-ḥayy*) or "precursors" (*sábiqún*), with a status that made them more than mere saints or intercessors between him and other believers. The Letters of the Living were "precursors," not only in the literal sense of their being the first believers in the Báb, but more importantly in their having been the first of mankind to respond to God's pre-eternal covenant in the "world of the first atom," that is, before the creation of the world.[63] Sẖí'í tradition identifies these *ṣábiqún* with Muḥammad and the Imáms (and often Fáṭima),[64] and in his later works the Báb describes the Letters of the Living explicitly as the return of the Prophet, the twelve Imáms, the four gates (*abwáb*) who succeeded the Twelfth Imám (later rejected in Bahá'í theory), and Fáṭima.[65]

The question of the status of the Letters of the Living became a crucial one for early Babism and produced considerable controversy. In 1848, the central Bábí community of Karbala in Iraq was split down the middle by a fierce argument between two factions centered on the persons of Qurratu'l-'Ayn Ṭáhirih and Mullá Aḥmad Kẖurásání respectively.[66] Kẖurásání's supporters objected particularly to the status accorded Mullá Ḥusayn Busẖrú'í and the Letters of the Living in general. Their opponents defended their position largely by extensive quotations from the Báb's writings, in which the *ḥurúfu'l-ḥayy* were extolled.[67] The details of this highly interesting but little-known debate cannot be entered into here: it is enough for our purpose to note that the pro-*ṣábiqún* faction, with its emphasis on hierarchy and obedience to charismatic authority, succeeded in forcing its opponents into the background, not only in Karbala, but throughout Iran as well.

As time went on, not only the original Letters of the Living, but later converts also were accorded exalted stations by the Báb. As his own claims became more elevated, those given to his followers rose accordingly. This development is not easy to trace with any precision, but fortunately that is not essential for our present course of enquiry. According to Muḥammad 'Alí Zunúzí, when the Báb abandoned the rank of *bábiyya* to take that of *dẖikru'lláh* (which on Dahají's reckoning would have been in the second year of his career), he gave the title of *báb* to his earliest convert, Mullá Muḥammad Ḥusayn Busẖrú'í,[68] who had already been identified by him as the return to earth of the prophet Muḥammad. This transfer of station is corroborated by the earliest Bábí history, the *Nuqṭatu'l-káf*.[69] The latter work also refers—with what degree of accuracy it is difficult to establish—to other shifts of status ascription between individual members of the Bábí hierarchy. Thus, the station of *bábiyya* was passed on Bushrú'í's death to his brother Muḥammad Ḥasan, also a Letter of the Living;[70] at Badasht, Mullá Muḥammad 'Alí Bárfurúshí, Quddús, claimed to be the return of the prophet Muḥammad, adducing in evidence of this his ability to produce verses, prayers, and homilies;[71] later, at the shrine of Shaykh Ṭabarsí, Quddús is said to have referred to Bushrú'í (originally understood to be the return of Muḥammad) as the Imám Ḥusayn.[72] More controversially, the *Nuqṭatu'l-káf* maintains that when, in the year 5, the Báb laid claim to the rank of Qá'im, "the Point of *qá'imiyya* manifested itself in the temple of his holiness the Remembrance [i.e., the Báb], who became the heaven of the (Primal) Will (*samá'-i mashiyatt*), while the earth of illumination and volition (*arḍ-i ishráq wa iráda*) was his holiness Azal (i.e., Mírzá Yaḥyá Núrí, Ṣubḥ-i Azal)."[73] In apparent —but not, as will be shown, necessarily real—contradiction to this, the same source elsewhere maintains that Quddús was himself the Qá'im and 'Alí Muḥammad his *báb*,[74] the former having advanced his claims in the fourth year after the period during which the latter had summoned men to God.[75] Quddús, it is said, made his claims independently and became the heaven of will, with the Báb the earth of volition.[76] Similarly, Quddús is described as "the origin of the point" (*aṣl-i nuqṭa*), 'Alí Muḥammad again being his *báb*. And, more confusingly, it is stated that the Báb and Quddús were both the Qá'im, in the same way that the Shí'í Imáms may all be referred to by this title.[77].

Lest these statements seem wholly idiosyncratic and be attributed to the unreliability of the *Nuqṭatu'l-káf* as a source (or indeed, be adduced as evidence of that work's unreliability), it will be worthwhile to note that there is independent corroboration of the fact that Quddús was regarded by some at least as the Qá'im (either independently of the Báb or in tandem with him and/or Mullá Ḥusayn Bushrú'í) and that he himself advanced claims of a messianic and theophanic nature. An important early history of the Shaykh Ṭabarsí siege, the *Waqáyi'-i mímiyya* (Events of the letter *mím*), consistently refers to Quddús as "the Qá'im of Jílán"[78] and cites a sermon by Mullá Ḥusayn in which he refers to Quddús as "the one whose advent you have awaited for one thousand two hundred and sixty (sic) years,"[79] a claim the latter is said to have advanced in his own behalf.[80] Another early account of the events at Shaykh Ṭabarsí, Luṭf 'Alí Mírzá Shírází's untitled history, notes, for example, that the Bábís at the shrine regarded Quddús as the point towards which prayers were to be directed and turned to him when they performed their devotions.[81]

The *Nuqṭatu'l-káf* (and, following it, the later Bahá'í *Táríkh-i Jadíd*) applies a number of Shí'í traditions to Quddús in connection with his identification as Qá'im. Among these are 'Alí's reference to events between the months Jumádá and Rajab,[82] and the prophecy that the Qá'im would be killed by a bearded Jewish woman named Sa'ída (who is identified with Quddús's executioner, the Sa'ídu'l-'Ulamá' Bárfurúshí).[83] The early attribution of this latter prophecy to Quddús and Sa'ídu'l-'Ulamá' is confirmed by its use in the same context in the *Waqáyi'-i mímiyya.*[84] Even a much later Bahá'í history, the *Táríkh-i Nabíl,* relates Quddús's arrival at the shrine of Shaykh Ṭabarsí to a well-known tradition concerning the Qá'im's arrival in Mecca and his leaning his back against the Ka'ba,[85] (a tradition which is not, curiously enough, related by Nabíl or other Bahá'í writers, as far as I know, to the Báb's pilgrimage to Mecca in

1844–5), while the number of Bábí participants in the Mázandarán conflict is given as exactly 313, the number of the companions of the Qá'im.[86]

Apart from Quddús, of course, other members of the Bábí hierarchy continued to be accorded important positions, including even that of *qá'imiyya*. Mullá Ḥusayn, as we have seen, was referred to by Quddús as the Imám Ḥusayn, an identification supported by Nabíl,[87] but is also described throughout the *Waqáyi'-i mímiyya* as the "Qá'im of Khurásán,"[88] a messianic role much enhanced in several accounts by his bearing of a black banner from Mashhad.[89] The Báb himself made it quite explicit that not only had the Prophet, the Imáms, and the *nuwwáb* (*abwáb*) returned to earth in the persons of the Letters of the Living, but other prophets and saints had reappeared in other of his followers: "The first to swear allegiance to me was Muḥammad the Prophet of God, then 'Alí, then those who were witnesses after him [i.e., the next eleven Imáms], then the Gates of Guidance, then those to whom God had accorded such grace of the prophets and holy ones and witnesses and those who believed in God and his verses."[90] This same view is expressed in a letter written by Mullá Shaykh 'Alí Turshízí, 'Aẓím (to whom the letter from which the above quotation is taken was addressed): "The Letters of the Living are true and are the tombs in which they [Muḥammad, the Imáms, and the four Bábs] have returned (*hum maráqid rujú'ihim*), and certain of the believers are the tombs of some of the prophets and saints and witnesses and holy ones; all have returned to the first life."[91] In the course of the Shaykh Ṭabarsí struggle, Quddús is said to have written a number of letters addressed to his followers in which he identified each one of them with a prophet or saint of the past. One of them, for example, is described as the return of Shaykh Aḥmad ibn Abí Ṭálib Ṭabarsí, the saint buried at the shrine itself.[92] Similarly, Zawára'í refers to the 313 companions of Quddús as *nuqabá'*,"[93] evidently a reference to the "directors" who were expected to return with the Qá'im.[94]

LATER CLAIMS OF DIVINITY

Nor was the extension of hierarchical status limited to the identification of individuals as the "return" (*raj'a*) of a particular holy figure of the past. In the last years of his career, the Báb bestowed on large numbers of his followers individual names of God numerologically equivalent to their original names. Thus, Mullá Muḥammad 'Alí Bárfurúshí was called "Quddús," Shaykh 'Alí Turshízí was "'Aẓím," Sayyid Yaḥyá Dárábí and Mírzá Yaḥyá Núrí both "Waḥíd" (the former being known as "Waḥíd-i A'ẓam," the "greater unity," the latter also being named "Azal"), Mírzá Asadu'lláh Khú'í "Dayyán," Mullá Rajab 'Alí Iṣfahání "Qahír," and so on.[95] Each such individual seems in some sense to have been understood as a manifestation of the particular attribute of God indicated by his name. It is in this sense, but with possibly wider implications, that Muḥammad 'Alí Bárfurúshí, Quddús, was called by the Báb "the last name of God" (*ismu'lláhu'l-ákhir*).[96]

Beyond this, certain individuals were seen as manifestations of the divinity in a broader and more explicit sense. One of the most compelling examples of this is the following statement of the Báb concerning Mullá Ḥusayn Bushrú'í: "And make mention of the first to believe, for if you should travel upon the Sea of Names, you will behold him to be the Primal Will, and if you should travel on the Sea of the first creation, you will behold the one who was the first to believe in him; and know that he has ever been and always will be alive. Whoever possesses might in the Bayán has become powerful through him, and whoever possesses knowledge in the Bayán has become knowledgeable through him. . . ."[97]

In an interesting passage of his "Lawḥ-i Siráj", Mírzá Ḥusayn 'Alí Núrí, Bahá'u'lláh, quotes in part and paraphrases in part words of the Báb concerning Ḥájj Sayyid Jawád Karbalá'í, in which he describes the latter as "the primal Mirror which has from all eternity reflected and will for all eternity reflect God," as "the Primal Cause" (*'illat-i awwaliyya*), and as "a prophet unto all the worlds." Bahá'u'lláh himself comments on the reference to Sayyid Jawád as the Primal Cause, saying that "this station is above all names, be they of the Essence of God (*dhátu'lláh*), or the Reality of God (*kaynú-natu'lláh*), or the Remembrance of God (*dhikru'lláh*), or the Mirror of God (*mir'átu'lláh*), for previously anyone who attributed such a station to the Prophet of God would have been declared an unbeliever, inasmuch as men believed the Primal Cause to be God Himself."[99]

As in the case of claims of *qá'imiyya*, it seem to have been Muḥammad 'Alí Bárfurúshí, Quddús, who was the Báb's chief rival in respect of claims to some form of divinity. 'Abbás Effendi, 'Abdu'l-Bahá, maintains that Quddús's commentary on the letter *ṣád* of the word *al-ṣamad* (Qur'án 112:2) which he "revealed" (*názil farmúdand*) at Shaykh Ṭabarsí, was "from beginning to end . . . (filled with the words) "Verily, I am God.'"[100] There certainly appears to be confirmatory evidence that, in the course of the Shaykh Ṭabarsí siege, Quddús did, in fact, make claims of this kind. Zawára'í refers to him as a "place of God's manifestation" (*maẓhar-i khudá*),[101] while a Bábí apostate who encountered him in Bárfurúsh after the end of the siege is said to have rebuked him with the words: "You claimed . . . that your voice was the voice of God."[102] Quddús's own claims to divine status for himself are reinforced by many of the Báb's statements about him. In a Tablet of visitation (*ziyára*) written at some point after Quddús's death in 1849, the Báb writes: "from all eternity you have existed in the exaltation of holiness and majesty, and unto all eternity you shall exist in the exaltation of holiness and majesty. You are the one who is manifested through the manifestation of your Lord (*anta 'l-ẓáhir bi-ẓuhúri rabbika*) and the one who is concealed through the concealment of your Lord. In the beginning when there was no beginning but you, and in the end when there will be no end save you; you ascended through all creation to a horizon unto which none preceded you."[103] In a section of the *Kitáb-i panj sha'n* written for Mullá Sha̲y̲k̲h̲ 'Alí Tur̲s̲h̲ízí, the Báb explicitly declares that "the last name of God has shone forth and flashed and gleamed and become manifest; well is it with him who sees in him nothing but God."[104]

Within the context of such statements, it may be possible to suggest a fresh dimension to our understanding of the events which occurred at the Bábí assembly at Bada̲s̲h̲t in 1848, which is generally associated with the abrogation of the Islamic laws (*s̲h̲arí'a*), the proclamation of the inauguration of a new age of inner truth (though not, I am inclined to think, at this stage the implementation of a Bábí *s̲h̲arí'a*), and the announcement of the imminent appearance of the Qá'im. (A secondary objective of the meeting was to draw up plans for the release of the Báb from prison in Azerbaijan.) In what is in some respects a curious letter, 'Abdu'l-Bahá states that "many have manifested divinity (*ulúhiyyat*) and lordship (*rubúbiyyat*). . . . At Bada̲s̲h̲t, her excellency Ṭáhirih raised to the highest heaven the cry of "Verily, I am God," as did many of the friends at Bada̲s̲h̲t."[105] Brief as it is and lacking in direct evidence, this theologically uncharacteristic statement is nonetheless extremely suggestive and may prove an important starting point for fresh enquiries into the significance of the Bada̲s̲h̲t gathering. It may well be the case, for example, that the recorded divisions between the participants in the meeting, in particular that between Qurratu'l-'Ayn and Quddús, relate in some way to the advancement of competing claims of this kind.

Certainly a number of Bábí texts of the post-Bada̲s̲h̲t period contain what would only a few years previously have been regarded as pure blasphemy. Some of the Báb's later writings, including numerous sections of the *Kitáb-i panj sha'n*, contain exordia such as "this is a letter from God, the Protector, the Self-subsisting, to God, the Protector, the Self-Subsisting,"[106] or "this is a letter from God to him whom God shall manifest."[107] Even more direct is the following passage from a letter of the Báb to Mullá Ibráhím Qazvíní, Raḥím: "'Alí before Nabíl [i.e., 'Alí Muḥammad, the Báb] is the Self of God (*nafsu'-lláh*) . . . and the name of Al-Azal, al-Wahid [i.e., Mírzá Yaḥyá Núrí, Ṣubḥ-i Azal] is the Essence of God (*dhátu'lláh*)."[108] In a letter also written to Qazvíní after the Báb's death, the latter's former amanuensis, Sayyid Ḥusayn Yazdí, declares "were it not for the existence of God in my beloved, the Eternal, the Ancient (*al-azal al-aqdam*) [i.e., Qazvíní],[109] I should not have addressed these words to you, my beloved," and goes on to refer to the Báb's death as "the disappearance of God" (*ghaybatu'lláh*) and "the ascension of God" (*ṣu'údu'lláh*)."[110]

I am of necessity selecting passages in order to get across a rather neglected point, and I would not wish to suggest that I have exhausted the possibilities of late Bábí theophanic doctrine or that I have necessarily offered the most reliable picture of it. What I wish to do is to lay a basis for the study of subsequent developments by showing that there was general acceptance in the Bábí community of widespread claims to theophanic status and authority and that no very systematic or consistent doctrine had been either developed or promulgated to resolve the issues such claims inevitably brought to the surface. It is, I think, important to do this in order to balance somewhat the view put forward by the Bahá'í writer Balyuzi and others to the effect that the doctrines contained in the *Nuqṭatu'l-káf* are merely "a reflection of the anarchy of the darkest days of the Bábí Faith" and that early Bábí leaders such as Dárábí, Zanjání, Mullá Ḥusayn, Quddús, and Qurratu'l-'Ayn could not possibly have held such opinions.[111]

I am willing to accept the view that the doctrinal situation following the death of the Báb and the core of the Bábí leadership was confused. But I think I have shown that the roots of later speculation lay incontrovertibly in theories and events close to the heart of the Bábí movement throughout its most coherent period. The notion of a united, doctrinally unobjectionable "Bábí Faith" is merely a reflection of the retrospective systematizing tendencies of modern Bahá'ís.

THE BÁBÍ HIERARCHICAL SYSTEM

Of paramount importance for our understanding of subsequent events, among which the Bahá'í/Azalí split is the most significant, is the hierarchical system of "mirrors" (*maráyá*), "glasses" (*bulúriyát*), "guides" (*adillá'*), and "witnesses" (*shuhadá'*) developed by the Báb in his later writings. This is not, in the strict sense, an organized system of hierarchical grades since the terms involved are, to a large degree, mutually interchangeable and imprecisely used in the texts. Nevertheless, hierarchy is certainly involved in the concept, and there are indications that definite roles were envisaged for individuals exercising the functions associated with the titles. In this respect, Bábí doctrine offers a clear continuation of the Shí'í theory of *ḥujiyya*, which is extended, not only to the prophet and the Imáms or their equivalents, but to other grades of a loose hierarchy as well.

In discussing the meaning of the term *nujabá'*, applied to the saints who will accompany the Qá'im on his return, Shaykh Aḥmad al-Aḥsá'í refers to variants on the well-known Ṣúfí hierarchy which includes, according to one version, a single "pole" (*quṭb*), four "pillars" (*arkán*), forty "replacements" (*abdál*), seventy "nobles" (*nujabá'*), and three hundred and sixty "righteous" (*ṣáliḥún*).[112] Such an arrangement, al-Aḥsá'í says, is not to be found in the works of Shí'í tradition, except for a statement by the Imám 'Alí ibn al-Ḥusayn referring to "the recognition of the meanings (*al-ma'ání*) in the second, the recognition of the gates (*al-abwáb*) in the third, the recognition of the Imám in the fourth, the recognition of the pillars (*al-arkán*) in the fifth, the recognition of the directors (*al-nuqabá'*) in the sixth, and the recognition of the nobles (*al-nujaba'*) in the seventh."[113] The first four of these (*al-tawḥíd* [in a common variant, *al-bayán*], *al-ma'ání, al-abwáb*, and *al-imáma*) are generally regarded as referring to the Imáms: as the stations (*al-maqámát*) in which God is known to men; as the "meanings" of God's acts; as his knowledge, power, wisdom, and so forth; as the "gates of God"; and as Imáms in the visible realm.[114] In al-Aḥsá'í's opinion, the four *arkán* are equivalent to the four *nuwwáb* of the Twelfth Imám, the *nujabá'* (whom he equates with the *abdál*) are the first ranks of the righteous in Shí'í Islam (*khiyár al-shí'a*), and the *nujabá'* are the second rank of these.[115]

This hierarchical grading is linked by al-Aḥsá'í to the degree of spiritual knowledge available to each of its ranks. The *nuqabá'* (or *khaṣísún*, "special ones"), for example, can know the Imáms in their highest stations of *maqámát, ma'ání*, and *abwáb*; whereas the *nujabá'* are capable only of knowing them in the rank of *imáma*.[116] From a different angle, it is said that the believers receive their knowledge of God from the prophets, who in turn receive theirs from Muḥammad and the Imáms, who are the first beings to whom God made himself known—a process which is compared to that of a series of mirrors reflecting the same original image in descending degrees (an analogy of importance in the present context).[117]

Implicit in this hierarchical system is the notion of intermediacy. The Imáms are, in the first place, the primary intermediaries between men and God, being the "gates" or "paths" that link the creation with the Creator.[118] There must, at the same time, be further intermediaries between the Imáms and the believers in general, since not all the latter possess the same capacity. Al-Aḥsá'í speaks of these latter intermediaries in the context of a much-commented quranic verse: "And we appointed, between them and the towns we blessed, manifest towns, and we measured the journey between them. Travel in them by night and by day securely." (34:18) According to a tradition related from the Imám Báqir, the "towns we blessed" are the Imáms, while the "manifest towns" (*quran ẓáhira*) are the messengers and transmitters from the Imáms to the believers (*shí'a*) and the scholars (*fuqahá'*)[119] of Shí'í Islam.[120]

The Bábí leader Qurratu'l-'Ayn Ṭáhirih also makes use of this quranic verse, referring to an alternative interpretation which identifies the "manifestations" with Shí'ís in general and the four "gates (*abwáb*) in particular.[121] She makes this identification in the course of a broader account of the continuing process of divine guidance through the ages, according to which God has sent a *maẓhar* and *ẓuhúr* in every age and period. Thus prophets were despatched until the coming of Muḥammad (who is, of course, their seal). After Muḥammad, men were tested through the Imáms until the disappearance of the last of them, after which the "gates" were appointed so that humanity should not be left without guidance. Following the "gates", pious ulama guided the Shí'ís[122] until the appearance of wicked scholars who made exalted claims for themselves and corrupted the faith. Since, however, the Hidden Imám wished to distinguish the good from the wicked, he chose a perfect man to whom he taught his inner knowledge and whom he preserved from sin and error.[123] Although she does not give his name, it is clear from subsequent references that Qurratu'l-'Ayn is here referring to Shaykh Aḥmad al-Aḥsá'í. On his death, she says, God appointed Sayyid Káẓim Rashtí to be the sign (*al-áya*) and proof (*al-ḥujja*) on behalf of the Imám to all men. After Rashtí,

'Alí Muḥammad S͟hírází was made the *báb* and *ḥujja*.[124] The Báb himself, she concludes, will be followed in his turn by the open appearance of the Imám in person.[125]

In another treatise, Qurratu'l-'Ayn links the concept of the "manifest towns" to the S͟hayk͟hí theory of the "fourth support" (*al-rukn al-rábi'*). This later theory is fairly complex, and I do not propose to discuss it in detail here. Suffice it to say that, where traditional S͟hí'í theology speaks of five "bases" (*uṣúl*) of religion (i.e., the oneness of God, prophethood, resurrection, the justice of God, and imamate), S͟hayk͟hí doctrine reduces these to three: knowledge of God, prophethood, and imamate. Added to these is a "fourth support," which is knowledge of the "friends" (*awliyá'*) of the Imáms, a term which includes the *nuqabá'* and *nujabá'*, together with *mujtahids* and the ulama in general.[126] In the course of a defence of the concept of four supports, Qurratu'l-'Ayn states that the "fourth support" may be identified with the "manifest towns."[127] She further argues that the meaning of the messenger (*rasúl*) in every age is the "bearer of the hidden sign," a branch of the tree that gives the fruit of true knowledge. This fruit is renewed in every age in order to put men to the test. This bearer of God's hidden knowledge is revealed at whatever time the will of God deems it proper.[128] In this age, she says, God has revealed the "fourth support" and sent a messenger (*rasúl*), who is the remembrance of the Imám —in other words, the Báb. This individual she then identifies as "the manifest town,"[129] later describing him as the "special *s͟hí'a* (*s͟hí'ay-i k͟haṣíṣ . . . az maqám-i ik͟htiṣáṣ*) and one of the *nuqabá'* or (echoing al-Aḥsá'í) "special S͟hí'a."[130] She also defends the Báb's use of the words "I am he who manifested himself to Moses on Sinai" (*man-am mutajallíy-i Músá dar Ṭúr*) by referring to a well-known S͟hí'í tradition to the effect that the one who appeared to Moses was a man from behind the throne of God, one of the *s͟hí'a* of the Imáms.[131] More widely, she states that, in this age, the *nuqabá'* are shining forth from the glory of the Imáms,[132] probably a reference to the Letters of the Living or other members of the Bábí hierarchy.[133]

The Báb himself makes use of the sevenfold concept of *tawḥíd, ma'ání, abwáb, imáma, arkán, nuqabá'*, and *nujabá'*. Although he does not identify them with any specific individuals, he does indicate that these last two groups exist on earth and go unrecognized by men.[134] He does, however, identify the Letters of the Living as the "manifest towns,"[135] an identification also made by Qurratu'l-'Ayn in a commentary on one of the Báb's letters.[136] Qurratu'l-'Ayn significantly precedes her own reference to the *sábiqún* as the "manifest towns" by describing them as "the paths and gates of the Remembrance" (*subul al-dhikr wa abwábuhu*),[137] epithets which draw attention to the role of the *sábiqún* as intermediaries between the primary manifestation of the Will and the rest of mankind.

Curiously enough, the Báb makes little use of the terms *nuqabá'* and *nujabá'*, preferring instead to employ the terms already mentioned (*maráyá, adillá'*, and *shuhadá'*). In the *Panj sha'n*, however, there occurs an important reference to the *nuqabá'* and *nujabá'*; in the context of an explanation of the Báb's theory of secondary mirrors. We have already noted that he often refers to the place of manifestation of the Will as a mirror, in which the sun of God (or of the Will) may be seen.[138] But this original mirror, as the representative of the hidden Essence, marks only the inception of a descending hierarchy, the grades of which are themselves described as mirrors reflecting it in a manner identical to that outlined by al-Aḥsá'í in his account of the hierarchy of knowledge.[139] "If," says the Báb, "unnumbered mirrors were to be placed before him [i.e., the *maẓhar*] and he were to decree prophethood [for them], they would be prophets (*rusul*); and if unnumbered mirrors were to stand in front of them and he were to decree guardianship [for them], they would be guardians (*awliyá'*); and if unnumbered mirrors were to stand before them and he were to decree directorship, they would be directors (*naqíb*); and if unnumbered mirrors were to stand before them and he were to decree nobility, they would be nobles (*najíb*); and likewise for every goodly name."[140]

This sequence of primary, secondary, tertiary, and other mirrors is, according to the Báb, an actual characteristic of every revelationary cycle, not only in the lifetime of the prophet (who is the primary mirror) but throughout the subsequent period, leading up to the reappearance of the Primal Will in another prophet. "Consider," he says, "the revelation of the prophet Muḥammad, how many mirrors appeared up until the time when God manifested the Point of the Bayán. . . . Similarly, behold in the Bayán, from the first moment that God sent it down upon the Primal Point until the time of the next resurrection, wherein God shall manifest him whom God shall manifest. . . all the pure glasses that have appeared, all the untouchable mirrors that have reflected. . . ."[141] In a lengthier passage, he describes the relationship between the primary and the other mirrors: God, he says, "has singled out from his creation a mirror indicating his firstness and his lastness, his appearance and his concealment, and has established it as his Will, inasmuch as it has only wished for that which he has wished. . . . In this mirror there is seen nothing but his most holy essence. . . . This mirror has appeared from the beginning that has no beginning in every revelation (*ẓuhúr*) with a (different) name, and in every period of concealment (*buṭún*) it has manifested itself on (different) thrones."[142] Although they are innumerable, these mirrors are but a single mirror in which God alone can be seen.[143] All other mirrors exist in the shadow of this single mirror and are all manifestations (*tajalliyyát*) of it.[144] This, however, raises the question of how there can be a multiplicity of mirrors in any one dispensation—to which the Báb replies that in each revelation the "speaker" (*náṭiq*, the primary manifestation of the divine Will),[145] which is a mirror showing the "manifest exaltation" of the *ẓuhúr*, summons men to the revelation, while all the secondary mirrors to be illumined in that *ẓuhúr* summon others to the primary mirror.[146] God, indeed, wishes to see innumerable secondary mirrors placed beneath the shadow of the first, all of them remaining entirely dependent on it.[147]

This hierarchical principle is precisely observed in the Bábí dispensation. God, says the Báb, created him and made him the mirror of his self, after which unlimited secondary mirrors were created from him. Out of these latter, God again selected a single mirror to be a mirror for himself, causing it to speak on his behalf and to act as a locus (*maqám*) for his revelation and concealment. From this secondary mirror in turn other mirrors are to be brought into existence, all of them calling men to God, informing them about him and guiding them to him.[148] This sequence is described in detail in a subsequent passage:

> God, praised be he, has singled out in this revelation an untouchable mirror and an exalted glass in which the sun of reality is reflected, upon which the point of divinity has shone, and in which the real being of eternity is displayed. . . . This mirror shall be reflected in (another) mirror, which mirror shall be reflected in (another) mirror, which mirror shall be reflected in (another) mirror, which mirror shall be reflected in (another) mirror. Even were I to make mention (of these mirrors) to the end that has no end, the accounting of my heart would not be free of those shining reflections, those ascending manifestations. But until now only that (original) mirror has appeared with pure innate capacity (*fiṭra maḥḍa*).[149]

This series of reflecting mirrors parallels and is in some ways closely linked to the better-known hierarchical system of Babism composed of "letters" (*ḥurúfát*), "unities" (*wáḥidát*), and "all things" (*kullu shay'*). Together with the Báb himself, the eighteen "Letters of the Living" formed the "first unity" (*al-wáḥid al-awwal*)[150] of the Bayán. It seems to have been the

Báb's intention to establish a complete and identifiable hierarchy based on the multiplication of "unities" (*wáḥid*), beginning with the Letters of the Living. According to Nabíl, the Báb instructed his first disciples to record the names of those whom they converted, lists of which were to be forwarded to him via his uncle in Shiraz. These lists were to be classified by the Báb into "eighteen sets of nineteen names each," each set constituting a single "unity" and the total, together with the first "unity" coming to 361, the number of "all things" (i.e., the numerical equivalent of the phrase *kullu shay'*).[151]

Although the Báb's later writings continue to contain complex references to this overall concept, there is no evidence that his original object was ever attained or that the classification of "unities" proceeded as planned. Nevertheless, there are references to a "second unity" (*al-wáhid al-thání*), which included the Bábí leader Sayyid Yaḥyá Dárábí, Vaḥíd,[152] and to "unities" other than the first,[153] and it seems likely that the Báb retained hopes of ultimately organizing his followers according to this scheme.

A related but more complex concept, which I cannot claim to understand or be able to explain fully at this point, is that of mirrors reflecting the letters of the unities or the unities in general. This idea is expressed simply (but unfortunately without any reference) by the Bahá'í writer Ishráq-Khávarí, who states that the Báb "established eighteen mirrors beneath the shadow of each of the Letters of the Living, in order that they might form the number of *wáḥid* (19) together with the Letters of the Living."[154] This seems to be related to the progressive development of the Báb's claims, as he himself indicates in the *Panj sha'n*: "I revealed myself in the gates for four years, and it is necessary that a mirror be found for each letter, that it may be a place of manifestation (*maẓhar*) for those letters.[155] This sense of progression is emphasized in the following passage:

"You revealed me in the name of your gates for that number [i.e., the number of years corresponding to them], 4; wherefore, create, O my God, for each unity an untouchable mirror that may reflect your essence, and an exalted glass that may guide (men) to your oneness. Then you removed the honor of that garment and raised me up from that inaccessible horizon and revealed me in the guides to your guardianship (*fi adillá' wiláyatika*) and the names of your unity. Wherefore, create O my God, in each year for each unity an untouchable mirror and an exalted glass that will reflect from my self in all the grades of your power and the manifestations of your glory,"[156]

Or again:

"I bear witness that God manifested me in the gates for the number of [the letter] *dál* [i.e., 4], in which we remained speaking; and since my self has recognized all things, it is necessary that that mirror be reflected by (another) mirror. . . , indeed it is necessary that there be found in each year a mirror for each manifestation of the guides of the unity (*adillá' al-wáḥid*)."[157]

What this appears to mean is that the Báb hoped a fresh mirror would be found to reflect each of the original Letters of the Living every year, in this way creating new unities, leading ultimately to the creation of one or more *kullu shay'*. It would, however, take a total of three hundred and sixty-one years to reach the first *kullu shay'* in this way. If, on the other hand, we think of an exponential progression, with each new unity generating subsidiary unities every year, numerous *kullu shay'* would rapidly come into being.

Possibly related to the above concept is that of the regular appearance throughout the Bábí dispensation of temples (*haykals*), apparently manifestations of each of the members of the first unity: "Nurture, O God, the tree of the Bayán until the day of him you will manifest; and cause to appear, O God, at the beginning of every (period of) sixty-six years a temple belonging to the temples of the unity, that they may raise up your paths in the Bayán [i.e., promulgate the Bábí laws] and take hold of what you decreed from your horizons in the Bayán until the day your heaven, your earth, and all that is between them shall be illumined by the appearance of him whom you will manifest."[158] The significance of this is somewhat clearer than that of the foregoing. In the course of his lengthy and complex discussion of the significance of "temples" in the last sections of the *Panj sha'n*,[159] the Báb says that every sixty-six years of the quranic era passed about one letter of the first "unity".[160] Significantly, the Báb compares the first temple (the locus of the Primal Will) and the eighteen temples beneath it to the sun and the mirrors reflecting it.[161] It is unclear what the relationship between the two ideas must be, but in the *Haykal al-dín* (Temple of religion), the Báb orders the renewal of all books every sixty-six years.[162] Perhaps the idea is that fresh knowledge will be revealed every sixty-six years and that, therefore, all previous books will become worthless.

It is far from clear to what extent the Báb wished to formalize this system. Many of the references to *adillá'*, *shuhadá'*, and *maráyá* seem quite general and open-ended. At the same time, there are hints that some sort of organization was to be introduced. In the Arabic Bayán and the *Haykal al-dín*, for example, the Báb describes the division of the spoils of war to various groups, including "the first letters" (*al-ḥurúf al-úlá*) and "the witnesses" (*al-shuhadá'*).[163] In the Persian and Arabic Bayáns the Báb lays down general rules for the distribution of tax revenue to the members of the unities, as well as the descendants of the Letters of the Living.[164] In one place, he instructs future Bábí kings to select twenty-five individuals from the ulama who are "horizons of the letters" (*matáli' al-ḥurúf*) to teach the people.[165]

LONG-TERM ESCHATOLOGICAL EXPECTATIONS

Whether organized or not, the concept of guides and witnesses is closely linked to the Báb's anticipation of the eschatological events related to the appearance of the next locus of the Primal Will, generally referred to in his writings as "he whom God shall manifest" (*man yuẓhiruhu 'lláh*). The Báb expected his laws and teachings to be preserved and promulgated in the long term by a succession of guides who would eventually lead men to the recognition of the next prophet. It is, as we have noted previously, a basic Shí'í principle that there must always be a divine proof (*ḥujja*) for creation. The Báb himself emphasizes this doctrine in a highly important passage of the *Panj sha'n*, which I shall quote almost in full:

> Know that [it is the case] in each manifestation (*ẓuhúr*) that, until the creation of that manifestation has reached the limits of perfection, the divine Will and eternal Volition of the Living One will not return to men. From the beginning of each manifestation to the day of the next manifestation, all the guides that appear always have affirmed and always will affirm the acceptance of that revelation; and they have been and will be the ornaments embellishing that period of concealment [*buṭún*; i.e., between revelations]. They are all mirrors reflecting the sun of oneness belonging to that manifestation and shining glasses displaying the Countenance of that concealment.
>
> And know that there has always been and always will be a proof on the part of the God unto his creation, for all things exist through the Will of God; indeed, it cannot be imagined that there should at any time be a thing and the proof for it on the part of God not be complete. . . . Just as the Living One has always existed, so there has ever been established the existence of the throne of reality among created beings. Throughout eternity his station has always existed, except that in the day of resurrection (*yawm-i qiyámat*) he

is manifest and shining above the horizon (*mushriq*), while in the days of his setting (*ghurúb*) he is knowing and hidden.

Yet during the period of his concealment, there have been and shall be guides to his cause in each manifestation who have preserved and shall preserve his religion. And there have been and shall be witnesses to creation on his part. These are the lights of guidance in the night of nights, through whom all (others) are guided.[166]

Referring to the questions of how long a period will elapse between his revelation and that of him whom God shall manifest, the Báb states that, in every manifestation God chooses for the locus of manifestation guides, witnesses, preservers (*ḥuffáz*), and forerunners (*ruwwád*)[167] who preserve God's laws from manifestation to manifestation and summon men to God from concealment to concealment.[168] It is men's duty to recognize the "throne of revelation" in each manifestation and cling, in each concealment, "to the guides of the one veiled in that manifestation.[169]

It is clear that this principle is also to obtain in the period between the manifestation of the Báb and that of him whom God shall manifest. "In the days of God," the Báb writes, "every glass that rises up will be a guide to him whom God shall manifest and all shall reflect him."[170] "While the sun is shining [i.e., while the Báb still lives], let you all obtain illumination from its light. But after that, he who recites[171] the verses of God in their true nature (*bi-fiṭratihá*), may you obtain illumination from their [the verses] light. And if after that there should shine forth one like him, then you shall be guided by one like him and shall shine with the light of God, until such time as the unity is complete, whereupon the affair shall return to God."[172]

This last passage seems to be made even clearer in the following lines from a letter of the Báb's to Mírzá Ibráhím Qazvíní, to whom he writes: "The cause shall reach the Name *al-Waḥíd* [i.e., Mírzá Yaḥyá Ṣubḥ-i Azal], for his appearance in himself is a proof; and after him, should God reveal one like him possessed of proof, it [the cause] shall reach him; otherwise the cause is in the hands of the witnesses in the Bayán, until the day of him whom God shall manifest in the next resurrection."[173] It seems evident, then, that the Báb anticipated some form of continuing *ḥujjiyya*, mediated at first through single individuals and then, if necessary, through the "witnesses" in general. That this was so is emphasized by his statement to the effect that "the creation shall be in the night of nights just as it was after Muḥammad, until you [God] show beneficence towards them through the manifestation of your self in the day of resurrection."[174]

A crucial question, of course, was that of how long the period of concealment between the Báb's death and the appearance of him whom God shall manifest would be. Although it cannot be proved, I am of the opinion that this did not actually become an issue until the mid-1860s, when conflicting Azalí and Bahá'í claims about the length or brevity of this period raised it to a central position in the debate between these two factions. The Báb's own writings, as we have seen, imply an interval similar to that between any two previous prophets. The reference to temples appearing every sixty-six years would seem to preclude any manifestation before at least one such period. More telling are the numerous passages that anticipate the appearance of Bábí kings,[175] ministers, governors, and ulama;[176] or the conquest of the entire earth by the Bábís;[177] or the general application of Bábí laws, including that of pilgrimage; or the construction of mosques and tombs; or the levying of taxes; or the regulation of trade—all of which necessitate the existence of a developed and stable Bábí state.

Indeed, some of the Báb's laws, such as the regulations that books must be renewed every 66 or 202 years[178] or that furniture must be replaced every 19 years,[179] of themselves imply a long-term outlook on his part. But perhaps the clearest indication of the minimum time-scale anticipated by the Báb is to be found in a passage of the *Haykal al-dín* which, in spite of its obscurities, is quite explicit as to the number of years involved.

> If he [God] wished, he could decree more than a "unity"; and if he desires he is capable [of revealing] until the day of resurrection thrones of the living (*a'rásh ḥayy,* sic); and if he wishes he will command you (to obey/follow?) one whose knowledge encompasses the laws of the Bayán after the sun has set. After six hundred and sixty-two years have elapsed of the Bayán, present yourselves before your ruler (*malíkikum,* God?) every eleven years (?, *fi iḥá'ashar sana,* sic), then praise [him?], that you may thus present yourselves before him whom God shall manifest.[180]

It is worth referring, even if only in passing, to the vexed question of the terms *aghyath* (of *ghiyath*) and *mustaghgháth,* which are used by the Báb in the Persian *Bayan* in connection with the appearance of him whom God shall manifest.[181] The most important passage in which the terms are used is in the sixteenth *báb* of the second *wáḥid*:

> I promise the people of the Bayán that if, at the time of the appearance of him whom God shall manifest, you should all attain to that mightier paradise [i.e., belief in him] and that greater meeting, you shall be blessed, you shall be blessed, you shall be blessed. Otherwise, should you hear that a revelation has appeared with the signs of the former (revelation), in the number of God the Most Succouring (*al-aghyath* = 1511), let you all enter in. If that should not take place and it has reached the number of the name of God the Beseeched (*al-mustagháth* = 2001), and if you should hear that a Point has appeared yet you have not all been convinced, have mercy on yourselves and all in your entirety enter beneath the shadow of that manifest Point. . . . If you do not hear [that he has appeared], then abase yourself and offer up supplications that the grace of God may not be cut off from you until [the time of] *mustagháth.* And if you hear between now and *mustagháth* that he

who is my beloved and your beloved, my sovereign and your sovereign, has appeared, do not hesitate even for a single second, but enter you all together beneath God's shadow. . . . O People of the Bayán, if anyone should hesitate even to take one breath after two thousand and one years, he shall without question no longer belong to the religion of the Bayán and shall enter hell.[182]

Bahá'í writers have, I think, been correct in pointing out that the two figures of 1511 and 2001 years represent the latest date at which the next manifestation was to appear, and in stressing that the Báb himself held that only God knew the time of the revelation[183] and that, whatever the date, all were obliged to recognize him whom God shall manifest when he came. At the same time, whatever later interpretations of these passages may suggest, it is highly unlikely that much or any early Bábí opinion anticipated the next manifestation before the passage of a considerable period of time, and certainly not as soon as the ninth or nineteenth year after the Báb's own appearance.[184]

It is also, I think, obvious that it is impossible to maintain that the Báb clearly foretold the year of the appearance of him whom God shall manifest or identified him with a living individual, and at the same time to hold that he set no time at all or, indeed, that he felt some need to refer to the latest date of the manifestation as 1511 or 2001 years in the future.

Early Bábí opinion as to the probable lateness of the next manifestation would have been reinforced by numerous statements of the Báb, particularly in the *Panj sha'n*, to the effect that, unless the creation begun under one manifestation has reached a state of completion (or perfection), the next manifestation will not arrive.[185] Such statements are almost without exception accompanied by references to the guides or mirrors who will appear to preserve the faith throughout the time of concealment. This principle of completeness preceding the recreation of all things in a new revelation[186] is stated explicitly to apply to the Bábí dispensation: "Unless the creation of the Bayán reaches perfection, God shall not manifest him—do you not see? All who shall appear before his appearance are guides to the fact that there is no god but him and that all are his servants."[187] "God knows the period (that will elapse) between the Point of the Bayán and him whom he shall manifest; but if the creation in any given manifestation does not reach perfection, God will not manifest the locus of the revelation of himself in the next manifestation.[188] "Today," he says, "the Bayán is in a state of seed; but at the beginning of the revelation of him whom God shall manifest, there will be the final perfection of the Bayán."[189]

Related in some way to this notion of increased perfection (which has important analogies in other aspects of Bábí doctrine)[190] is the concept that, as a revelation progresses, time becomes increasingly thin or subtle to the point that a fresh locus of manifestation has to appear. This idea may have been derived by the Báb from Shaykh Aḥmad al-Aḥsá'í, who employs it in relation to the appearance of the Twelfth Imám. According to al-Aḥsá'í, the beginning and end of time are both subtle (*laṭíf*), while its middle is dense. As men draw closer to the time of the Imám's appearance, time becomes increasingly subtle until he finally returns.[191] This appears to be linked to the theory that the heavens move quickly during a time of injustice and slowly during a period of justice, so that, when the Qá'im appears, a year will equal ten normal years.[192] Al-Aḥsá'í also believed that, when the Qá'im appeared, the heavens would return to their original position and commence their second revolution. [193] It certainly seems that al-Aḥsá'í conceived of time as essentially single, beginning with the creation and culminating in the appearance of the Hidden Imám. The Báb, however, while borrowing the idea that time becomes increasingly fine, sees this as a process that recommences with every fresh revelation of the Primal Will. "In every manifestation, when the era (*kúr*) has reached the extremity of fineness and the cycle (*ṭúr*) [has reached] the utmost degree of thinness, he [God] has manifested himself to his creation in the throne he has chosen from among men, the seat he has selected from among his servants."[194] Thus, time became increasingly subtle through the 1,270 years of the Islamic era until God revealed the Báb,[195] so that time is now in a state of subtlety.[196] Since the Báb elsewhere states that God nurtured men for 1,270 years,[197] it seems evident that the processes of temporal refinement and gradual perfecting are assumed to go hand in hand during the period of concealment.

Finally, it is worth noting in passing that the Báb hinted more than once that the time of the appearance of him whom God shall manifest could, in fact, be calculated in advance: "The length of time from this revelation to the revelation of him whom God shall manifest is known to God. But it is possible for men to know it from what they deduce through the science of letters [gematria]. Should God give anyone that knowledge in its entirety, he will make his deduction just as those who deduced [the time of] the revelation of the Point of the Bayán from poems."[198] "The period separating one manifestation from another," he says, "is known only to God or to those to whom God has given the science of letters in its entirety ."[199] Among other things, the final sections of the *Panj sha'n* are devoted to the revelation of the science of letters, with the aim of enabling men to recognize him whom God was to manifest on his appearance. And it seems to be the case that specualtion employing gematria was used by many Bábís in an attempt to "decipher" the rather abstruse statements found in these passages.[200]

SHORT-TERM ESCHATOLOGICAL EXPECTATIONS

If, as I think is correct, the vast majority (if not all) of the Bábís in the period after the Báb's death regarded the next manifestation as an event that would occur in the distant future, possibly as much as 2001 years away, what did they expect to happen in the immediate future—in the next ten or twenty years, let us say? I should like to look at one or two indications that there was some kind of messianic expectation in primitive Babism, even after the Báb's own claims had reached their highest point. This was, as I propose to demonstrate, largely rooted in Shí'í eschatological theory and in various allusions in the writings of the Báb himself. But I think it can also be attributed in part to the actual conditions of Babism in the 1850s.

The sharp contrast between Shí'í messianic expectations relating to the earthly triumph of the Qá'im and the rapid establishment of a reign of justice under his government, on the one hand, and the physical destruction of the Báb and his leading followers, on the other, must have been a tremendous shock to the large numbers who had put their faith in the Báb as their messiah. In such a situation, the failure of prophecy will provoke a variety of responses: the abandonment of belief, more intense faith, or readjustment or rationalization of the content of the prophecy that has been deemed to have failed. Rather than simply resign themselves to the failure of their immediate hopes and patiently await the coming of him whom God shall manifest, it is probable that a large part of the Bábí community would have looked for further eschatological events and personages in the present.

Shí'í prophecy relating to the events surrounding the appearance of the Qá'im, Muḥammad, and the other Imáms is extremely flexible and open to varying interpretation. Even such a devout believer in the validity of Shí'í traditions as Shaykh Aḥmad al-Aḥsá'í was forced to admit that the prophetic traditions were full of irreconcilable contradictions.[201] It is, therefore, possible to create a variety of scenarios for events to come, each of which can be justified by reference to different prophecies. I do not wish to enter into a detailed discussion of these prophecies here—the interested reader may find adequate information in the standard works[202]—but instead to draw attention to one or two that may be particularly relevant to our present discussion.

According to a number of traditions, the Qá'im will be the first of the Imáms to return to earth,[203] after which he will rule for seven or nine years, each of which will be the equivalent of ten normal years.[204] Al-Aḥsá'í expresses a definite preference for the figure seven (seventy).[205] After fifty-nine years of the Qá'im's rule have passed, the Imám Ḥusayn will come forth; he will remain silent (*ṣámit*) for eleven years (i.e., until the year seventy), whereupon the Qá'im will be killed and his place taken by Ḥusayn for nineteen years until the appearance of 'Alí.[206]

Now, it was true that the Qá'im (i.e., the Báb) had been put to death in the sixth (thus, sixtieth) year of his "reign." The logical conclusion must, therefore, have been that the Imám Ḥusayn would now appear to take over the task he had begun. However, this did not tally very well with strict Bábí theory. The Báb had, as we have seen, stated categorically that the Imám Ḥusayn had already returned to earth along with Muḥammad, Fáṭima, the other Imáms, and the four Gates. In at least one place, moreover, he had gone on to say that "whoever awaits, after this, the appearance of the Mahdí or the return (*raj'a*) of Muḥammad or one of those who have believed in God or his verses, is of those who possess no knowledge— [this shall be so] until the day when God causes me and those who have believed in me to return. That shall be the day of resurrection, when all shall be in a new creation."[207] Since the letter in which this passage occurs is known to have been widely spread among the Bábís, we must assume that this clear rejection of further "returns" was reasonably well known within the community.

And yet it must have been tempting to ignore it or interpret it away, for the Shí'í prophecies did not speak of all the sacred figures of Islam returning at once, and it was well known that 'Alí in particular was expected to have "two returns."[208] There were, moreover, hints in the Báb's writings that further eschatological events could after all be anticipated in the very near future. These hints are far from easy to disentangle, but I shall attempt to give some idea of what they involved.

Let me begin by looking at a passage of the *Dalá'il-i sab'a* where the Báb commences by quoting part of the well-known Shí'í tradition, the "Ḥadíth Kumayl," interspersing his citations with references to each of the first five years of his prophetic mission. Thus, in the first year there occurred "the uncovering of the veils of glory, without any indication," in the second "the extinction of what was doubtful and the clarification of what was known," in the third "the rending of the veil through the overcoming of the mystery," in the fourth "the attraction of oneness to the attribute of singleness," and in the fifth "a light shone out of the morning of eternity (*ṣubḥ ul-azal*) upon the tabernacles of oneness."[209] He concludes by telling his correspondent that he will indeed see the light from the morning of eternity if he does not despair.[210]

Immediately after this, the Báb turns to examine a phrase in a morning prayer (*du'a al-saḥar*) written by the Imám Báqir, which begins with the well-known words "O God, I beseech you by your beauty (*bahá'ika*) in its most beautiful [aspect], and by all your resplendent beauty. O God, I beseech you by all of your beauty."[211] According to the Báb's interpretation, this first section of the prayer refers to Muḥammad, the next to 'Alí, up to the fifth section (which begins, "I beseech you, O my God, by your light [*núrika*] in its most luminous aspect"), is a reference to the Imám Ḥusayn.[212] Identification of the word light (*núr*) with Ḥusayn occurs elsewhere in the Báb's writings[213] and can, therefore, be regarded as entirely normal in the present context. Although he does not say so explicitly, it is clear that he is linking the light that occurs in the fifth phrase of the "Ḥadíth Kumayl" (and hence in the fifth year of his mission) with the light that is mentioned in the *du'á al-saḥar* and which is identified with the Imám Ḥusayn. In other words, the Imám Ḥusayn is the light that "shone out of the morning of eternity."

Following this, the Báb quotes a short passage from a letter written by Shaykh Aḥmad al-Aḥsá'í to Sayyid Káẓim Rashtí, ending with the words: "You shall know his call after a time (*ba'da ḥin*)."[214] This is not the first time the phrase *ba'da ḥin* occurs in the *Dalá'il-i sab'a*: several pages earlier, the Báb cites two passages from the *Khuṭba al-tuṭunjiyya* attributed to the Imám 'Alí, in the second of which the following words occur: "After a time you shall possess a new thing (*ṭurfa*) through which you shall know part of the explanation. Thereupon the regions shall be tongue-tied through men summoning others to every vanity. Beware, beware, and expect the appearance of the greatest relief."[215]

In spite of its obvious meaning of "after a while," *ba'da ḥín* has been interpreted numerologically, the word *ḥín* being taken as a reference to the year 1268 A.H.[216] In other words, *ba'da ḥín* may be read as "after 68," namely the year 69 or, within the context of the Bábí dispensation beginning in 1260, the year 9. In order to get a little closer to what the Báb is trying to say in the *Dalá'il-i sab'a*, let us look at a number of passages in the *Panj sha'n*. Here, he refers to the year 9 and to what will precede and follow it. Thus, for example, he says: "This is what we promised you a time ago (*min qabli ḥín* [lit. "from before a time"]), when we replied to you: "Wait until nine has elapsed of the Bayán, then say "blessed be God, the best of creators.""""[217] Immediately after this, he says (again, it appears, referring to an earlier reply) that "before nine (*al-ṭá'*), there must appear in six (*al-wáw*) two signs from God in the book from the early ones (*al-awwalín*)."[218] I shall come back to these two "signs" in a moment, but first let me quote a later section of the *Panj sha'n* addressed, like the first, to Mullá Shaykh 'Alí Turshízí 'Aẓím: "Before the maturity (*bulúgh*) of the Primal Point in the wombs of existence 'before nine' (*qabla 'l-tis'a*), [which is] the equivalent of 'before a time' (*qabla ḥín*), it is necessary that two mirrors reflect God."[219]

It would seem that the 'two signs' and the 'two mirrors' mentioned in these passages are to be regarded as identical. But what are they references to? After the first of the passages quoted, the Báb continues as follows: "Say: the first of them [i.e., the two signs] is Yaḥyá the prophet [i.e., John the Baptist], and the other is the son of 'Alí."[220] After the second, he goes on: "for from the beginning of creation (*min badí' al-awwal*) until this time, no one was born after the passage of six months except Yaḥyá the prophet and Ḥusayn the son of 'Alí."[221]

Both the second passages from the *Panj sha'n* and a similar passage quoted by Bahá'u'lláh in his *Lawḥ-i Shaykh*[222] speak in terms of "maturing" or of the development of an embryo (a common Islamic and Bábí image). The lines just quoted explicitly bring in the notion of an embryo reaching maturity in the brief period of six months. Could, therefore, the appearance of the "two signs" (or "two mirrors") in the year 6 (1266 A.H./1849–50A.D.) be intended to indicate the actual birth of the Bábí revelation, which had previously been in a state of gestation? The Báb may have anticipated that "before nine," which seems to mean "in the year six" (nine months being, of course, the normal period of gestation), the Bayán would reach maturity in the appearance of two mirrors representing Ḥusayn and John the Baptist. As far as Ḥusayn is concerned, this would certainly correspond to the prophecies referring to his appearance in the sixtieth (thus, the sixth) year of the reign of the Qá'im.

But what of the "year nine" itself? There are clear references to it in some of the Báb's writings. In the Arabic *Bayán*, for example, he writes: "When you hear the mention of the one we shall manifest in the name of the Qá'im, anticipate the difference between *al-qá'im* and *al-qayyúm*. Then you shall attain to all good in the year nine."[223] This statement is echoed in somewhat different words in the *Haykal al-dín*: "Rise up[224] when you hear the name of the Qá'im and when you mention [it]. And you shall witness all good between the difference of *al-qá'im* and *al-qayyúm* numerically (*'adadan*) in nine years."[225] One of the problems posed by the use of the terms *al-qayyúm* (meaning something like "self-sufficient") in these passages is that it is not a normal eschatological term in Shí'í literature and cannot readily be identified with an expected eschatological figure. Normally, in fact, the word occurs as a title of the divinity. In a letter to his uncle, Ḥájí Mírzá Sayyid 'Alí Shírází, the Báb identifies it numerically with the name Yúsuf (=156) and says that "it means the Qá'im of the family of Muḥammad," which is, of course, himself.[226] Nor is the numerical difference between *al-qá'im* and *al-qayyúm* of much help, since this may amount to 5, 9, or 14, depending on the value given to the third letter (either *yá'* or *hamza*) of *qá'im*.

The reader—if he has persevered this far—will by now have reached the conclusion that none of this is very clear. I suspect that many early Bábís may have felt the same way. Nevertheless, it is apparent that references of this kind must have encouraged interest in the years around 1268, 1269, and 1270 A.H. (1851–54 A.D.) and suggested the possibility of the initial appearance of John the Baptist and Ḥusayn in 1266/1848–49, possibly followed by their later activity in 1269/1852–53. And the question of *ḥusayniyya*—the claim to be the return of Ḥusayn—did indeed come to be of more than passing interest around this period.

NOTES

This paper is an expanded version of a paper written for the Second Annual Los Angeles Bahá'í History Conference, August 1984. It is only part of a larger study of authority claims in middle Babism (c. 1850–1866) that I have undertaken. The purchase of many of the materials used in the preparation of this paper was made possible through a grant from the Research Committee of Newcastle University, to whom I wish to express my thanks.

1. The following are among the more important recent studies of the subject: D. MacEoin, "From Shaykhism to Babism: A Study in Charismatic Renewal in Shí'í Islam" (Ph.D. thesis, Cambridge University, 1979); idem., "Early Shaykhí Reactions to the Báb and His Claims," in M. Momen (ed.), *Studies in Bábí and Bahá'í History* Vol. I (Los Angeles: Kalimát Press, 1983); idem, "the Bábí Concept of Holy War," *Religion* (1982) 12: 93–129; M. Momen (ed.), *The Bábí and Bahá'í Religions, 1844–1944: Some Contemporary Western Accounts* (Oxford: George Ronald, 1981); idem, "The Trial of Mullá 'Alí Bastámí: A Combined Sunní-Shí'í Fatwá against the Báb," *Iran* (1982) 20: 113–43; idem, "The Social Basis of the Bábí Upheavels in Iran (1848–53): A Preliminary Analysis" in *IJMES* (1953) 15:157–83; A. Amánat, "The Early Years of the Bábí Movement: Background and Development" (Ph.D. thesis, Oxford University 1981); P. Smith, "Millenarianism in the Bábí and Bahá'í Religions," in R. Wallis (ed.), *Millennialism and Charisma* (Belfast: Queen's University, 1982); idem, "A Sociological Study of the Bábí and Bahá'í Religions" (Ph.D. thesis, Lancaster University, 1982); Mangol Bayat, *Mysticism and Dissent: Socioreligious Thought in Qájár Iran* (Syracuse, N.Y.: Syracuse University Press, 1982) ch. 4 "The Politicization of Dissent in Shia Thought: Babism."

2. On this figure, much lower than that generally given in Bahá'í sources, see D. MacEoin, "From Babism to Baha'ism: Problems of Militancy, Quietism, and Conflation in the Construction of a Religion," *Religion* (1983) 13: 219–55, p. 236.

3. See letter of Sayyid Ḥusayn Yazdí to Mullá 'Abdu'l-Karím Qazvíní (dated possibly late 1850 or 1851) in [Sayyid 'Alí Muḥammad Shírází, the Báb and Sayyid Ḥusayn Yazdí] *Qismatí az alwáḥ-i khaṭṭ-i Nuqṭay-i Úlá wa Áqá Sayyid Ḥusayn Yazdí* (n.p. [Tehran], n.d.) p. 39; Mírzá Ḥusayn 'Alí Núrí, Bahá'u'lláh, "Lawḥ-i warqá," in 'Abdu'l-Ḥamíd Ishráq-Khávarí (ed.), *Má'iday-i ásmání*, 10 vols. (Tehran, 1971–72—1972–73) vol. 4, p. 150; idem, *Kitáb-i íqán* (Cairo, 1352/

1933) pp. 168–69; Shoghi Effendi [Rabbani], *God Passes By* (Wilmette, Ill.: Bahá'í Publishing Trust, 1944) pp. 90–91.

4. MacEoin, "Early Shaykhi Reactions"; idem, "From Shaykhism to Babism." ch. 5.

5. See idem, "Nineteenth-century Bábí Talismans," paper delivered at the annual conference of the British Society for Middle East Studies, Cambridge, 1983, published in *Studia Iranica* (1985) 14:1, pp. 77–98.

6. Sayyid Mahdí Dahají, *Risálay-i Sayyid Mahdí Dahají*, MS F57, E. G. Browne Or. MSS, Cambridge University Library, p. 38.

7. Dahají is at this point attempting to prove that the phrase "the light that dawns from the morn of eternity upon the temples of unity" (*núr ashraqa min ṣubḥ al-azal 'alá hayákil al-tawḥíd*) refers to the Báb's appearance as the Qá'im and not to the emergence of Ṣubḥ-i Azal in the fifth year. There is in existence, however, a statement by the Báb's contemporary, Mírzá Muḥammad 'Alí Zunúzí, to the effect that, in the beginning, the Báb claimed to have been sent by the Hidden Imám and that his words were below those of the Imám but superior to those of al-Aḥsá'í and Rashtí; after that he adopted the title *dhikru'lláh*, then Qá'im, and finally the station of *rubúbiyyat* (lordship, divinity)—see text quoted Mírzá Asadu'lláh Fáḍil-i Mázandarání, *Kitáb-i ẓuhúr al-ḥaqq*, vol. 3 (n.p. [Tehran ?], n.d.) pp. 31–33. On the later claim to *rubúbiyya*, see the Báb, *Bayán-i fársí* (n.p. [Tehran], n.d.) exordium, p. 4.

8. See, for example, idem, *Qayyúmu'l-asmá'*, MS F11, E. G. Browne Or. MSS, Cambridge University Library, ff.2a, 19a, 32b, 36a, 69, 96a, 103b, 114a. In this and other early works, the term *ḥujja* is generally reserved for the Twelfth Imám and for the writings of his *báb*, Sayyid 'Alí Muḥammad. But for an apparently early description of the Báb as *al-ḥujja al-kubrá* (the greatest proof), see Qurratu'l-'Ayn, *risála* printed in Mírzá Abú'l-Faḍl Gulpáygání and Mírzá Mahdí Gulpáygání, *Kashf al-ghiṭá 'an ḥiyal al-a'dá'* (Ashkhabad, n.d.) appendix, p. 2. The same writer refers to the Báb as "the Proof of God." (*Risála* printed in Mázandarání, *Ẓuhúr al-ḥaqq*, vol. 3, p. 361)

9. See the Báb, *Kitáb-i panj Sha'n* (n.p. [Tehran], n.d.) pp. 11, 184, 256, 280. See also idem, *Dalá'il-i sab'a* (n.p. [Tehran], n.d.) p. 29.

10. A passage quoted from this letter in the *Kitáb-i nuqṭatu'l-káf* identifies it with that printed in the Báb and Yazdí, *Qismatí az alwáḥ*, p. 14 (transcription pp. 13–12 [sic]); see Ḥájí Mírzá Jání Káshání, *Kitáb-i-Nuqṭatu'l-Káf*, ed. by E. G. Browne (Leyden and London, 1910) p. 209. The text is also printed in Mázandarání, *Ẓuhúr al-ḥaqq*, vol. 3, pp. 164–66.

11. Two main facts point to this date: the first is the Báb's own references to a period of four years elapsing before his elevation to the rank of Qá'im, the second his explicit announcement of *qá'imiyya* in the pages of the *Dalá'il-i sab'a*, a book certainly written in Mákú (see the Báb, *Dalái'il*, pp. 25, 29, 30). The Báb left Mákú on 9 April 1848 (see Mullá Muḥammad Nabíl Zarandí, *The Dawn-Breakers*, ed. and trans. by Shoghi Effendi [Wilmette, Ill.: Bahá'í Publishing Trust, 1932] p. 259).

12. The Báb, *Bayán-i fársí*, exordium, p. 4 (*básiṭ* = 72 = Máh-kú [a variant of Mákú]; the Báb himself gives the spelling "Mákú"; ibid., 4:12, p. 136; idem, *Dalá'il*, p. 67).

13. The link between *qá'imiyya* and the inauguration of a new dispensation (and not merely a new era) is to some extent indicated by a number of messianic traditions that state the Qá'im will appear with "a new day, a new religion, and a new creation," or "a new book" given to him by Muḥammad and 'Alí, of "a new cause, a new book, a new *sunna*, and a new heaven." (See texts quoted by Shaykh Aḥmad ibn Zayn al-Dín al-Aḥsá'í in "Risála fi 'l-'iṣma wa 'l-raj'a," in idem, *Jawámi' al-kilam*, 2 vols. [Tabriz, 1856, 1860], vol. 1, part 1, pp. 62, 64, 66.)

14. The Báb, *Bayán-i fársí*, exordium, p. 1; 3:7, p. 81; 4:1, p. 105; 4:2, p. 110, and passim; idem, *Panj sha'n*, pp. 31–32, 62, 114, 125–26, 155, 165–66, and passim; idem, *Dalá'il*, pp. 1, 31; idem, *al-Bayán al-'arabí* (n.p. [Tehran], n.d.), section 1, p. 3; 3:7, p. 10.

15. The Báb, *Panj sha'n*, p. 92.

16. Ibid., p. 245.

17. See ibid., pp. 23, 40, 102, 125, 161, 277; idem, *Dalá'il*, pp. 2, 3, 20 (*payghambar*); idem, *Bayán-i fársí* 2:1, p. 12 and passim.

18. In an important passage of the *Kitáb-i panj sha'n*, the Báb states that "this revelation [*ẓuhúr*] is the fifth revelation in two thousand seven hundred and seventy (years)." (*Panj sha'n*, p. 289) Elsewhere,

he breaks this figure down into portions, as follows: from Moses to David: 500 years; from David to Jesus: 500 years; from Jesus to Muḥammad: 500 years more or less; and from Muḥammad to himself 1270 (Or 1271) years. (See ibid., pp. 66, 199, 315, and cf. passage quoted by Mullá Rajab 'Alí Qahír Iṣfahání, *Risálay-i Mullá Rajab 'Alí*, MS F24, E. G. Browne Or. MSS, Cambridge University Library, f78a–78b.)

This calculation seems to be based largely on a tradition from the *Tafsír* (Qur'án commentary) of 'Alí ibn Ibráhím [ibn Háshim al-Qummí], in which it is stated that five hundred years passed between Moses and David, and one thousand between David and Jesus (quoted by Shaykh Aḥmad ibn Zayn al-Dín al-Aḥsá'í, *Sharḥ al-ziyára al-jámi'a al-kabíra*, 4th. ed., 4 vols. [Kerman, 1355 sh./1976–77], vol. 1, p. 195).

The Báb was not, however, wholly consistent in his use of this schema. In the passage just referred to as quoted in Rajab 'Alí Qahír's *risála*, for example, he places David before Moses. There is a well-known contradiction in the *Dalá'il-i sab'a* which at one point places Moses one thousand years before David, with the space between David and the Báb as 2,270 years (p. 18), and at another puts Moses 2,270 years in the past, as in the *Panj sha'n* (p. 38). In one passage of the *Panj sha'n*, however, the Báb speaks of Moses, Jesus, Muḥammad, and himself as coming together in a single succession without David (p. 335).

Elsewhere, the Báb returns to a schema closer to that found in the Qur'án, referring to the revelation of God in Noah, Abraham, Moses, Jesus, and Muḥammad. (See *Panj sha'n*, pp. 384, 396–97; *Dalá'il*, p. 66.) In one passage he speaks of prophets prior to Adam. (*Panj sha'n*, p. 241) The notion of five dispensations seems, however, to be related (albeit idiosyncratically) to the well-known Islamic theory of five major prophets, the *úlú 'l-'azm* or "possessors of constancy," namely Noah, Abraham, Moses, Jesus, and Muḥammad. (See al-Aḥsá'í, *Sharḥ al-ziyára*, vol. 2, p. 155.)

19. The related verb *tajallá* (to become clear, manifest) and its derivatives (especially *tajallí*), with strong echoes of the theories of Ibn al-'Arabí, are frequently used by the Báb. (See, for example, *Panj sha'n* pp. 31, 54, 195.) On Ibn al-'Arabí's use of this term, see Muḥyí

'l-Dín ibn al-'Arabí, *Fuṣús al-ḥikam,* ed. by Abu'l-'Alá 'Afífí (Cairo, 1946) pp. 12–21; idem, *The Bezels of Wisdom,* trans. by R. W. J. Austin (London, 1980) pp. 149–50; T. Izutzu, *A comparative study of the Key Philosophical Concepts in Sufism and Taoism: Ibn al-'Arabi and Lao-Tzu, Chuang-Tzu* (Tokyo, 1966) pp. 37–38.

It is impossible to tell how far, if at all, the Báb may have been directly influenced by the ideas of Ibn al-'Arabí. There is no evidence that he had read any of the latter's works, although we do know that Shaykh Aḥmad al-Aḥsá'í was familiar with some of them, even though he strongly disapproved of Ibn al-'Arabí (see Shaykh Aḥmad ibn Zayn al-Dín al-Aḥsá'í, *Sharḥ al-'Arshiyya,* 2nd. ed., vol. 1 [Kerman, 1361/1982], pp. 26–27; idem, *Sharḥ al-ziyára,* vol. 1, pp. 71, 219, vol. 3, p. 219).

20. The Báb, *Panj sha'n,* p. 40.

21. Ibid., p. 102.

22. Ibid., p. 125.

23. Idem., *Bayán-i fársí,* exordium, p. 3.

24. Ibid., p. 4.

25. On the notion that God's *ẓuhúr* to his creation can only take place metaphorically, see al-Aḥsá'í, *Sharḥ al-'Arshiyya,* vol. 1, p. 61.

26. The Báb, *Panj sha'n,* p. 31; cf. ibid., p. 390; idem, *Dalá'il,* p. 2. On the Imáms as loci of the Primal Will, see al-Aḥsá'í, *Sharḥ al-ziyára,* vol. 2, p. 192.

27. The Báb, *Bayán-i fársí* 4:6, pp. 120–21.

28. Idem, *Panj sha'n,* p. 23 ("the *rusul* are the thrones of his manifestation"). For "thrones," see passim. 'Arsh *al-ḥaqíqa,* "the throne of reality," is often used (e.g., ibid., pp. 21, 31). On the primary application of 'arsh to the "Reality of Muḥammad" (*al-ḥaqíqa al-muḥammadiyya*) and "Absolute Guardianship" (*al-wiláya al-muṭlaqa*), of which the Imáms are the loci, see al-Aḥsá'í *Sharḥ al-ziyára,* vol. 4, p. 245. On Bábí usage, see further, 'Abdu'l-Ḥamíd Ishráq-Khávarí, *Raḥíq-i makhtúm,* 2 vols. (Tehran, 130–131 *Badí'*/1974–76) vol. 2, pp. 157–60.

29. The Báb, *Panj sha'n,* p. 24 and passim.

30. Ibid., p. 423 and passim. This *haykal* is particularly described as "the temple of man": "The Will is in the temple of man ('alá haykal al-insán) from the beginning that has no beginning to the end that has

no end" (ibid., p. 388) and, more interestingly: "For the Will has always been in the temple of God ('alá haykal alláh, which is the temple of man, and all things have been created from it" (ibid., p. 389). On the Imáms appearing in different *hayákil*, see al-Aḥsá'í, *Sharḥ al-ziyára*, vol. 2, p. 160. On the wider implications of the term *haykal* and its relationship to talismans and the science of letters, see my paper "Nineteenth-century Bábí talismans."

31. The Báb, *Panj sha'n*, pp. 34, 132–33, 149–50, and passim. On the concept of the Imáms appearing in their bodies like images in mirrors, see al-Aḥsá'í, *Sharḥ al-ziyára*, vol. 3, p. 128.

32. The Báb, *Panj sha'n*, p. 23 and passim. On the Imáms as *maẓáhir*, see al-Aḥsá'í, *Sharḥ al-ziyára*, vol. 2, p. 48.

33. The Báb, *Bayán-i farsí*, 2:8, p. 37 and passim. *Shajarat al-ẓuhúr* also occurs (*Panj sha'n*, p. 42).

34. Ibid., p. 104 and passim. In this context, the *maẓhar* of the Will is often referred to as the "horizon" (*mashriq*) or "dawning-point" (*maṭla'*)—see ibid., p. 51.

35. Idem., *Bayán-i fársí*, 3:7, p. 81 and passim.

36. Ibid., 1:1, p. 4 and passim. On the use of the titles "first point" and "last point" for the legendary saint Khiḍr by 'Abdu'l-Karím Jílí, see H. Corbin, *Terre celeste et corps de resurrection* (Paris, 1960) p. 244.

For some other terms used for the Primal Will, see the Báb, *Panj sha'n*

37. Idem, *Bayán-i fársí* 1:1, p. 4; 3:8, p. 84.

38. Ibid., 2:8, p. 37.

39. Al-Aḥsá'í, *Sharḥ al-ziyára*, vol. 4, p. 269. Cf. ibid., vol. 2, p. 316.

40. The Báb, *Panj sha'n*, p. 423.

41. Ibid., p. 102.

42. Ibid., p. 23.

43. See al-Aḥsá'í, *Sharḥ al-ziyára*, vol. 2, pp. 108 233; vol. 3, pp. 29, 242.

44. See the Báb, *Panj sha'n*, p. 195: "If he did not reveal himself to the prophets in their own selves, how could God be known?"; ibid., p. 313: "Bear witness that the knowledge of God is not made manifest save by the knowledge of the place in which his self is manifested."

45. Ibid., p. 54; cf. idem, *Dalá'il*, p. 65.

46. Idem, *Panj sha'n*, p. 242.

47. Ibid. On the Imáms as both human and divine, see al-Aḥsá'í, *Sharḥ al-ziyára*, vol. 2, p. 200.

48. The Báb, *Panj sha'n*, p. 40; cf. p. 314: "His inward aspect is the words "no god is there but God," while his outward aspect in the Qur'án was Muḥammad, the messenger of God, and in the Bayán the Essence of the Seven Letters [i.e., 'Alí Muḥammad], and in the Gospel Jesus, the Spirit of God, and in the Psalms David, the Friend of God, and in the Torah Moses, the Interlocutor of God, and after the Bayán he whom God shall manifest."

49. Ibid., p. 391.

50. Ibid., p. 31.

51. See ibid., pp. 24, 31, 59, 63–64, 156, 162, 314, 320; cf. idem, *Dalá'il*, p. 3.

52. Idem. *Panj sha'n*, p. 133.

53. Ibid., pp. 141, 228, and passim. The idea that a single spirit manifests itself in an ever-changing variety of human forms is fundamental to Ismá'ílí and Twelver (Imámí) Shiism. For the Ismá'ílís, the Imáms "are like one and the same person, only appearing in different bodies and states although being in spirit one and the same all through the ages." (W. Ivanow, *Studies in Early Persian Ismailism* [London, 1948], p. 2) Al-Aḥsá'í says of the Imáms that "although they have appeared in numerous forms (*hayákil*), despite their being a single entity, there is no multiplicity in this other than from the point of view of an alteration of place, time, direction, and station." (*Sharḥ al-ziyára*, vol. 2, p. 160)

54. See previous note.

55. *Ḥadíth al-Saḥába*, quoted al-Aḥsá'í, ibid., vol. 2, p. 54. Cf. ibid., p. 115, where the Imáms are said to have spread all the revealed religious systems (*shará'i'*). Al-Aḥsá'í comments that, although the Imáms were created after Muḥammad, they are like him in their essences. Ibid., vol. 4, p. 173)

56. For discussion of this complex problem, see Henri Corbin, *En Islam iranien*, 4 vols. (Paris, 1971–72), vol. 1, chapter VI; idem, *Histoire de la philosophie islamique*, vol. 1 (Paris, 1964), pp. 62–79. See comments of al-Aḥsá'í, *Sharḥ al-ziyára*, vol. 4, p. 64.

57. See A. A. Sachedina, *Islamic Messianism* (Albany, N.Y., 1981) p. 68 and passim.

58. See, for example, al-Aḥsá'í, *Sharḥ al-ziyára*, vol. 2, pp. 41, 56–57, 114, 200 ("God created one thousand thousand worlds and one thousand thousand Adams; in each one of these worlds he caused the Prophet of God [i.e., Muḥammad] to rise up, together with his offspring 'Alí'), 279; vol. 3, pp. 243, 257, 301–02, 361–62; vol. 4, pp. 173, 174.

59. Ibid., vol. 4, p. 188.

60. Ibid., vol. 2, p. 115; cf. ibid., p. 54.

61. Ibid., p. 54.

62. *Ḥadíth* from Imám Ja'far Al-Ṣádiq relating to the Twelfth Imám, quoted in al-Aḥsá'í, "Risála fi 'l-'iṣma wa 'l-raj'a," in *Jawámi'*, vol. 1, part 1, p. 85; also quoted idem, *Sharḥ al-ziyára*, vol. 3, p. 92, and the Báb, *Dalá'il*, pp. 3–4.

63. For the use of *ṣábiqún* in this context, see Sayyid Káẓim Rashtí, *Uṣúl al-'aqá'id* (Iran Bahá'í Archives, xerox collection, 4) pp. 57, 58.

64. See ibid., pp. 90–91; Ḥájí Muḥammad Khán Kirmání, *al-Kitáb al-mubín*, 2nd. ed., 2 vols. (Kerman, n.d.), vol. 1, pp. 304–05; al-Aḥsá'í, *Sharḥ al-ziyára*, vol. 2, pp. 53, 305 (pre-creation).

65. The Báb, *Bayán-i fársí*, 1:2, pp. 6–7; 1:3, pp. 8–10; idem, letter to Ḥájí Sayyid 'Alí Shírází, quoted Mázandaráni, *Ẓuhúr al-ḥaqq*, vol. 3, pp. 223–24; idem, letter to 'Alí [Mullá Shaykh 'Alí Turshízí?], in the Báb and Yazdí, *Qismatí az alwáḥ*, p. 14 (transcription, pp. 13–12 [sic]); idem, letter in ibid., p. 18 (transcription, p. 17); idem. *Panj sha'n*, p. 88 (where Mullá Ḥusayn is identified as the "throne of the Point of the Qur'án [i.e., Muḥammad]"). At a later period, the Báb, while retaining this identification, stated that the Letters of the Living (*ḥurúf-i wáḥid*) possess two stations: that in which they themselves are seen, in which they are but creatures of God, and that in which only God can be seen, in which they are the "letters of truth." (*Bayán-i fársí*, 5:17, p. 180)

66. For a discussion of the main details of this dispute, see MacEoin, "From Shaykhism to Babism," chapter 6, section "Division within the Bábí community," pp. 203–07.

67. The main issues of this debate and some of the circumstances

surrounding it have been fortuitously preserved for us in three manuscript *risálas*, one by Mullá Aḥmad (printed in 'Alí al-Wardí, *Lamaḥát ijtimá'iyya min ta'ríkh al 'Iráq al-ḥadíth*, vol. 2 [Baghdad, 1969] pp. 159 ff.), another by Shaykh Sulṭán al-Karbalá'í (ms. in *Nivishtiját wa áthá-i aṣḥáb-i awwaliyya yi amr-i a'lá ki dar ithbát-i amr-i badí' nivishta-and* [Iran Bahá'í Archives, xerox collection, 80] pp. 310–32; printed in Mázandaráni, *Ẓuhúr al-ḥaqq*, vol. 3, pp. 245–59), and one which can, I think, be attributed to Qurratu'l-'Ayn (ms. in *Nivishtiját wa áthár*, pp. 212–82).

68. Text quoted Mázandaráni, *Ẓuhúr al-ḥaqq*, vol. 3, p. 32. See also ibid., p. 121 and idem, (Mázandaráni), *Asrár al-áthár*, 5 vols. (Tehran, 1967/8—1972/73), vol. 2, p. 12.

69. Káshání, *Nuqṭatu'l-káf*, p. 181. I have discussed the vexing question of the authorship and authenticity of the *Nuqṭatu'l-káf* (a point much contested by Bahá'í authors) in an earlier work ("A Revised Survey of the Sources for Early Bábí History and Doctrine," unpublished dissertation, Cambridge, 1977, pp. 168–194) and will not return to it here. Suffice to note my conclusion that, although the bulk of this work is unlikely to be by the hand of Mírzá Jání Káshání, it is undeniably early and, whatever its theological peculiarities from a later viewpoint, remarkably reliable. It is certainly not an Azalí "forgery." For issues such as those under discussion in the present paper, it is often much more useful than many later historical works.

70. Káshání, *Nuqṭatu'l-káf*, p. 181.

71. Ibid., p. 152.

72. Ibid., p. 169. This obviously had much to do with Mullá Husayn's name, as in the case of some later claimants to the station of *ḥusayniyya*.

73. Ibid., p. 208. On *iráda* as the origin of all worlds but itself created by the *mashi'a*, see the Báb, *Bayán-i fársí*, 2:16, p. 57; on the *iráda* as a mirror of the *mashi'a*, see ibid., 3:7, p. 82.

74. Káshání, *Nuqṭatu'l-káf*, p. 202; cf. ibid., p. 208.

75. Ibid., p. 207.

76. Ibid., p. 202.

77. Ibid., p. 207. On this broader use of the term *qá'im*, see al-Aḥsá'í, *Sharḥ al-ziyára*, vol. 3, p. 75, Sachedina, *Islamic Messianism*, p. 15.

78. Sayyid Muḥammad Ḥusayn Zavára'í, *Waqáyi'-i mímiyaya* (Cambridge University Library, E. G. Browne Or. MSS, F.28, item 1) p. 3 and passim.

79. Ibid., p. 54.

80. Ibid., p. 70.

81. Luṭf 'Alí Mírzá Shírází, untitled history (Cambridge University Library, E. G. Browne Or. MSS, F.28, item 3) p. 71.

82. Káshání, *Nuqṭatu'l-káf*, p. 208. For the original *ḥadíth* and its relationship to the appearance of the Qá'im, see al-Aḥsá'í, *Sharḥ al-ziyára*, vol. 3, pp. 79, 88, and (in particular) 223.

83. Káshání, *Nuqṭatu'l-káf*, pp. 90; Mírzá Ḥusayn Hamadání, *The New History (Tárikh-i-Jadíd) of Mírzá 'Alí Muḥammad, the Báb*, ed. by E. G. Browne (Cambridge University Press, 1893), p. 91 (where Quddús is incidentally referred to as the "Lord of the Dispensation"). For the original prophecy, see *Sharḥ al-ziyára*, vol. 3, pp. 60, 75.

84. Zavára'í, *Waqáyi'*, p. 48.

85. Nabíl, *Dawn-Breakers*, p. 352. For the original prophecy, see al-Aḥsá'í *Sharḥ al-ziyára*, vol. 3, pp. 84–85.

86. Nabíl, *Dawn-Breakers*, p. 354. For the original prophecy, see al-Aḥsá'í, *Sharḥ al-ziyára*, vol. 3, p. 48.

87. Nabíl, *Dawn-Breakers*, p. 344.

88. Zavára'í, *Waqáyi'*, p. 1 and passim.

89. Nabíl, *Dawn-Breakers*, pp. 324–25. References in the tradition literature to various banners are numerous and confused, but the most significant in this context is undoubtedly to the banner presented by the Prophet Muḥammad to the Qá'im (see al-Aḥsá'í *Sharḥ al-ziyára*, vol. 3, pp. 81, 82, 83). On the appearance of black banners from Khurasan (which is, of course, related to the Abbasid revolt of the eighth century), see ibid., p. 113.

90. The Báb, letter to Mullá Shaykh 'Alí Turshízí, in the Báb and Yazdí, *Qismatí az alwáḥ*, p. 13. Cf. letter (also to Turshízí?), ibid., p. 17; the Báb, *Haykal al-dín* (n.p. [Tehran], n.d. [with *al-Bayán al-'arabí*]), pp. 1–2. On the return of all former prophets and saints in the *raj'a*, see al-Aḥsá'í, *Sharḥ al-ziyára*, vol. 3, p. 69. On various meanings of *raj'a*, see Káshání, *Nuqṭatu'l-káf*, p. 170. The identification of the first and second to swear allegiance to the Qá'im as

Muḥammad and 'Alí, followed by the other Imáms, is based on prophetic traditions to this effect (see, for example, text quoted al-Aḥsá'í, "'Isma wa raj'a," in *Jawámi'*, vol. 1, part 1, p. 66).

91. Turshízí, letter printed in Mázandarání, *Ẓuhúr al-ḥaqq*, vol. 3, p. 166. Cf. generally letter from Qurratu'l-'Ayn to Turshízí, printed in Hamadání, *New History*, p. 436 (with facsimile, p. 435; this section of the letter is not translated by Browne). The "tomb" analogy is used later by Mullá Rajab 'Alí Qahír when he refers to Turshízí as the tomb of Mullá Ḥusayn Bushrú'í (*marqad-i awwal man ámana—risála*, f. 25a) and to Ṣubḥ-i Azal as the tomb of Mullá Muḥammad 'Alí Bárfurúshí, Quddús, (*marqad-i ḥarf-i ákhir*—ibid., f. 44a).

92. Zavára'í, *Waqáyi'*, p. 47.

93. Ibid., p. 55.

94. On the *nuqabá'*, *nujabá'*, etc., see below.

95. See Dahají, *Risála*, pp. 32, 151–52. Cf. Mírzá Yaḥyá Núrí, Ṣubḥ-i Azal, *Kitáb-i mustayqiẓ* (n.p. [Tehran], n.d.) p. 17.

96. Sayyid 'Alí Muḥammad Shírází, the Báb, *Ziyára* for Mulla Muḥammad 'Alí Bárfurúshí, in Muḥammad 'Alí Malik Khusraví, *Táríkh-i shuhadá'-i amr*, 3 vols. (Tehran, 1974) vol. 2, p. 412.

97. The Báb, *Panj sha'n*, p. 104.

98. Ḥusayn 'Alí Núrí, Bahá'u'lláh, "Lawḥ-i Siríj," in Ishráq-Khávarí (ed.), *Má'ida*, vol. 7, p. 86.

99. Ibid.

100. 'Abbás Effendi, 'Abdu'l-Bahá', *Makátíb-i 'Abdu'l-Bahá'*, vol. 2 (Cairo, 1330/1912), p. 254; cf. P. 252. No copy of the *tafsír* on the *ṣád* of *al-Ṣamad* is, to my knowledge, extant. According to Nabíl, the original, along with other writings, was entrusted to a certain Mullá Muḥammad Ḥamza [Sharí'atmadár Bárfurúshí], an 'álim resident in Bárfurúsh (*Dawn-Breakers*, p. 409). Sharí'atmadár (who was sympathetic to the Bábís and who lived until 1281/1864–65) wrote a work entitled *Asrár al-shaháda* in 1272/1856, in which he mentions having seen a *tafsír* by Quddús on the *Súrat al-tawḥíd*, consisting of five thousand or six thousand verses (see Mázandarání, *Ẓuhúr al-Ḥaqq*, vol. 3, p. 438). This does not, of course, necessarily imply that this work remained in Sharí'atmadár's possession, but it may prove a useful starting-point for the task of locating it. In 1977, I saw briefly what seemed to me to be an autograph copy of the *Asrár al-shaháda* which had recently come into the possession of the Iranian National

Bahá'í Archives in Tehran, but I have no way of knowing whether or not other materials belonging to Sharí'atmadár also came into their possession at the same time.

101. Zavára'í, *Waqáyi'*, p. 48.

102. Nabíl, *Dawn-Breakers*, p. 412.

103. The Báb, *ziyára* for Bárfurúshí, in Malik Khusraví *Táríkh-i shuhadá'*, vol. 2, p. 413.

104. Idem, *Panj sha'n*, p. 280.

105. 'Abbás Effendi, *Makátíb*, vol. 2, pp. 254–55. Unfortunately, the writer presents no documentary or testimonial evidence for this statement, although we may assume he had an eye-witness account from his father, Mírzá Ḥusayn 'Alí, Bahá'u'lláh. What is interesting—and theologically controversial—is that 'Abbás Effendi goes on to refer to claims to divinity made in his father's *Qaṣída 'izz warqá'iyya* without distinguishing these in any way from those made by Qurrat-u'l-'Ayn, Quddús, or other Bábís at Badasht. On the use of the phrase "Verily, I am God" (*innaní aná 'lláh*) by the mirrors of the divine Will, see the Báb, *Panj sha'n*, pp. 133–34.

106. (*Hádhá kitáb min 'inda 'lláh 'l-muhaymini 'l-qayyúm ilá 'lláhi 'l-muhaymini 'l-qayyúm*), in a letter to Ṣubḥ-i Azal, in the Báb and Yazdí, *Qismatí az alwáḥ*, p. 1 (facsimile of original on previous unnumbered page); also printed in [Sayyid 'Alí Muḥammad Shírází, the Báb and Mírzá Yaḥyá Núrí, Ṣubḥ-i Azal] *Majmú'a'í az áthár-i Nuqṭay-i Úlá wa Ṣubḥ-i Azal* (n.p. [Tehran], n.d.) p. 38, and Hamadání, *New History*, p. 427 (hand of Ṣubḥ-i Azal).

107. (*Hádhá kitáb m in alláh ilá man yuẓhiruhu 'lláh*), *Panj sha'n*, pp. 2, 24, 33, 57, 104, 207. Cf. Dahají, *Risála*, p. 113 ("the Point of the Bayán [i.e., the Báb] revealed the words "from God to God" in numerous tablets").

108. The Báb and Ṣubḥ-i Azal, *Majmú'a'í az áthár*, p. 37. On the application of the term *dhátu'lláh* to both the Báb and his "mirrors," see [Mullá Muḥammad Ja'far Naraqí], *Tadhkirat al-gháfilín* (Cambridge University Library, E. G. Browne Or. MSS, F.63), p. 32. (On the authorship of this work, see introduction to 'Izziyya Khánum, *Tanbíh al-ná'imín* [n.p. (Tehran), n.d.] p. 3.) For the Báb as *dhátu'lláh*, see the Báb, *Haykal al-dín*, 1:18, p. 5.

109. Qazvíní is known by a number of names: "Raḥím" (numerically equivalent to "Ibráhím"), "Khalíl" (the epithet of the prophet

Abraham), and the codename "Mírzá Aḥmad." The divine name *al-qadím* and its derivatives (especially *al-aqdam*) are used in the section of the *Panj sha'n* written for him. (See ibid., pp. 327ff.)

110. Yazdí, letter in the Báb and Yazdí, *Qismatí az alwáḥ*, p. 38.

111. H. M. Balyuzi, *Edward Granville Bowne and the Bahá'í Faith* (London: George Ronald, 1970) p. 73.

112. Al-Aḥsá'í, "'*Iṣma wa raj'a*," in *Jawámi'*, vol. 1, part 1, p. 59. For further details on the Sufi grades of *awliyá*, see J. S. Trimingham, *The Sufi Orders in Islam* (Oxford, 1971) pp. 163–65; A. A. Nicholson, "Badal," *The Encyclopedia of Islam*, 1st ed.

113. Al-Aḥsá'í, "'*Iṣma wa raj'a*," *Jawámi'*, vol. 1, part 1, p. 59. This tradition is also quoted by al-Aḥsá'í in a similar context in *Sharḥ al-ziyára*, vol. 3, p. 215. The Báb discusses these seven stages of *ma'rifa* in his *Ṣaḥífay-i 'adliyya* (n.p. [Tehran], n.d.; pp. 18–33), where the *arkán* are identified as the four *úlú 'l-'azm* before Muḥammad (i.e., Noah, Abraham, Moses and Jesus) and as four prophets who acted as pillars of God's grace after Muḥammad (Jesus, Khiḍr, Elias, and Idrís).

114. On this central concept, see al-Aḥsá'í *Sharḥ al-ziyára*, vol. 1, pp. 20–27, 121; vol. 2, pp. 353, 363–64 (where he places *nubuwwa* before *ma'ání* and *af'ál* after *imáma*); vol. 3, pp. 29–30, 38, 144, 149; vol. 4, pp. 171, 250, 269. For a much more detailed exposition, see Ḥájí Mullá Muḥammad Karím Khán Kirmání, *Irshád al-'awámm*, 4th ed., 4 vols. in 2 (Kerman, 1380/1960) vol. 3, pp. 96–262.

115. Al-Aḥsá'í, *Sharḥ al-ziyára*, vol. 3, p. 215.

116. Ibid., p. 216.

117. Ibid., p. 243. The knowledge of God vouchsafed to the Imáms themselves differs from one to the next, although all possess sufficient knowledge to perform the function of *hujja*, which requires fulfilling men's needs in respect to knowing God. (See ibid., vol. 2, pp. 311–12)

118. See, for example, ibid., vol. 2, pp. 64, 201, 203, 364; vol. 3, p. 11.

119. Assuming this to be a reasonably early tradition, *fuqahá'* here must be taken in its original wider sense of "scholars" (equivalent to *'ulamá'*), rather than "jurisprudents."

120. Ibid., vol. 2, p. 265.

121. Qurratu'l-'Ayn, *Risála* in Gulpáygání and Gulpáygání, *Kashf al-ghiṭá'*, appendix, pp. 5–6.

122. Qurratu'l-'Ayn here quotes a version of a well-known tradition to the effect that in every age there is an arbiter (*'adúl*) who rejects from the faith the corruptions of the errant and thus preserves it from error. For other references, see MacEoin, "From Shaykhism to Babism," p. 14.

123. Qurratu'l-'Ayn, *Risála* in Gulpáygání and Gulpáygání, *Kashf al-ghiṭá'*, appendix, pp. 3–8.

124. Ibid., pp. 11–14.

125. Ibid., p. 15. This reference indicates that the *risála* must predate the Báb's claim to *qá'imiyya*.

126. For fuller details, see MacEoin, "From Shaykhism to Babism," pp. 168–71.

127. Qurratu'l-'Ayn, *Risála* (MS in private hands, Tehran; copy in possession of author) pp. 8–9.

128. Ibid., p. 12.

129. Ibid., pp. 13–14. On the Báb as the "fourth support," cf. p. 30.

130. Ibid., pp. 18, 19. On the Báb as one of the *nuqabá'*, cf. p. 30. The Báb himself refers to al-Aḥsá'í as a "pure Shí'a" (*shí'ay-i kháliṣ*) in his *Ṣaḥífay-i 'adliyya.* (p. 33)

131. Qurratu'l-'Ayn, *Risála* (in private hands) pp. 30–31. For details of this tradition, see al-Aḥsá'í, *Sharḥ al-ziyára*, vol. 3, pp. 361–62; vol. 4, pp. 195, 200–201; idem, *Sharḥ al-'Arshiyya*, vol. 1, p. 21.

132. Qurratu'l-'Ayn, *Risála* (in private hands) p. 34.

133. The later Bahá'í writer Mullá Muḥammad Zarandí, Nabíl, appears to identify the Letters of the Living as *nuqabá'* under the looser title "Men of the Unseen" (presumably *rijál al-ghayb*)—see *Dawn-Breakers*, p. 70.

134. The Báb, *Ṣaḥífay-i 'adliyya*, pp. 20–33, especially pp. 29–31.

135. Idem, quoted Qurratu'l-'Ayn (?), *Risála*, in Mázandarání, *Ẓuhúr al-ḥaqq*, vol. 3, p. 250. (This *Risála* is also reproduced in *Nivishtiját*, pp. 310–332; this reference p. 317.)

136. Quoted al-Karbalá'í, *Risála*, in Mázandarání, *Ẓuhúr al-ḥaqq*, vol. 3, p. 248.

137. Quoted ibid.

138. See note 31. See further Rajab 'Alí Qahír, *Risála*, f. 30b–31a.

This theory may owe something to the frequent use of the mirror analogy by Ibn al-'Arabí. See Ibn al-'Arabí, *Bezels*, pp. 50–51, 233; cf. Austin's comments, ibid., p. 48.

139. See note 117.

140. The Báb, *Panj sha'n*, p. 102.

141. Ibid., pp. 162–63.

142. Ibid., p. 133. On God's singling out a mirror from all creation, see ibid., pp. 120, 132, 141, 149. On the significance of the *buṭún*, see below.

143. Ibid., p. 133.

144. Ibid., p. 134.

145. The term *náṭiq*, together with its corollary *al-sámiṭ*, ("the silent one"), is, of course, well known in Ismailism, although it finds a certain usage in Imámí Shiism as well. Al-Aḥsá'í speaks of the appearance of a *náṭiq* and *sámiṭ* in each age (*Sharḥ al-ziyára*, vol. 3, p. 151).

146. The Báb, *Panj sha'n*, p. 134.

147. Ibid., p. 135. On the dependence and indirectness of the secondary and subsequent mirrors, see ibid., p. 217 and idem, *Bayán-i fársí*, 6:7, p. 208.

148. Idem, *Panj sha'n*, pp. 149–50.

149. Ibid., pp. 199–201. It is unclear from the context whether the first mirror here refers to the Báb himself or to another individual, possibly Ṣubḥ-i Azal. There are certainly references elsewhere to the latter's possession of *fiṭra*.

150. On the use of *al-wáḥid al-awwal*, see the Báb, *al-Bayán al-'arabi*, 1:1, p. 3; idem, *Haykal al-dín*, 1:12, p. 3.

151. Nabíl, *Dawn-Breakers*, p. 123. Cf. A. L. M. Nicolas (trans.), *Le Béyan Persan*, 4 vols. (Paris, 1911–1914), vol. 1, pp. 7–9, f.n., 13, f.n. On the relationship of this system to the Bábí calendar, see the Báb, *Bayán-i fársí*, 5:3, p. 153. There are parallels to the *kullu shay'* total in various Sufi theories, including Rúzbihán Baqlí Shírází's concept of 366 saints linked to the hearts of various prophets. (See H. Corbin, *L'homme de lumière dans le Soufisme Iranien* [Paris, 1971], p. 83.

152. Rajab 'Alí Qahír, *Risála*, f. 43b.

153. The Báb, *al-Bayán al-'arabí*, 8:16, p. 38.

154. 'Abdu'l-Ḥamíd Ishráq-Khávarí, *Raḥíq-i makhtúm*, 2 vols. (Tehran, 1974–75), vol. 1, p. 338.

155. The Báb, *Panj sha'n*, p. 280. The sentence following this seems to me extremely significant, but it is, I fear, very difficult to interpret owing to the vagueness of verbs and pronouns in it. A tentative translation would continue the passage as follows: "for after I stripped off that garment [i.e., *bábiyya*] and revealed myself in the name of messiah-hood (*al-maqṣúdiyya*) and the status of the promised one (*al-maw'údiyya*), it was necessary that one of its temples (*min hayákilihá* [reading *há* as a pronoun, although it is written as if separate—"one of the temples of *'há'*"?]) should put it (*al-bábiyya*?] on." Mullá Rajab 'Alí Qahír omits the *há* (or *há'*) in his quotation of this passage. (*Risála*, f. 76b)

156. The Báb, *Panj sha'n*, pp. 184–85.

157. Ibid, pp. 256–57. Also quoted Rajab 'Alí Qahír, *Risála*, f. 76b.

158. The Báb, *Ṣalát al-hayákil*, quoted ibid, f. 58a; also quoted 'Izziyya Khánum, *Tanbíh al-ná'imín*, p. 50. The number 66 equals the word *alláh*. There may be eschatological significance in the period of sixty-six years. Shí'í tradition refers to the "year 66" in an eschatological context. (See al-Aḥsá'í, "'iṣma wa raj'a," *Jawám'*, vol. 1, part 1, p. 84.)

159. On which see my paper, "Nineteenth-century Bábí talismans."

160. The Báb, *Panj sha'n*, p. 408. The passage is obscure. Sixty-six years for each letter comes to only 1254, which does not seem to be a significant year.

161. Ibid., p. 412. Cf. idem, *al-Bayán al-'arabí*, 5:10, p. 11, where the *hayákil al-ḥayy* (i.e., Letters of the Living) are described as mirrors before the "sun of the point" (*shams al-nuqṭa*).

162. The Báb, *Haykal al-dín*, 7:1, p. 27.

163. Ibid., 5:6, p. 6; idem, *al-Bayán al-'arabí*, 5:6, p. 19.

164. Ibid., 8:16, p. 38; idem, *Bayán-i fársí*, 8:16, p. 300.

165. Idem, *al-Bayán al-'arabí*, 11:2, p. 54.

166. Idem, *Panj sha'n*, p. 209. On the *ḥujja* as single with other *ḥujaj* in its shadow, see ibid., p. 136.

167. He also mentions *qunnád* (?), the meaning of which is unclear.

168. The Báb, *Panj sha'n*, p. 199. Cf. ibid., p. 247.

169. Ibid., p. 381.

170. Ibid., p. 258. Cf. ibid., p. 176.

171. Reading the *nún* of the verb as emphatic, in order to provide a singular for the imminent pronoun *hu*.

172. Passage from untitled word of the Báb, quoted Rajab 'Alí, *Risála*, f. 60a.

173. Letter to Mírzá Ibráhím Qazvíní, in the Báb and Núrí, *Majmú'a'i az á*th*ár*, p. 38. On the use of "al-waḥíd" as a title of Ṣubḥ-i Azal, see Browne, "The Babis of Persia. II," *Journal of the Royal Asiatic Society* 21 (1889) pp. 996–97.

174. The Báb, passage from *Kitáb al-asmá'* (?), quoted Rajab 'Alí Qahír, *Risála*, f. 20b.

175. See, for example, the Báb, *Bayán-i fársí*, 4:5, pp. 119–20; 5:5, pp. 157, 158; 7:16, p. 262; idem, *al-Bayán al-'arabí*, 9:3, p. 41; 11:2, p. 54; 11:13, p. 58; 11:16, p. 60; idem, *Haykal al-dín*, 1:16, p. 4; 5:19, p. 9; 3:11, p. 11; 4:9, p. 15; 7:9, p. 29; 7:16, p. 31.

176. See, for example, the Báb, *al-Bayán al-'arabí*, 10:16,p. 50; 10:17, p. 51; 11:2, p. 54; idem, *Haykal al-dín*, 3:11, p. 11; t:16, p. 31.

177. See, for example, ibid., 5:5, p. 6; 5:19, p. 9; 4:9, p. 15.

178. Ibid., 7:1, p. 27.

179. Idem, *al-Bayán al-'arabí*, 9:14, p. 43.

180. Idem, *Haykal al-dín*, 1:16, p. 4.

181. This topic has been discussed previously by several writers, including E. G. Browne (*Nuqṭat al-káf*, pp. XXV–XXVI) *Ishráq-Khávarí (Raḥíq*, vol. 2, pp. 514–25) and Mázandarání (*Asrár*, vol. 4, pp. 427–28).

182. The Báb, *Bayán-i fársí*, 2:16, pp. 61–62. See also ibid., 2:17, p. 71; 3:15, p. 100; 7:10, p. 252.

183. Ibid., 3:15, p. 100; 7:10, p. 252.

184. There is evidence that Bahá'u'lláh himself may have originally held this view. In the *Lawḥ kull al-ṭa'ám* he writes "O Kamál, were I to explain this verse to you from today until the days reach *al-mustagháth*, the day when men shall stand before the face of the Living, the Creator, I would be able to do so through what God has given me of his grace and bounty." (In Ishráq Khávarí, *Má'ida*, vol. 4, pp. 272–73.) The implication seems to be that the time-span involved is one of great duration.

185. The Báb, *Panj sha'n*, pp. 162, 198, 208, 315.

186. "In every *ẓuhúr*. God renews the creation of all things." (Ibid., p. 352)

187. Ibid., p. 176; cf. p. 194. Cf. idem, *Kitáb al-asmá'*, quoted by Rajab 'Alí Qahír, *Risála*, f. 58b.

188. The Báb, *Panj sha'n,* p. 315.
189. Idem, *Bayán-i fársí,* 2:7, p. 31.
190. Thus, he states that all things culminate in the form of man and that man progresses from level to level until he reaches perfection as a prophet (*Bayán-i fársí,* 2:1, pp. 14–15); men are singled out from the rest of creation and purified by the prophets (*Panj sha'n,* p. 205); the Báb himself has been raised through increasingly exalted stations (ibid., pp. 184–85); clay will progress to stages of increasing refinement through the alchemical process (ibid., p. 337); the inhabitants of hell in a subsequent revelation possess a station higher than those of paradise in the one before (ibid., p. 426—but cf. p. 403); divine knowledge is revealed progressively (ibid., p. 100); the words of the manifestation in each revelation are more exalted than in the previous one (*Bayán-i fársí,* 3:1, p. 79); each revelation is the same as the one before, but nobler (ibid., 3:1, pp. 79–80; cf. 4:11, p. 136); the successive manifestations resemble a child at various states of its growth (ibid., 3:12, p. 95); the paradise of each thing lies in its perfection (ibid., 5:3, p. 155); each thing has its degree of perfection in which a divine name may be applied to it (ibid., 5:6, p. 164); as the ages progress, the time will come when nothing is named save by a divine name (ibid., 5:4, p. 155); if it be in anyone's power to do a thing to perfection, he must not leave any shortcomings in it (ibid., 6:3, p. 192.
191. Al-Aḥsá'í, "Al-risála al-Rashtiyya," in *Jawámi',* vol. 1, part 2, p. 103. Al-Aḥsá'í states elsewhere that time (*zamán*) may be subtle (*laṭíf*), dense (*ghalíẓ*), simple (*basíṭ*), or compound (*murakkab*). (See *Sharḥ al-ziyára,* vol. 3, p. 305.)
192. Idem, "'Iṣma wa raj'a," in *Jawámı',* vol. 1, part 1, p. 82. This idea is in itself linked to Ibn Síná's theory that the measurement of time depends upon motion, time being the quantity or measure of motion. (See Sayyed Hossein Nasr, *An Introduction to Islamic Cosmological Doctrines,* [Cambridge, Mass., 1864], pp. 224–25.)
193. Al-Aḥsá'í, "'Iṣma wa raj'a," in *Jawámí',* vol. 1, part 1, p. 62.
194. The Báb, *Panj sha'n,* p. 248.
195. Ibid., p. 319. The Báb consistently dates the Islamic era, not from the *hijra* in 622, but to the prophet's *ba'tha,* ten years previously.
196. Ibid., p. 215.

197. Ibid., p. 311.
198. Ibid., p. 199.
199. Ibid., p. 315. Cf. idem, *Bayán-i fársí*, 7:10, p. 252.
200. See my paper "Nineteenth-century Bábí talismans." For example of prophetic interpretation of some passages in this part of the *Panj sha'n*, see Mírzá Ḥusayn 'Alí Núrí, Bahá'u'lláh, letter to Muballigh-i Shírází, Iran National Bahá'í Archives, MS 3003C (incorrectly catalogued as a work of the Báb).
201. Al-Aḥsá'í, *Sharḥ al-ziyára*, vol. 3, pp. 63, 87, 115, 120.
202. See ibid., vol. 3, pp. 54–121; idem., "'Iṣma wa raj'a," in *Jawámı'*, vol. 1, part 1, pp. 38–111; Muḥammad Báqir Majlisí, *Biḥár al-anwár*, 102 vols. (Tehran, 1384/1964), vol. 53; Sachedina, *Islamic Messianism*, chapter 5.
203. Al-Aḥsá'í, *Sharḥ al-ziyára*, vol. 3, p. 57.
204. Ibid., pp. 57–58. Other figures are also given, including 203, 309, 19, and 70.
205. Ibid., pp. 58, 60.
206. Ibid., p. 60.
207. The Báb, letter to Mullá Shaykh 'Alí Turshízí, 'Aẓím, in the Báb and Yazdí, *Qismatí az alwáḥ*, p. 13.
208. See, for example, al-Aḥsá'í, *Sharḥ al-ziyára*, vol. 3, p. 60.
209. The Báb, *Dalá'il*, p. 58.
210. Ibid.
211. Ibid.
212. Ibid. This is explained metaphorically in terms of light as a lamp burning itself in order to give illumination to others (just as Ḥusayn sacrificed himself), pp. 58–59. It also appears to be numerologically true, since "Ḥusayn" (128) when doubled equals *núr* (256). It is conceivable that the doubling in this case is an allusion to Ḥusayn's return. For the text of the *Du'á al-saḥar* together with a commentary, see Ḥájí Muḥammad Karím Khán Kirmání, *Sharḥ du'á al-saḥar* (Kerman, n.d.). Kirmání identifies the *núr* outwardly with the Fourth Support (*rukn al-rábi'*) and inwardly with the Qá'im. (See ibid., pp. 61, 62)
213. See the Báb, *Panj sha'n*, pp. 294, 321.
214. Idem, *Dalá'il*, p. 59. Although the text differs slightly, this is almost certainly the letter quoted in part by Rashtí himself in his *Dalíl*

al-mutaḥayyirín (n.p. [Tabríz?], 1276/1859–60), p. 37. The phrase quoted, with a slight variation, is from the Qur'án (38:88).

215. Quoted in the Báb, *Dalá'il* p. 46.

216. See Shoghi Effendi, in Nabíl, *Dawn-Breakers*, p. 18, f.n. 1.

217. The Báb, *Panj sha'n*, pp. 255–56. A garbled version of this passage is given by Mírzá Ḥusayn 'Alí Núrí, Bahá'u'lláh in his *Lawḥ-i Shaykh* (Cairo, 1338/1920) pp. 104–05 (trans. by Shoghi Effendi, *Epistle to the Son of the Wolf* [Wilmette, Ill.: Bahá'í Publishing Trust, 1941], p. 142); cf. ibid., pp. 113–14 (trans. *Epistle*, p. 152).

218. The Báb, *Panj sha'n*, p. 256.

219. Ibid., p. 280. The term *qabla ḥín* occurs frequently in the phrase "in every time and before a time and after a time' (*fí kulli ḥín wa wabla ḥín wa ba'da ḥín*), much used in Bábí writing. See, for example, passages in Mázandarání, *Ẓuhúr al-ḥaqq*, vol. 3, pp. 70, 167 (last line), 168 (last two lines); Káshání, *Nuqṭatu'l-káf*, pp. 429–30; the Báb, *Dalá'il*, p. 72; idem, letter in the Báb and Yazdí, *Qismatí az alwáḥ*, p. 9, 35.

220. Idem, *Panj sha'n*, p. 256.

221. Ibid., p. 280.

222. Bahá'u'lláh, *Lawḥ-i Shaykh*, pp. 113–14 (trans. *Epistle*, p. 152).

223. The Báb, *al-Bayán al-'arabí*, 6:15, p. 27.

224. Reading the opening verb as an imperative, by analogy with the corresponding passage in the *Bayán-i farsí*, 6:15, p. 230.

225. The Báb, *Haykal al-dín*, 6:15, p. 25.

226. Letter quoted in Mázandarání, *Ẓuhúr al-ḥaqq*, vol. 3, p. 223. Bahá'í doctrine, however, explicitly identifies *al-qayyúm* as a prophetic title of Bahá'u'lláh. (See Ishráq-Khávarí, *Raḥíq*, vol. 2, pp. 316–17; Mázandarání, *Asrár*, vol. 4, pp. 259–31; Mírzá Ḥusayn 'Alí Núrí, Bahá'u'lláh, letter to Shaykh Káẓim Qazvíní Samandar, in *Alwáḥ-i ḥaḍrat-i Bahá'u'lláh . . . shámil-i Iqtidárát* . . . (n.p., n.d.), p. 61; idem, letter in Ishráq-Khávarí, *Má'ida*, vol. 4, pp. 173–74.) The term appears to be used for Ṣubḥ-i Azal in the *Nuqṭatu'l-káf*, p. 253.

ANGEL STANDING ON LAND AND SEA
Revelation 10:1–7

A UNIQUE ESCHATOLOGICAL INTERFACE: BAHÁ'U'LLÁH AND CROSS-CULTURAL MESSIANISM

by Christopher Buck

Religions decline in fortune over time, between heyday and renaissance. Whether due to oppression from foreign conquerors, or to eclipse from the rise of a more popular movement, or to the threat of encroaching secularism, or to the decay of the social order itself, a religion will eventually face crisis. It is during such crucial periods that a peculiar type of scripture dawns on the historical horizon, that which we call apocalyptic.

The 1979 International Colloquium on Apocalypticism at Uppsala and the 1983 Princeton Conference on Maitreya Studies are two instances which show how interest in the apocalyptic is still quite alive.[1] Most religions, if not all, develop future-oriented "visions of the end." In such eschatological dramas, cosmology is applied to the future, and these prophecies, often modelled on past events, may be regarded as a kind of projected or inverse history.[2] Central to most apocalypses is the messianic savior whose function is to effect a deliverance from oppression, after which will be the revitalization of religion—from lowest ebb to restored power.

The morphological and historical nucleus of messianism is, on comparative grounds, defined by Lanternari as follows: "A messianic movement is, in general, a collective movement of escape from the present and of expectation of salvation, promoted by a prophet-founder, following a mystico-ecstatic inspiration: a movement which intends to start a renewal of the world which will be realized in an eschatological perspective as a return to a primordial and paradisical age."[3]

In all apocalyptic traditions eschatological associations are proclaimed by the charismatic aspirant to messianic office. Prophecy is drawn on for purposes of legitimation. This phenomenon repeats itself over and over in history. But when a new religion or messianic movement encounters diverse traditions beyond its own ideological milieu, what kind of cross-fertilization occurs?

The case of the Bahá'í Faith demonstrates the process, since it is both well-documented and ongoing. Bahá'u'lláh (1817–1892), prophet-founder of the Bahá'í cause, has been heralded by his followers as the eschatological Imám Ḥusayn (Shiism), S͟háh Bahrám Varjávand (Zoroastrianism), the Spirit of Truth or Comforter (Christianity), Kalki Viṣṇuyaśas (Hinduism), Maitreya (Buddhism), as well as Viracocha (Peruvian Incan tradition). Other instances of messianic dignity conferred upon Bahá'u'lláh augment this eschatological constellation.[4]

The only important historical parallel to this example of what one might call a "multiple messiahship" is afforded by the prophetology of Mání. In a passage preserved by al-Bírúní from Mání's now-lost *S͟háhpúragán*, Mání proclaims:

> Wisdom and deeds have always from time to time been brought to mankind by the messengers of God. So in one age they have been brought by the messenger of God called Buddha to India, in another by Zoroaster to Persia, in another by Jesus to the West. Thereafter this revelation has come down, this prophecy in this last

age, through me, Mání, the Messenger of the God of Truth to Babylonia.[5]

Mání, who evidently styled himself "the seal of the prophets"[6] (as later Muḥammad likewise would), was regarded by early followers (according to the newly discovered *Cologne Mání Codex*) as a manifestation of the "True Prophet" whose spirit enlightens a succession of revelators throughout the ages. Such prophetology echoes Elkasaite doctrine (as Mání was raised among Elkasaite baptists), and is strikingly evocative of the True-Prophet Christology of Ebionite Christianity as developed in the Pseudo-Clementine Romance.[7]

Thus a unique contribution of Mání to religious thought is the way in which he universalized prophetology through a federal ideology adapted to embrace wisdom-traditions outside the Abrahamic thought-world. So successful was Mání that during his own lifetime, the religion spread to Ctesiphon, Babylon, Armenia, India, Mesene, Susiana, and Edessa.[8]

Although Mání was probably the first person in history ever to have consciously pursued the role of a world-prophet, nineteenth-century civilization proved a far more auspicious time for such a figure. Like Mání, Bahá'u'lláh was a Persian, yet both transcended their own cultural boundaries. However, Bahá'u'lláh succeeded where Mání failed. Through a comparable, though perhaps more august proclamation, Bahá'u'lláh was a superior organizer of an optimistic rather than pessimistic spirituality. By formulating a code of laws replete with a clear structure for the future development of his community of believers, Bahá'u'lláh founded a Faith with the potential for becoming a world religion.[9]

As the "World-Reformer," through whose "new World Order"[10] the peoples of the world would be universalized, Bahá'u'lláh began to articulate an ideology which relativizes all past apocalyptic visions as expressive of the same theme, hope, mandate, and promise. Within a single vision, legitimated through Bahá'u'lláh's federal prophetology, is developed a concept referred to as "progressive Revelation":

> Contemplate with thine inward eye the chain of successive Revelations that hath linked the Manifestation of Adam with that of the Báb [Bahá'u'lláh's forerunner]. I testify before God that each one of these Manifestations . . . hath each been the bearer of a specific Message, that each hath been entrusted with a divinely-revealed Book and been commissioned to unravel the mysteries of a mighty Tablet . . . And when this process of progressive Revelation culminated . . . He hath arisen to proclaim in person His Cause unto all.[11]

Bahá'u'lláh taught as "fact that all the Prophets of God . . . have invariably foretold the coming of yet another Prophet after them, and have established such signs as would herald the advent of the future Dispensation."[12] Such tension of eschatological expectancy belonged to past religions, but in this age: "The Prophetic Cycle hath, verily, ended."[13] Bahá'u'lláh announces: "Say: He Who is the Unconditioned is come, in the clouds of light, that He may . . . unify the world."[14]

Of universal movement in Bahá'í prophetic history is Bahá'u'lláh's advent as the "Promise of all the Prophets of God, . . . heralded in all the sacred Scriptures."[15] Augmenting the great announcement are the specific eschatological claims advanced by Bahá'u'lláh himself. Taking each eschatological association separately, Bahá'u'lláh proclaimed himself to be four messianic figures, correlative of course to the four religious traditions which then predominated in nineteenth-century Persia. This is the point of departure for the Bahá'í process of cross-acculturation of its own universal messianism.

Bahá'u'lláh's fourfold messiahship is interesting to document, since this proclamation in effect originated a Bahá'í teaching technique. Through these specific eschatological bridges, built to appeal to various apocalyptic traditions, potential converts were enabled to make the crucial connexion of faith between Bahá'u'lláh and an expected deliverer foretold in prophecy.

This eschatological interface was expanded through the missionary endeavors of Bahá'u'lláh's followers, and to some extent by the official pronouncements of the successive heads of the Faith. Now, as the Bahá'í teachings are increasingly promulgated among the world's tribal and minority cultures, new apocalyptic expectations are encountered by Bahá'í teachers, who seek to build appropriate eschatological bridges. A closer look at Bahá'u'lláh's inaugural role in this "Diffusion of the Bahá'í Faith" (which topic was discussed by panelists at two conferences of the American Academy of Religion in 1984) is in order and calls for a systematic description.

Quite public about his intentional role as a universal apocalyptic figure, Bahá'u'lláh directed his proclamations to specific religious communities, informing us that:

> At one time We address the people of the Torah and summon them unto Him Who is the Revealer of verses, Who hath come from Him Who layeth low the necks of men. . . . At another, We address the people of the Evangel. . . . At still another, We address the people of the Qur'án saying: "Fear the All-Merciful, and cavil not at Him through Whom all religions were founded." . . . Know thou, moreover, that We have addressed to the Magians Our Tablets. . . . We have revealed in them the essence of all the hints and allusions contained in their Books.[16]

To examine Bahá'u'lláh's specific claims within each of the four aforenamed traditions illustrates the appeal to prophecy which a charismatic aspirant to messianic office necessarily makes for purposes of legitimation. Such *testimonia* are naturally enlarged upon by later followers. Before we proceed to this secondary process, let us look at Bahá'u'lláh's appeal to messianic expectations then current in Persia and elsewhere among Shí'í Muslims, Christians, Jews, and Zoroastrians.

Shí'ih Islam: Bahá'u'lláh first acknowledges a popular belief in Imami Shiism: that of the appearance or emergence (*ẓuhúr*) of the Hidden Twelfth Imám, who is called *qá'im*, followed by the return (*raj'át*) of other Imáms to eventually establish their rule. The return of the third, Imám Ḥusayn, represents an apocalyptic vision which has been at times a very passionate longing in Shí'í folk beliefs. Among the bewilderingly numerous apocalyptic traditions in Shiism, the exegesis of the Quranic passage: "Then, returned We unto you the turn [to prevail] against them and aided you . . . ," (Qur'án 17:6) attributed to the sixth Imám, Ja'far-i-Ṣádiq, was quite influential. Here, by "returned" is meant the return of Imám Ḥusayn, who will be flanked by the seventy-two of his companions who were martyred with him on the field of Karbala. These companions will announce the return of Ḥusayn. At the same time, the Qá'im will be among the people. When the people have truly recognized Ḥusayn, the Qá'im will die, and Ḥusayn will perform the funeral rites and burial.[17] With this all-too-slight background, the relevant messianic claim is advanced by Bahá'u'lláh as follows:

> Consider the eagerness with which certain peoples . . . have anticipated the return of Imám-Ḥusayn, whose coming, after the appearance of the Qá'im, hath been prophesied, by the chosen ones of God, exalted be His glory. These holy ones have, moreover, announced that . . . all the Prophets and Messengers, including the Qá'im, will gather together beneath the shadow of the sacred Standard which the Promised One will raise. That hour is now come. . . . The seal of the choice Wine of His Revelation hath, in this Day . . . been broken. Its grace is being poured out upon men. Fill thy cup, and drink.[18]

Both Shí'í and Sunní Islam anticipate two expected deliverers, the first being the Mahdí (the "Divinely Guided One")—whom Shí'í tradition identifies with the hidden Twelfth Imám. Following the Mahdí is to be (in Sunní tradition) Jesus Christ, who returns to break crosses and to kill swine. In Shí'í tradition, this tradition is replaced by belief in the return of Imám Ḥusayn, the Prince of the Imáms. The martyrdom of Ḥusayn has moved the Persian psyche as powerfully as has the crucifixion of Jesus Christ for Christians down through the centuries. There is a particularly striking passage in the writings of Bahá'u'lláh, where his identification as the Return of Ḥusayn is achieved through an allusion to the martyrdom of this heroic figure. This passage is translated below, from a Tablet (the *Lawḥ-i Naṣír*) mostly in Persian and which was revealed during the Adrianople period (1863–68).

> By God! This is He Who hath at one time appeared in the name of the Spirit [Jesus Christ], thereafter in the name of the Friend [Muḥammad], then in the name of 'Alí [the Báb], and afterwards in this blessed, lofty, self-subsisting, exalted, and beloved Name. In truth, this is Ḥusayn, Who hath appeared through divine grace in the dominion of justice, against Whom have arisen the infidels, with what they possess of wickedness and iniquity. Thereupon they severed His head with the sword of malice, and lifted it upon a spear in the midst of earth and heaven. Verily, that head is speaking from atop that spear, saying: "O assemblage of shadows! Stand ashamed before My beauty, My might, My sovereignty and My grandeur. Turn your gaze to the countenance of your Lord, the Unconstrained, so that you may find Me crying out among you with holy and cherished melodies."

Christianity: Since the chronological sequence of Bahá'u'lláh's initial proclamations is difficult to establish, apart from the extant datable writings, the order of the four religions given here is arbitrary. Wherever dates occur they will be noted. In Stiles's study of the conversion of religious minorities to the Bahá'í Faith in Iran, she notes that while a significant Jewish conversion movement began in Hamadan around 1877, and while in the early 1880s Zoroastrians were drawn to the Bahá'í Faith, no conversions among Persian Christians appear to have taken place.[19]

Yet this should not obscure the fact that Bahá'u'lláh and his followers were engaged in dialogue with Christians at an early date, as well as during later stages of contact. Stile's intriguing observation awaits further documentation.

> While the psychological and theological changes which occurred in the Bábí/Bahá'í community between 1850 and 1875 prepared Bahá'ís to receive non-Muslims, those changes did not in themselves cause the conversions. Were this the case we might expect a close correspondence between conversion and Bahá'í outreach to certain groups. I did not find this to be the case. Of all non-Muslim religions, Christianity was addressed most frequently in Bahá'u'lláh's writings, and much earlier than Judaism and Zoroastrianism. Early Bahá'ís often approached Christians and requested their scriptures.[20]

Momen's survey of early relations between Christian missionaries and Bábí/Bahá'í communities is particularly interesting in this context.[21]

Returning to Bahá'u'lláh, we find him addressing a number of epistles or "Tablets" to Christians during the 'Akká period of his ministry (1868–1892).[22] Of these Tablets, the most important was the one to Pope Pius IX, written around 1869. In it there is what one might call a dual messianic claim. Specificially, it is:

> This is indeed the Father (*al-wálid*), whereof Isaiah gave you tidings [Isa. 9:6b] and the Comforter (*al-mu'azzí*) whose coming was promised by the Spirit.[23]

In Bahá'u'lláh's *Lawḥ-i Aqdas,* often referred to as the Tablet to the Christians (late 1870s?), this dual claim is reaffirmed:

> This is an Epistle from Our presence unto him whom the veils of names have failed to keep back from God. . . . Say, O followers of the Son! . . . Lo! The Father is come, and that which ye were promised in the Kingdom is fulfilled! . . . Verily, He Who is the Spirit of Truth is come to guide you unto all truth.[24]

The same passage (Isa. 9:6b) again appears to be alluded to here, since Isaiah is the only Old Testament prophet explicitly referred to in the entire Tablet. Of the two, the Comforter/ Spirit of Truth declaration seems to be the more important for Bahá'u'lláh, not only for establishing a prophetic relationship to, but also claiming an actual parallel with Jesus. This is intimated by such texts as follow:

> The Comforter Whose advent all the scriptures have promised is now come that He may reveal unto you all knowledge and wisdom.[25]

> This Day Jerusalem hath attained unto a new Evangel, for in the stead of the sycamore standeth the cedar.[26]

> O concourse of Christians! Verily, He (Jesus) said: 'Come ye after Me, and I will make you to become fishers of men.' In this day, however, We say: 'Come ye after Me, that We may make you to become quickeners of mankind.'[27]

As Riesenfeld has pointed out,[28] currents in early Christianity looked upon Jesus as the Comforter. Evidence for such identification is found in I John 2:1, where Jesus is called *paráklétos* (albeit in a juridical sense). A further witness occurs in a fragment from the Acts of John discovered in one of the Oxyrhynchus papyri: "O Jesus, the Comforter . . ." (POxy 850, *verso*

10).[29] It would make sense, therefore, that Bahá'u'lláh, far removed from Pentecostal presuppositions, could interpret the Johannine Jesus' promise of "another Comforter" (John 14:16) to be transparently a reference to a future advent of a Prophet like unto Jesus, parallel to Moses' promise of a Prophet like unto himself (Deut. 18:15–19).[30]

What is unclear, however, and deserves further enquiry, is how the Father is associated by Bahá'u'lláh with the messianic Spirit of Truth. The mere juxtaposing of two prophecies is possible, but does not account for Bahá'u'lláh's deliberately consistent juxtapositions in Christian contexts. Did Bahá'u'lláh see, in the subordinationist Christology of John 14:28, a prophecy of the coming of the Father, indicated as an eschatological event in verse 30 (as a possible reading), when "the prince of this world cometh"? One could see, however unconvincingly, how the occurrence of the term "Father" in the verse immediately following the later Spirit of Truth prophecy (John 16:12–14) could be viewed as a name for the second Comforter.[31] "For the Son of Man shall come in the glory of his Father" (Matt. 16:27) also associates the name of the Father with the second Advent in glory.

Bahá'u'lláh's proclamation was not just theological; and its impact must be explained otherwise. Charismatic power was what rendered his claim to be the "Father" plausible. A case in point surrounds the conversion of the first Christian Bahá'í, Fáris Effendi, the Syrian Protestant who was won over to the Faith by the Bahá'í poet and historian Nabíl-i-A'zam. This event took place in Egypt (rather than Persia, where a few Armenian Christians would later convert) in the year 1868. Fáris and Nabíl were cellmates in a prison in Alexandria. Like Ḥakím Masíḥ, the first Jewish Bahá'í, Fáris was a physician; but he was a priest as well (hence his title, *Qasís-i Súrí*). Naturally, both of the prisoners tried to convert the other. Since Fáris was a priest, he must have encountered the claim that Bahá'u'lláh was the

"Father" with some astonishment, but he was able to make the eschatological connexion to become a Bahá'í.

It happened that Bahá'u'lláh, himself a prisoner, was anchored in the port of Alexandria in August 1868, en route to exile in the prison-city of 'Akká. So close was the steamer that it was visible from the rooftop of Fáris's prison. Fáris took this opportunity to dispatch a special messenger to deliver a letter to Bahá'u'lláh. The messenger was a Christian watchmaker named Constantine who, upon returning from Bahá'u'lláh's ship, exclaimed, "By God! I saw the Father of Christ."

Zoroastrianism: Given the despised minority status of nineteenth-century Persian Zoroastrians, Bahá'u'lláh's open recognition of Zoroaster as a great Prophet (*yik-i az payghambarán-i buzurg*) assumes considerable significance. Moreover, Bahá'u'lláh wrote directly to Persian Zoroastrians in a manner sympathetic to their traditions. Again, the leading Bahá'í teacher Mírzá Abú'l-Faḍl Gulpáygání was at pains to demonstrate that Bahá'u'lláh's lineage could be traced back to Yazdigird III, the last Zoroastrian monarch to occupy the throne of Persia.

Bahá'u'lláh wrote to particular Zoroastrians of prominence and to the *dasturs* (or high priests) as well. Cambridge Orientalist E. G. Browne published partial texts of three epistles of this kind.[32] The most celebrated Zoroastrian to whom Bahá'u'lláh wrote was Manakji Limji Hataria, known in Iran as Mánakjí Ṣáḥib, who had met Bahá'u'lláh in 1854, while passing through Baghdad en route to Persia from India. As emissary from Parsi India, Manakji did more for the amelioration of oppressive conditions for Zoroastrians in Persia than any other nineteenth-century figure. For several years Manakji corresponded with Bahá'u'lláh through Mírzá Abú'l-Faḍl Gulpáygání, a newly-won Bahá'í who was in Manakji's employ from early 1877 to late 1882, years between two major imprisonments for being a Bahá'í.[33]

As with other letters from Bahá'u'lláh to Zoroastrians, some of the Tablets to Manakji were composed in pure Persian, without a trace of Arabic. This was considered by all to be a literary feat. One of these Tablets advances a veiled messianic claim: "When the world was environed with darkness, the sea of generosity was set in motion and divine illumination appeared . . . This is the same illumination which is promised in the heavenly books."[34]

To Zoroastrian *dasturs* Bahá'u'lláh wrote: "O High Priests! . . . The Incomparable Friend is manifest. . . . Whatsoever hath been announced in the Books hath been revealed and made clear."[35] But the most specific of Bahá'u'lláh's proclamations to Zoroastrians was penned in a Tablet known as *Shír-Mard* (Lion of a Man) or *Lawḥ-i Haft Pursish* (Tablet of seven questions), to Ustád Javán-Mard, principal of the Zoroastrian school of Yazd. In response to Javan-Mard's question, Bahá'u'lláh explicitly identifies himself as the eschatological Sháh Bahrám Varjávand, the expected Zoroastrian deliverer.[36]

Judaism: To the religious leaders of Christendom, Bahá'u'lláh shows preference for Isaianic imagery in messianic context: "O concourse of bishops! . . . He Who is the Everlasting Father calleth aloud between earth and heaven."[37] This preference is made clear in Bahá'u'lláh's direct declaration: "I am the One Whom the tongue of Isaiah hath extolled."[38] Allusion to Isaiah 9:6b has been indicated in the Tablet to the Pope (above). Appeal as well to the following verse (Isa. 9:7) is transparent from a call to the "people of the Torah" along with related passages which would no doubt be communicated to many Jews by Bahá'ís who would cull such of Bahá'u'lláh's claims as:

> The Most Great Law is come, and the Ancient Beauty ruleth upon the Throne of David.[39]
>
> The Promised Day is come and the Lord of Hosts hath appeared.[40]

> O concourse of the divines! The heaven of religions is split and the moon cleft asunder and the peoples of the earth are brought together in a new resurrection. . . . The episode of Sinai hath been reenacted in this Revelation.[41]

> Behold . . . all the testimonies of the Prophets in My grasp. . . . I am He Who feareth no one. . . . This is Mine hand which God hath turned white for all the worlds to behold. This is My staff; were We to cast it down, it would, of a truth, swallow up all created things.[42]

Moses/Sinai typology is strong throughout Bahá'u'lláh's writings; in many other places, moreover, he is "the Voice of the Lord . . . coming from the Burning Bush."[43] This led to accusations that his followers believed in his "Divinity and Godhood," but Bahá'u'lláh responded: "O Shaykh! This station is the station in which one dieth to himself and liveth in God. Divinity, whenever I mention it, indicateth My complete and absolute self-effacement. This is the station in which I have no control over mine own weal or woe nor over my life nor over my resurrection."[44]

Bahá'u'lláh's denial of any personal claim to "Divinity and Godhood" did not preclude him from speaking in the voice or persona "of the Lord," however. Metaphors abound in his writings to express the unique position he affords at the intersection of the human and divine realms as the Theophany, or Manifestation of God:

> Consider the goldsmith: Verily, he makes a ring, and although he is its maker, yet he adorns his finger with it. Likewise, God the Exalted appears in the clothing of the creatures. (*Lawḥu'ẓ-Ẓuhur*)

> I am the royal Falcon on the arm of the Almighty. I unfold the drooping wings of every broken bird, and start it on its flight. (*Lawḥ-i Maqṣúd*)

And elsewhere Bahá'u'lláh speaks of himself as the:

> Youth who is riding high upon the snow-white She-Camel betwixt earth and heaven. (Tablet of the Hair)

Relative to past prophets, Bahá'u'lláh designates Muḥammad as the "Seal of the Messengers," the Báb as the "King of the Messengers" (*sulṭán al-rusul*), and refers to himself as the "Sender of the Messengers" (*mursil al-rusul*). Since all past prophets were sent to progressively prepare the world for its eventual unity, the spirit which propels mankind toward its own unification is the same spirit that has empowered messengers of the past to fulfill their preparatory roles. Bahá'u'lláh's fourfold messiahship, therefore, functions not only as an ideology which can create eschatological bridges for winning converts, but also serves as a kind of theory of religious relativity.

Conclusions: Bahá'í messianism's cross-cultural expression at first appears to be an eschatologically eclectic and adaptive syncretism, with a messianic mixing of various apocalyptic traditions. Such a view has influenced both scholar and polemicist in various assessments of the Bahá'í Faith. Recalling E. G. Browne once again:

> From what has been said above, the Western reader may be tempted to think of the Bábí [Bahá'í] doctrine as embodying, to a certain extent, the modern Western rationalistic spirit. No mistake could be greater. The belief in the fulfillment of prophecies; the love of apocalyptic sayings culled from the Jewish, Christian, and Muhammadan scriptures . . .[45]

And Browne goes on. Our purpose is not to prove this view wrong, but rather to refine it. Without a History of Religions perspective, the perceived necessity of such cross-cultural expression is not so obvious; but parallels in Christian and Islamic missionary enterprise are clear. Since the rational spirit is strongly cultivated, with science given a status complementary in function to that of religion in Bahá'í principle, the superficiality of Browne's analysis comes into focus once the Bahá'í worldview is grasped. With Bahá'u'lláh's pronouncement that "all the Prophets of God proclaim the same Faith,"[46] Bahá'ís are oriented towards a kind of *praeparatio messianica* appreciation of all past apocalyptic urges.

There is some validity to Browne's criticism, on the other hand, since Bahá'í appeal to prophecy to date has tended to be somewhat uncritical. This is characteristic of *testimonia* in all religious apologetics which in argument depend on apocalyptic proof-texts. As I have shown in two earlier papers, where I subjected Bahá'í appeals to prophecy within Hindu and Zoroastrian traditions to critical analysis, apocalyptic literatures are predominantly "prophecies from past events" when it comes to messianic predictions, are of priestly redaction, with typological dependence on past prophet/warrior deliverers, tend to be religiously and culturally ethnocentric (often with vengeful attitudes toward oppressors), and are discordant in their lack of uniformity.[47]

Positively, Bahá'ís have fostered renewed interest in past traditions. This in itself helps break down religious prejudices, since Bahá'ís embrace earlier world monotheisms as a part of a global heritage. Thus, Bahá'u'lláh, perhaps more than any other religious figure, has not only integrated eschatologies as convergent, but has cultivated a unific awareness of the parallel and complementary integrity of all faiths.

NOTES

1. Vide: *Apocalypticism in the Mediterranean World and the Near East: Proceedings of the International Colloquium on Apocalypticism, at Uppsala, Sweden, August 1979,* D. Hellholm, ed. (Tübingen: Mohr, 1983). Papers from the 1983 Princeton Conference on

Maitreya Studies were kindly provided by Prof. D. Overmyer (University of British Columbia).

2. The projection of the past into the future, so often the model for apocalyptic prophecy, was styled "inverse history" by historian F. Kazemzadeh of Yale.

3. V. Lanternari, "Messianism: Its Historical Origin and Morphology," *History of Religions* 2 (1962) p. 70.

Relevant also is J. Collins' definition of apocalypse: "'Apocalypse' is a genre of revelatory literature with a narrative framework, in which a revelation is mediated by an otherworldly being to a human recipient, disclosing a transcendent reality which is both temporal, insofar as it envisages eschatological salvation, and spatial insofar as it involves another supernatural world." ("Introduction," *Apocalypse: The Morphology of a Genre, Semeia* 14 (1979) p. 9.

Towards a definition of "revelation," see G. Widengren, "Phenomenology of Revelation", *Studia Missionalia* 20 (1971) pp. 301–319.

4. The classic Bahá'í position on the relation of past apocalyptic promises to Bahá'u'lláh was expressed by Shoghi Effendi, Guardian of the Bahá'í Faith and Bahá'u'lláh's great-grandson: "To Israel He [Bahá'u'lláh] was neither more nor less than . . . the 'Everlasting Father', the 'Lord of Hosts' come down 'with ten thousands of saints'; to Christendom Christ returned 'in the glory of the Father'; to Shí'ah Islám the return of the Imám Ḥusayn; to Sunní Islám the descent of the 'Spirit of God' (Jesus Christ); to the Zoroastrians the promised Sháh Bahrám; to the Hindus the reincarnation of Krishna; to the Buddhists the fifth Buddha." (*The Bahá'í World* 14 (1963–1968) p. 31.)

Association of Bahá'u'lláh with Viracocha is documented in a photograph in *The Bahá'í World* 16 (1973–1976) pp. 445, where Andean Quechua Indians are pictured beside a placard which reads: "Bahá'u'lláh el Returno de Viracocha." This proclamation took place in Cuzco, Peru at the 1975 All-Quechua Bahá'í Conference.

5. Cited in E. G. Browne's *A Literary History of Persia* (Cambridge University Press, 1902) vol. 1, p. 163.

6. For sources, see F. Mojtabai, "Mani and Shapur," *Journal of the K. R. Cama Oriental Institute* 46 (1978) p. 100.

7. A. Henrichs, "Mani and the Babylonian Baptists: A Historical Confrontation," *Harvard Studies in Classical Philology* 77 (1973) pp. 45–55. Also, E. Rose, *Die Manichaische Christologie* (Wiesbaden:

Otto Harassowitz, 1979), reviewed in *Numen* 29 (1982) pp. 273–75 H. Klimkeit).

8. A. Bausani, *The Persians* (London: Elek, 1971) p. 55.

9. No formal comparison between the two religious systems has been undertaken. Clear documents designating succession, administrative structure, individual and social laws, come from Bahá'u'lláh's own pen.

10. Bahá'u'lláh, *Epistle to the Son of the Wolf* (Wilmette: Bahá'í Publishing Trust, 1979) p. 63; Shoghi Effendi, *The World Order of Bahá'u'lláh* (Bahá'í Publishing Trust, 1982) p. 146.

11. Bahá'u'lláh, *Gleanings from the Writings of Bahá'u'lláh* (Bahá'í Publishing Trust, 1971) pp. 74–75.

12. Bahá'u'lláh, *Kitáb-i-Iqán. The Book of Certitude* (Wilmette: Bahá'í Publishing Trust, rev. ed., 1974) pp. 12–13.

13. Bahá'u'lláh, *Gleanings,* p. 60.

14. Bahá'u'lláh, *Epistle to the Son of the Wolf,* p. 46.

15. Bahá'u'lláh, *Gleanings,* p. 5.

16. Bahá'u'lláh, *The Proclamation of Bahá'u'lláh to the Kings and Leaders of the World* (Haifa: Bahá'í World Centre, 1967) p. 87.

17. A. Sachedina, *Islamic Messianism: The Idea of Mahdi in Twelver Shi'ism* (Albany: State University of New York Press, 1981) pp. 168–69.

18. Bahá'u'lláh, *Gleanings,* p. 12; L. Vaglieri, who contributed the entry on Ḥusayn for *Encyclopaedia of Islám,* singles out an eschatological account which approximates the tradition to which Bahá'u'lláh refers: "Among the eschatological accounts is the following: Ḥusayn went to the Raḍwá mountains where he will remain on a throne of light, surrounded by the Prophets, with his faithful followers behind him, until the coming of the Mahdi [Qá'im]; then he will transfer himself to Karbalá', where all the celestial and human beings will visit him."

19. S. Stiles, "The Conversion of Religious Minorities to the Bábí Faith in Írán: Some Preliminary Observations" (unpublished paper, 1983) p. 1. See also: W. Fischel, "The Jews in Persia," *Jewish Social Studies* 12 (1950) p. 156; Fischel, "The Bahá'í Movement and Persian Jewry," *The Jewish Review* (1934) pp. 47–55; H. Cohen, *Jews of the Middle East* (1973) p. 201.

20. Stiles, pp. 6–7.

21. M. Momen, "Early Relations Between Christian Missionaries and the Bábí and Bahá'í Communities," *Studies in Bábí and Bahá'í History, Vol. 1*, ed. by Momen (Los Angeles: Kalimát Press, 1983).

22. S. Lambden, 'A Tablet of Bahá'u'lláh to George David Hardegg: The *Lawḥ- Hirtíq*," *Bahá'í Studies Bulletin*, vol. 2, no. 1 (1983) pp. 32–62.

23. Ibid., p. 47, rendered from the text of *Lawḥ-i Páp*, in [Bahá'u'lláh], *Alváh-i názilay-i khitab bi muluk va ru'asáy-i arḍ* (Tehran: Bahá'í Publishing Trust, 124 Bahá'í Era [1967–68] p. 85.

24. Bahá'u'lláh, *Tablets of Bahá'u'lláh revealed after the Kitáb-i Aqdas* (Haifa: Bahá'í World Centre, 1978) pp. 9, 12.

25. Bahá'u'lláh, cited in *The Bahá'í World* 14 (1963–1969) p. 45.

26. Bahá'u'lláh, *Epistle to the Son of the Wolf*, p. 145.

27. Bahá'u'lláh, *The Proclamation of Bahá'u'lláh*, p. 91.

28. H. Riesenfeld, "A Probable Background to the Johannine Paraclete," *Ex Orbe Religionum: Studia Geo Widengren Oblata* (Leiden: Brill, 1972) vol. 1, pp. 266–76.

29. "O Jesus, the Comforter . . ." cited in ibid., 273.

30. Parallelism of Paraclete to Jesus has recently been examined by M. Isaacs, "The Prophetic Spirit in the Fourth Gospel," *The Heythrop Journal* 24 (1983) pp. 391–407. In the section, "Prophetic Functions ascribed to the Spirit-Paraclete" (393–99), the Spirit of Truth serves as: 1) Divine Messenger; 2) One who glorifies Jesus; 3) Teacher; 4) Witness; 5) Predictor; 6) One who is rejected; 7) The Abiding Spirit. Isaacs' parallelism is brought into bolder relief in the section, "Jesus as the Model for the Paraclete-Prophet" (pp. 402–404).

31. Isaacs prefers the term "Counsellor" to "Comforter" in her rendering of John 15:26: "But when the Counsellor comes, whom I shall send to you from the Father, even the Spirit of Truth, who proceeds from the Father, he shall bear witness to me." Might not the cluster of titles, *Counsellor/Father/Prince* evoke Isaiah 9:6?

32. Browne, "A Catalogue and Description of 27 Bábí Manuscripts," *Journal of the Royal Asiatic Society* 24 (1892), "Three Epistles to Zoroastrians" pp. 671–76. (To be precise, Browne provides the full text of the first epistle.) See also, J. C. Katrak, "Professor E. G. Browne's Reminiscences of the Zoroastrians of Iran," *Browne Centenary Volume* (Calcutta: Iran Society, 1963) pp. 38–45.

Browne documented the apocalyptic fervor of the Zoroastrians in Persia in his classic, *A Year Amongst the Persians*. (See S. Seawright's evaluation of the work, *The British in the Middle East* [New York: Atheneum, 1970] pp. 141–42). Browne recorded: "Their relations to one another [Zoroastrians and Bahá'ís] are of a much more friendly character than the relations of either of them towards the Muhammadans, the Zoroastrians . . . regarding 'the virtuous of the seven climes' as their friends, and the Bábís [Bahá'ís] being commanded by Behá [Bahá'u'lláh] to associate with men of all religions with spirituality and sweet savour". . . Moreover the Bábís recognise Zoroaster as a prophet . . . and are at some pains to conciliate and win over his followers to their way of thinking, as instanced by the epistles addressed by Behá from Acre to certain of their number; while some few at least of the Zoroastrians are not indisposed to recognize in Behá their expected deliverer, S͟háh Bahrám, who, as Dastur Tir-andaz informed me, must appear soon if they were to be rescued from their abasement, and 'the Good Religion' re-established. The Dastur himself, indeed, would not admit that Behá could be this promised saviour, who, he said, must come before the next Naw-Rúz [Persian New Year] if he were to come at all . . ." (*A Year Amongst the Persians* [Cambridge University Press, 1970 (1893)] pp. 431–32).

33. G. Aidun, "Manekji Limji Hataria and the Bahá'í Faith," *Bahá'í Studies Notebook* 1 (1980) pp. 47–62; M. Boyce, "Manekji Limji Hataria in Iran," *Golden Jubilee Volume* (Bombay: K. R. Cama Oriental Institute, 19) pp. 21–26; M. Momen, "Abu'l-Fazl Golpaygání," *Encyclopaedia Iranica*.

34. Bahá'u'lláh, Tablet to Mánackjí Sáhib, *Star of the West* 1 (1910) 5ff.; *Bahá'í Scriptures*, pp. 130–33.

35. Bahá'u'lláh, *The Proclamation of Bahá'u'lláh*, pp. 105–106.

36. S. Stiles, *Zoroastrian Conversions to the Bahá'í Faith in Yazd, Írán* (M.A. Thesis in Oriental Studies, University of Arizona, 1983) p. 20; 27. H. Balyuzi, *Bahá'u'lláh: The King of Glory* (Oxford: George Ronald, 1980) p. 10. The text of *Law͟h-i Haft Pursis͟h* (or S͟hír-Mard) was most recently published in Bahá'u'lláh, *Majmú'ihy-i maṭbú'ihy-i alváḥ-i mubárakihy-i ḥaḍrat-i Bahá'u'lláh* (Wilmette: Bahá'í Publishing Trust, 1978) where one finds the explicit association with S͟háh Bahrám on p. 240.

37. Bahá'u'lláh, cited in Shoghi Effendi, *The Promised Day is Come* (Wilmette: Bahá'í Publishing Trust, 1961) pp. 104–5.
38. Bahá'u'lláh, cited in *The Promised Day is Come*, p. 34.
39. Bahá'u'lláh, *The Proclamation of Bahá'u'lláh*, p. 89.
40. Bahá'u'lláh, *Tablets of Bahá'u'lláh*, p. 239.
41. Bahá'u'lláh, *Tablets of Bahá'u'lláh*, pp. 247–48.
42. Bahá'u'lláh, *Lawḥ-i Mubáhilih*, cited in A. Taherzadeh, *The Revelation of Bahá'u'lláh: Adrianople, 1863–68* (Oxford: George Ronald, 1977) p. 293.
43. Bahá'u'lláh, *Tablets of Bahá'u'lláh*, p. 265. A parallel proclamation is ventured by Bahá'u'lláh when he writes: "O people! The Sun of Utterance beameth forth in this day, above the horizon of bounty, and the radiance of the Revelation of Him Who spoke in Sinai flasheth and glisteneth before all religions." (*Epistle to the Son of the Wolf*, p. 65)
44. Bahá'u'lláh, *Epistle to the Son of the Wolf*, p. 41. An illuminated tablet in Bahá'u'lláh's own cursive, a facsimile of which forms the frontispiece to *The Bahá'í World*, Vol. 14 (1963–68), reinforces this important distinction: "When I contemplate, O My God, the relationship that bindeth me to Thee, I am moved to proclaim to all created things, 'Verily I am God!'; and when I consider my own self, lo, I find it coarser than clay!"
45. Browne, *Encyclopaedia of Religion and Ethics*, ed. by J. Hastings: (Edinburgh, 1908–14) vol. 2, p. 306. Broadcast proclamation of the advent of Bahá'u'lláh on the part of Bahá'ís has led one critic's evaluation of the Faith to include negative as well as positive assessment. Bahá'ís are taken to task for having bordered on creating "a magnified cult of the founder." (J. Nijenuis, "Bahá'í: World Faith for Modern Man?" *Journal of Ecumenical Studies* 10 [1973] p. 532.)

In contrast, the personality inventory of Bahá'ís, conducted by J. Keene, deserves notice: "Bahá'í World Faith: Redefinition of Religion," *Journal for the Scientific Study of Religion* 6 (1967) pp. 221–35.

46. Bahá'u'lláh, *Iqán*, pp. 135–54. The full text states: ". . . all the Prophets are Temples of the Cause of God, who have appeared clothed in divers attire. If thou wilt observe . . . , thou wilt behold them all abiding in the same tabernacle, soaring in the same heaven,

seated upon the same throne, . . . and proclaiming the same Faith. . . . Wherefore, should any one of these Manifestations of Holiness proclaim, 'I am the return of all the Prophets', He verily speaketh the truth."

Also: "Know thou assuredly that the essence of all the Prophets of God is one and the same. Their unity is absolute. God, the Creator, saith: There is no distinction whatsoever among the Bearers of My Message. They all have but one purpose; their secret is the same secret. To prefer one in honor to another, to exalt certain ones above the rest, is in no wise to be permitted. Every true Prophet hath regarded His Message as fundamentally the same as the Revelation of every other Prophet gone before Him. (Bahá'u'lláh, *Gleanings*, pp. 78–79.)

47. Buck, "The Mystery of the Sworded Warrior in Hindu Apocalypse: Was Kalki Viṣṇuyaśas Bahá'u'lláh?" AAR/SBL, PacNW Region, 1981; Buck, "Was Bahá'u'lláh S͟háh Bahrám Varjávand despite Zoroastrian 'Prophecies'?" AAR/SBL PacNW Region 1982. For the summary of a further study in Bahá'í prophetology, see Buck, "Illuminator vs. Redeemer: A 'Trajectory' of Ebionite Christology from Prophet Messianism to Bahá'í Theophanology" *Abstracts: American Academy of Religion/Society of Biblical Literature Annual Meeting 1983* (Scholars Press, 1983) p. 86.

Other references to specific messianisms include: *Kalki Viṣṇuyaśas*: K. Jayaswal, "The Historical Position of Kalki and his Identification with Yasodharman," *The Indian Antiquary* 46 (1917) pp. 145–53; H. Bhide, "Is Kalkirája an Historical Personage?" *The Indian Antiquary* 48 (1919) pp. 123–28; D. Mankad, "Kalki— The Earliest Check to Buddhism," *The New Indian Antiquary* (1942) pp. 337–43; D. Kosambi, 'The Avatára Syncretism and Possible Sources of the Bhagavad-Gita," *Journal of the Bombay Branch of the Royal Asiastic Society* 24–25 (1948–49) pp. 121–34; P. Eggermont, "The Ṡaka Era and the Kaniṣka Era," *Papers on the Date of Kaniṣka*, ed. by A. Basham; (Leiden: Brill, 1968) pp. 87–93 (89).

S͟háh Bahrám Varjávand: K. Czeglédy, "Bahrám Ċóbín and the Persian Apocalyptic Literature," *Acta Orientalia Academiae Scientarum Hungaricae* 8 (1958) pp. 21–43; M. Bíró, "Bahrám Ċóbín and the Establishment of the Principality in Kartli," *Acta Orientalia* 33

(1979) p. 177; Czegledy, "Bahrám Ċóbín," *Antik Tanulmányok* 4 (1957) p. 301; R. Frye, *Neue Methodologie in der Iranistik* (Wiesbaden: Otto Harrassowitz, 1974) p. 66; Frye, "The Charisma of Kingship in Ancient Iran," *Iranica Antiqua* 6 (1964) pp. 36–54; S. Eddy, *The King is Dead: Studies in the Near Eastern Resistance to Hellenism, 334–331 B.C.* (University of Nebraska, 1961) pp. 343–49 (343; 348 n 45).

Maitreya: Papers from the 1983 Princeton Conference on Maitreya Studies: P. Jain, "Stages in the Bodhisattva Career of the Tathagáta Maitreya"; J. Barbaro, "On the Meanings of the Maitreya Myth: A Preliminary Typology." J. Kitagawa, "The Career of Maitreya," *History of Religions* 21 (1981) pp. 107–25; P. Eggermont, "The Origin of the Saka-Era," *Indo-Iranian Journal* 2 (1958) pp. 225–28; H. Ui, "Maitreya as an Historical Personage," *Indian Studies in Honor of C. R. Lanman* (Harvard, 1929) pp. 95–102. On all three (Saoŝyant/Kalki/Maitreya) messianisms: Abegg, *Der Messiasglaube in Indien und Iran* (Berlin, 1929).

Persian Imámí Shí'ih Messianism: I. Friedländer, "The Heterodoxies of the Shí'ites," *Journal of the American Oriental Society* 29 (1908) esp. pp. 23–30 (on *al-raj'a*); D. Halperin, "The Ibn Ṣayyád Traditions and the Legend of al-Dajjál," JAOS 96 (1976) pp. 213–25; A. Sachedina, *Islamic Messianism: The Idea of Mahdi in Twelver Shí'ism* (State University of New York, 1981); J. Husain, "The Role of the Imámite *Wikála* with Special Reference to the First *Safír*," *Hamdard Islamicus* 5 (1982) pp. 25–52; P. Smith, "Motif Research: Peter Berger and the Bahá'í Faith," *Religion* 8 (1978) pp. 210–34.

Christian Messianism: F. Gardiner, "The Description of Spiritual Phenomena under the Figure of Natural Convulsions," *The Old and New Testament Student* I (1889) pp. 162–69; E. Renan, *Antichrist* (London, 1890); S. Giet, *L'Apocalypse et l'Histoire* (Paris: Universitaires de France); J. Collins, "Pseudonymity, Historical Reviews and the Genre of the Revelation of John," *Catholic Biblical Quarterly* 39 (1977) pp. 329–43; Pesch, "Markus 13," and, F. Neirynck, "Marc 13: Examen critique de l'interpretation de R. Pesch," *L'Apocalypse Johannique et l'Apocalyptique dans le nouveau Testament*, ed. by J. Lambrecht (Leuven University, 1980); T. Callan, "Psalm 110:1 and the

Origin of the Expectation that Jesus Will Come Again," CBQ 39 (1982) pp. 622–36.

Jewish Messianism: E. Osswald, "Zum Problem der *Vaticinia Ex Eventu*," *Zeitschrift für die Alttestamentliche Wissenschaft* 75 (1963) pp. 27–44; P. Casey, "Porphyry and the Origin of the Book of Daniel," *Journal of Theological Studies* 27 (1976) pp. 15–33; N. Wieder, "The Idea of a Second Coming of Moses," *Jewish Quarterly Review* 46 (1956) pp. 356–64; H. Teeple, *The Mosaic Eschatological Prophet* (SBL, 1957); J. Fossum, "Jewish-Christian Christology and Jewish Mysticism," *Vigiliae Christianae* 37 (1983) pp. 260–87.

DR. SUSAN I. MOODY (1.) WITH MISS ELIZABETH STEWART

AMERICAN BAHÁ'Í WOMEN AND THE EDUCATION OF GIRLS IN TEHRAN, 1909–1934

by R. Jackson Armstrong-Ingram

In 1909, the Protestant women of the United States were represented in "heathendom," after fifty years of effort, by 1,948 unmarried women missionaries whom they supported through 44 missionary societies which collectively contributed four million dollars that year. In the same year, the first representative of the Bahá'í women of the United States to be sent to that vast realm of missionary activity, Dr. Susan Moody, arrived at her post in Tehran. Moody was joined over the next few years by Elizabeth Stewart, a nurse; Dr. Sarah Clock; and Lillian Kappes, a teacher. These four women formed the first resident embassage of Western Bahá'í women in the East.

The Bahá'í women had much in common with their Protestant compatriots: they were unmarried; they were products of a nineteenth-century North American socialization and education; they were fired with an urgent need to enlighten and to succor; and they would be faithful to their calling unto death. But they had also much that set them apart.

For most of the missionaries who came bearing the lantern of Western Protestantism, their main wish was to light the way to faith, however important the work of health and education along the way. The Bahá'í women came to the homeland of their faith. The members of the community they joined there were themselves bound up, as were their recent forebears, with the early history of that faith, and they had among them some of its most illustrious propounders. The ultimate goal of the Protestant missionaries was an accomplished fact for the Bahá'í women—an established and operating community of faith. The latter's attention could be more confidently concentrated on goals that were more socio-political then overtly religious. To convert was not their chief aim, but rather to assist the already converted. The expansion of the host community was primarily its own concern, theirs was largely the welfare and prestige of that host community. To be sure, their activities were not limited to the Bahá'í community in Tehran: indeed, their influence outside that community was considerable. But that outside activity was only indirectly linked to spreading their faith: they might teach it by example, by preparing the ground, but they did so without expectation of any immediate harvest.

The Protestant missionaries were often, with varying degrees of formality and actuality, under the supervision of American men. The Bahá'í women were independent of such control. Certainly, the official authority structure of the Bahá'í community in Tehran was male, but as Westerners these women functioned largely as honorary men within that structure, rather than filling any available female role. That is, although not eligible for elected offices and while associating freely with women, they otherwise participated in men's social and religious activities and had personal friendships with men.

Western Bahá'í men had visited and continued to visit Tehran (as did other Western Bahá'í women), but the only American man who had become a resident member of the Tehran Bahá'í community, the teacher Sydney Sprague, left as the group of women was becoming established. The Western Bahá'í presence in Tehran was female and was largely supported by a female constituency in the United States. Thus, though it operated with reference to a male host community, it had no immediate need to refer to, confer with, or defer to a male incursionary element parallel to itself; and in their interaction with that male host community these women knew, as did their hosts, that their concerns and efforts had the fervent support of the then head of their common faith, 'Abdu'l-Bahá.

The careers of these Western Bahá'í women in Tehran are of interest, not only as features of both Western and Eastern Bahá'í history, but also as being part of, yet distinct from, the general missionary effort being supported by American women at the time. My concern in this essay is to present some selected aspects of their careers—in particular, their work as change agents in the field of the education of girls in Tehran, in respect to both general education and religious education within the Bahá'í community.

This group of women was active in Tehran from the period of their arrival (1909–1911) to the mid-1920s. By then both Clock and Kappes had died, the latter being replaced for a time by Genevieve Coy. In 1925, Moody and Stewart arrived back in the United States for the sake of their health and to encourage support for the work they had been doing in Tehran. During this visit, Stewart died in October 1926, one month before Shoghi Effendi wrote to the American Bahá'í community asking that competent teachers be sent to assist the schools in Tehran, with Moody accompanying them if possible. In 1928, Moody left the United States for Iran accompanied by Adelaide Sharpe. They were later joined in Tehran by Sharpe's mother, Clara Sharpe. This "second wave" of American Bahá'í women is linked to the first by the presence of Moody and by its overt social intent: but in considering it, we find some differences between the attitudes that Moody and the Sharpes had about their posts. As a complement to the discussion of the activities of the early group, I will discuss the tensions inherent in the later one.

Moody went to Iran in 1909, in answer to an appeal that an American woman doctor join with a small group of Iranian Bahá'í doctors in starting a hospital in Tehran, so that the new institution's services could be made available to women. After her arrival in Tehran on 25 November, Moody established her own practice as well as working with the group of Bahá'í doctors and other Iranian doctors. On 26 December 1909, she wrote:

> My sign was swung below the window yesterday. So imagine me hanging there in both English and Persian. I think the news of my being here spread rapidly over the city and the sign serves to locate the office and dispensary of Dr. Moody, the American.[1]

Her services were evidently in considerable demand and she was consulted by men as well as women:

> There is work for 20 women doctors in Teheran. I wish you could have seen into my house to-day—crowds, and when a hurry call came from a distance where a woman had been poisoned—I had to turn away 5 women and three men and rush off in a carriage.[2]

And on the following day she had to, "turn away ten patients, time and strength cannot be stretched further."[3]

Despite her heavy schedule Moody found time to visit and be visited. From the day she arrived, she had frequent visitors from among the Bahá'í community and their friends, and was taken to various homes. The Tehran Bahá'ís did their best to make her feel welcome and appreciated, including giving her Christmas (1909) presents of rose water, nougat, pomegranates, etc. She gave a special dinner for three guests:

> Christmas day was a pleasant one for me. Ismail did his level best and served our little feast well. I was a little uneasy when I saw the small size of a Persian turkey, but it went the rounds. He stuffed it

with pistachio nuts, figs, thin slices of cocoanut, etc., and it tasted delicious. Our drink was a sherbet made of quince juice. We had nuts and fruit, as well as some of Mrs. Lundberg's gift of fruit cake, and "American chocolate creams" for desert.[4]

As Moody knew some Persian (*fársí*) before coming to Iran, she was able to converse directly with her new friends. Also, in some of the homes she exchanged visits with, various members of the family spoke English or French. As might be expected, a number of the homes that Moody saw belonged to the more prominent members of the Tehran Bahá'í community. On the afternoon of Sunday, 28 November 1909, she was collected at her hotel to visit the Varqá home:

I knew I was to go there, so put on my hat again and went down to find their carriage and a fine team of greys at the door. Was driven rapidly to Arbab Jemshid, the Varga home, where Mr. Sprague lives. It is a beautiful home. Walls hung with fine rugs and exquisite Japanese embroideries. Lemon trees loaded and plants and flowers in the drawing room. Fine banquet lamp. Tables of fine brass openwork. Luxurious chairs and sofas and the floor covered with the choicest rugs. Mirza Azizullah Khan and Mirza Valiollah Khan both took me to the door of the women's apartments. When the former turned back and the younger took me in to see his wife and mother. The latter is the wife of Varga and mother of young Ruhullah, the martyr. She had a sweet sad look, born of sorrow. . . .

Then came one of the deep experiences of my life. I hardly dare to write of it. They have the most precious mementoes of the Bab and of the Blessed Perfection [Bahá'u'lláh], as well as their own loved ones, and of Abdul Baha and these treasures they opened and showed to me. My dear friends, I cannot describe them. It is impossible. Enough to say we four were sobbing together. It was a long time before we could again converse.

We had tea and real sponge cake, the first I have seen since I ate it in America.

Later they asked me to go back to the drawing room where Mirza

Azizullah Khan was teaching the head Mollah of Teheran. His secretary was with him. The Mollah had read but did not believe and easily became irritated. I could see that his discomfiture was making a Bahai of his secretary and was sure of it when the latter took my hand in parting for that is unheard of from a devout Mussulman. It was most interesting to listen, though I could follow but little. I could see the Mollah's weakness. Mirza Azizullah Khan brought me back to the hotel . . .[5]

In January 1910, she met "the son of the Regent of Persia" at another home:

His title is Sirdar. He spoke of his pleasure in having an opportunity of meeting the two Americans of whom he had heard and expressed delight that Mr. Sprague, who was also there, had adopted the "kola" (Persian hat).

This family are advanced, the women are educated and do not veil before the men visitors; that is, the older ones do not, but the young married daughter of the doctor's, who had been playing both European and Persian music for us on the tar, left the room as the Sirdar came in. She had not veiled for Mr. Sprague. The doctor's sister has lived in Paris, going there with a daughter of Muzaffar-ed-Din-Shah, sixteen years ago.[6]

This issue of veiling was one of great symbolic significance for Western Bahá'í women and their progressive Eastern sisters. It functioned as a symbol of all that they felt to be wrong with the position of women in Iranian society, while being unveiled was taken as evidence of progress. Also in January 1910, Moody sent a photograph of a group of unveiled Bahá'í women of Tehran to the United States to be duplicated and spread there at the women's request:

I think I mentioned that this is an important event in their lives; they have thrown down one rule, for once, that is, to show their faces to the world. I cannot describe to you how they are deprived.

Again to-day I was in a home—The wife's mother was closely veiled because the husband's young brother was in the room; and later all the women left the room because two men, friends of the family, were coming. I could stay and enjoy hearing the newcomers tell of a recent trip to Russia, etc. On leaving I went to say good bye to the women—their rooms are in an entirely separate court, as if in another house. A man servant passed just as I raised the heavy curtain to leave, and all the women screamed and pulled down their veils, or drew the "chadur" up over their mouth and nose. The husband we met in Paris and since being on the continent, he is anxious to help free the women from their dreary life.[7]

Among the women Moody met in Tehran were those who had been leaders in advancing women's education in the Bahá'í community, and she found that one of her main roles was to reinforce and legitimize their efforts. Moody felt that her work for women's health was inextricably linked to the developing of women's education. The conditions she found when visiting the sick, even in quite affluent homes, were not conducive to her work as a doctor:

. . . how often I long for dear Miss Stewart, as the need for good nursing becomes more and more evident. The women seem so ignorant and incapable of the simplest hygienic measures, and my own strength is often overtaxed in giving douches, enema and rubbing. I try to teach a midwife, if present, these things, but younger women would take it up easier. I discussed this with two of the men yesterday and find there is a barrier still to be surmounted—a false pride . . . only education can set these dear sisters free.[8]

In these homes I must do all the work myself, and so little to do with; not a piece of flannel, nor rags enough to put on a compress; they know so little about nursing that they think I should stay and do everything day and night. I just have to break away when I feel that the patient is out of danger. Wouldn't your tender hearts ache if you could see some of these homes? One room, the only sign of

> furniture is the "corsi", . . . a table covered by a quilt, beneath is a brazier of charcoal. It is about two feet or 18 inches high and they sit or lie with feet under it. The walls and floors are mud, the ceiling is rafters which show the straw covering. The poor are very poor.
>
> In the better class homes they still use the "corsi" and sleep on the floor. I was called the other night to a wealthy home, the owner of the electric light plant here. Several courts and several separate dwellings enclosed within the grounds. The wife, who was ill, is a beautiful woman; her mattress was on the floor, but there was a fire in the chimney place. Everything showed wealth. This dear woman has hysteria, beside physical ailments, and her brother who talks French, told me that he knew it came from living in the harem. No exercise, no outside interest.
>
> Well, my American sisters, I am sure your hearts would ache in this home as well as in the other. Nothing but education can free them and it cannot come too soon.[9]

Some Bahá'í women in Tehran had conducted small schools for girls, an exercise that could sometimes be hazardous due to the combined prejudice against Bahá'ís and against the education of girls on the part of the majority of the population. For several years the Bahá'í community of Tehran had maintained a boys school, and in 1910 Moody persuaded the school committee to adopt one of these fledgling girls school as a separate department under the aegis of the boys school committee. This girls department began with 30 Bahá'í girls from poor homes. But by the time it was closed in 1934, it had grown to around 750 students of various religious backgrounds and had the reputation of being the best girls school in Tehran, drawing pupils from all levels of society.

The other strand of education that Moody found herself involved with was religious education within the Bahá'í community itself. As with secular education, the Bahá'í community of Tehran had provided organized religious education for its boys for some time, but no comparable program for girls. There were study meetings held for interested women in the houses of certain Bahá'í teachers, but there was no graduated program to prepare girls for participation in their religious community. Moody, and the other American Bahá'í women, assisted in the establishment of a religious education program for the community's girls comparable to that provided for the boys.

These two strands of education that the Western Bahá'í women became involved with were central to their concerns. Although three of the women were theoretically concerned primarily with medicine, and most of their time was devoted to health care, the main thrust of their correspondence is the development of girls' education and the need to support it. Their attitudes toward and activity in education, as well as those of the succeeding group of women, had a significant impact on the development of the education of girls in the Bahá'í community of Tehran, and more generally on the education of girls in Iran as a whole. (It should be borne in mind throughout this essay that the focus is on the attitudes and perceptions of the American women. This is not a rounded account of the education of girls in the Bahá'í community in Tehran, but a detailed look at only one facet of that topic. On many of the issues discussed, there were no doubt other points of view which must be taken into account in any attempt to paint a broader picture.)

The change from small independent schools run by individual women to a department of the boys school was not an unmixed blessing as it put the education of girls under the direction of the boys school committee. Relations between the American women and this committee were not entirely happy for several years. Even when relations improved because of changes in the composition of the committee, there was a feeling that the girls school did not receive the same level of consideration that the boys school did. This was particularly felt in regard to the accommodation made available for it. In 1916, Clock decided that it was time for the Bahá'í women in the United States to know the problems their representatives had been facing with the committee:

> Yesterday Miss K. [Kappes] was simply abused by the meeting of 5 men, came home in perfect nervous collapse & was awake all night from sheer nervousness & worry. Until now we have kept all our troubles to ourselves & I do not know what will come of my having told this, but I have not asked any one's advice about it. I only hope all the Bahai women will know but not Miss K's family, of course it will turn out right some way, we don't know how. . . .
>
> Not long ago a tablet [i.e., a letter from 'Abdu'l-Bahá] came to a Persian here praising Miss K & her work in the school, the improvement among the teachers as well as pupils & she has the moral support of many of the best men, all the women who in an excited meeting all stood by her.[10]

> . . . if Miss Kappes were not a Bahai or not less than a saint she would not have put up with all she has, for five years her hands have been tied, that is they have not allowed her to use her own advanced ideas as to a school, she is exceedingly clever, the only reason was because one man had power but no sense. last year the school committee turned him out & another man was put in his place, who having been educated in Europe is advanced & the school came up wonderfully. . . . At the time Miss K took her vacation July & Aug. (the schools were all closed during July) the entire committee disbanded & a smaller one of 5 men attempted to put things in shape, one of these 5 is the one they forcibly turned out. he is Miss K's enemy. They put in two teachers whom everyone knows cannot teach & when Miss K returned to school everything was in terrible shape, now they want her to take full charge of the finances, a thing they failed in themselves, besides all the other management, she has refused to take the financial responsibility. . . . some of the good men are entirely with her. They offer to open another school for her & several of the nicest of the girls will teach for nothing.[11]

By 1918, Clock was able to report that things were going better:

> The working affairs of the school are being much better conducted than last year when through personal enmity among themselves the schools were made a target, but this year both the boys and girls schools have been put in the hands of a society of young men who follow all Miss K's suggestions even in the working of the boys school where she taught English until last year when they permitted her to devote all her time to the girls . . .[12]

Apart from the basic issue of who should control the girls school, the committee or those who were actually running the school, the main bones of contention were finances and the curriculum. The premises provided for the girls school were much inferior to those provided for the boys, and the women who taught there were paid a pittance. The American women felt that some of the school's financial problems were due to the committee having "put in many pupils as free who can afford to pay."[13] They wanted the decision as to whether or not a pupil should be subsidized to be in the hands of those capable of judging the pupil's ability. Clock wrote to Mrs. Platt:

> Miss K & I are agreed on the question of free pupils & what we really think from practical experience would startle most people. Miss K took on a little girl as your pupil [Platt was providing a scholarship], tried her for a year & she did not make good progress either she was lazy or lacked in brain capacity & so Miss K said, 'How can I keep that child & let money from Mrs P go toward her?' she notified the family if they want her kept in school they must pay for her & so now they do. almost without exception the girls who are free pupils are the ones who cause disturbance & we think they should be made to pay even a part of the regular fee, but the fees are so small it is not enough to pay proper teachers for good work, building rent, coal & the ordinary incidentals, & provide materials such as is often needed, school furniture, materials for teaching. there may be & have been exceptions to this idea of ours & if Miss K finds a girl whom she thinks bright & ambitious whose parents are not able to pay for her she will tell you, but most of the

charity children come from the lower class who have not brain capacity & the money spent on them is wasted.[17]

The American women ameliorated what they saw as the inadequate financial management of the committee by keeping control of certain funds in their own hands. Scholarship funds from the United States for both the boys and girls schools came through Moody. But aside from these funds, some women wished to send further support specifically to the girls school. At first they were asked to send educational materials that were difficult to obtain in Iran, but later quite considerable sums of money were sent.

In July 1919, a bank account was opened in the name of the girls school into which such contributions could be paid. And Iranian Bahá'í women were encouraged to contribute directly to it also. The main aim for this account was that it should grow into a building fund to permit the erection of a purpose built girls school. This effort was seen as being equivalent to the effort of the American Bahá'ís to raise money for the Mashriqu'l-Adhkár (Bahá'í House of Worship) in Wilmette, Illinois. It not being possible at that time to contemplate building a public place of Bahá'í worship in Tehran, to work for the realization of what would become a dependency of such a place of worship was regarded as of equal importance. After Kappes died in 1920, the fund that she had started continued as the "Lillian Kappes Memorial Fund," and into the 1930s it was an important source of auxiliary funding for the school. The expansion of the school was aided by this fund: for example, when new grades were added, it often paid for the desks and chairs.

On the matter of the girls school curriculum, Kappes felt that: "The feeling here is more in sympathy with domestic & child training work than higher instruction . . ." Her view was that the necessity was for a "solid academic basis" to be given in the school, so that there would be a growing core of capable women teachers to make a good education for girls more widely available. The "domestic arts" she felt would be more adequately raised by developing "a modified 'girl-scout' movement" that took account of conditions in Iran.[15] Her feeling that the teaching of the "domestic arts" needed to be adapted to Iranian conditions was based on experience, as Kappes had tried teaching them in the school:

> . . . giving cooking lessons to the 7th class as well as sewing and housekeeping, the latter is very difficult to teach here, since all the furniture in many houses consists of the rugs on the floors, and then very simple cooking utensils, a very small proportion of people have tables and chairs and much smaller still have bedsteads, they sleep on the floor on often a very thin mattress.[16]

(In fairness to the Bahá'ís of Tehran, it should be mentioned that after Godseah Ashraf arrived in the United States in 1911, as the first Iranian Bahá'í woman to be sent there to study, her pursuit of a lengthy education, including graduate work in educational philosophy and psychology, was looked upon as unnecessary and wasteful by some American Bahá'í women who felt that all she needed to assist her in teaching the girls of Iran was a quick diploma in home economics.)

The American women's view of a suitable curriculum was that of an "advanced" Western school, but with some adaptation to local circumstances. Character moulding was to be an important goal, in particular as the "Oriental" character was held to be severely flawed:

> You may think as I did the Persian children are very docile & lamb-like but if you were here you might call some of them lambs but many of them would have to be called by another name. I believe it is Abdul Baha who says "now they are the most depraved people in

the whole world", BahaUllah also speaks of their degradation etc. We must be most charitable with them but in the school small things cannot be overlooked & any one is fortunate who has a girl under the care of Miss Kappes to be trained. They have an inborn sense of disregard for the truth, all of them, I do not know one single person upon whose word you may rely, not excepting one, but I think some of the girls at least will learn to tell the truth for Miss K washes their mouths well with good strong laundry soap & it has worked wonders. No matter where you go in a meeting or anywhere else you can always pick out a girl from The Tarbiat school from her behavior & general conduct. . . .

In general there is no such thing as a sense of necessity of discipline in a Persian home, if a child wants anything it has but to cry & everything comes its way. No such thing as self control is even dreamed of & the great lack in the Persian character is Sincerity. I do not wish to give you an exaggerated idea or put them in a false light to you, but if some of these things were not true why were we sent here to work among them? I am sorry that we did not know more of the truth of the people before we came . . .[17]

The harshness of these comments is typical of observations by many Americans on the members of cultures distinct from their own among whom they have lived for any length of time. The American women in Tehran did make friends for whom they had considerable respect, but these were mainly from among those who also filled roles as change agents within the community.

The women also felt that the girls were handicapped by their native language, in that traditional texts and their associated pedagogical methods were so inadequate. They felt that: "there is only one way in which they can be taught, that is by learning another language & teaching them in it."[18] One of the principal aims in making a wider range of educational materials available to the girls through another language was to broaden their worldview, both literally and figuratively. Clock reported that,

"Miss K's ambition has been to have the girls have enough knowledge of English to teach them proper geography."[19] Thus there was an early concern to acquire good geography teaching aids for the school, maps of the world and the continents and texts. Clock also reported that by 1916, "many of the girls know enough English to be taught all sorts of subjects in English"[20]; and among these were anatomy, physiology and first aid.

The girls' horizons were also expanded by the regular use of pictures cut from American magazines (the *Ladies' Home Journal* was particularly available) as rewards and as stimuli for English lessons. It must not be thought that there was a conscious effort to "Americanize" the pupils, however. On the contrary, there was a conscious attempt to instill in them a sense of Iranian national identity and a consideration of their own roles in the progress of their country. This blend of elements may be clearly seen in the commencement ceremonies held by the school from 1917 onwards.

The 1917 commencement was held in a garden adjoining the school and was attended by about three hundred women. The decorations for the occasion were planned by Clock as, "the Persians know nothing about what we call decorations, their only idea is to hang up rugs on the walls."[21] Clock's idea was to festoon the verandah of the garden, which was used as the stage, with garlands of ivy and to place a picture of the shah, inside a heavy ivy wreath, as the centerpiece. This somewhat somber motif was lightened by a liberal use of Iranian flags. The girls entered the garden in a procession and all from the third through sixth grades carried flags: "each one was made by hand by the little girl who carried it & she even drew the 'Lion & the Sun' herself. Some of the sewing is very good & some very bad." As the girls reached the stage the teachers collected the flags and hung them on the ivy. Before making the flags, the girls had not even known the colors used in it. Their sense of the national colors was reinforced by all "displaying the Persian colors, green, red & white," in some way in their dress except the graduates who wore white.[22]

The program continued with a mixture of poems and songs in Persian and English, with one recitation in French, and the reading of several essays, including one on hygiene and one on the "duty of extending the work of the school by opening higher grades." The climax of the program was the recitation by the entire school of a poem to the flag that had been commissioned for the occasion. This was followed by a group of five third-grade girls from various states singing "Our Native Land," with the school joining in the refrain, and then the fourth grade singing "Iran." The program represented an amalgam of "advanced" ideas, including a display of gymnastics ("because some talk had gone abroad that I try to teach dancing which here is regarded as something akin to a sin"),[23] and an effort to infuse a national consciousness. The amalgam seems to have been well received:

> At the end of the program one of the princesses who occupied one of the front seats, called Miss K down from the platform & took a beautiful gold ring with her own initials from her finger & put it on hers. She also wrote a little speech which was read by one of the teachers thanking the Americans in a very nice manner. Everybody everywhere is praising Miss K for her work . . .[24]

The making of the flags became a regular feature of the school curriculum for the next several years, and was one of the features of Kappes' regime copied by other girls schools. However, the staffs of these other schools were often unaware of the rationale behind what Kappes did and could introduce quirks into their copying that defeated the original point. This was the case in one school with the idea of the flags:

> To show you how silly some of the women are one of the schools has imitated Miss K's idea of making flags by the pupils but not of Persian colors, of blue & pink. Many of them imitate her methods in school work but in such a crude way you hardly realize the original plan, they think they improve on the ways of the Tarbiat school.[25]

Kappes influenced other schools also by her pupils going to them as teachers. Once a girl had taken the Board of Education examination, she was technically qualified to teach in any girls school in Iran. Girls who had passed that exam under the tutelage of Kappes were widely regarded as the cream of potential teachers. Indeed, not only schools but mothers of marriageable sons attempted to recruit through Kappes, although she declined to take advantage of this latter testimony to the reputed quality of her product.

A useful assessment of what had been achieved by the school during this early period is given in a report by Kappes' successor, Dr. Genevieve Coy. As a highly trained educationalist, and as someone who had not had ties to the school during the Kappes regime, Coy's assessment is the nearest to neutral expert testimony available. After her arrival in 1922, Coy found that the school had 255 pupils, of which around a quarter were not Bahá'ís. By this time, the school had expanded to nine grades and a further grade was expected to be added shortly. Most of the teachers had been trained in the school, and Coy felt that the success with which the school had continued to operate between Kappes' death and her own arrival was due to the quality of the training they had received there. However, she also believed them to be very underpaid and mostly "working entirely for the love of the work and the Bahai Cause," and she was eager that their salaries should be raised. The building used for the school was still not a satisfactory one, either. She thought that the girls were, "on the whole, a happy, merry, well-behaved group," who had, "learned to play, in the last few years." As to the opinion of Tehran at large:

> The school is recognised as the best Persian Girls' school in the city. Not long ago the City Director of Education said the Girls' Tarbiat School was the best girls' school in the city, that all their work was excellent,—but alas, that they were Bahais![26]

During this early period, then, we may say that the Western Bahá'í women had a large part in establishing a creditable educational institution that catered to the secular educational needs of some of the girls of the Tehran Bahá'í community and that was sufficiently non-sectarian for the quality of the education it offered to be recognized and utilized by a number of non-Bahá'ís. They do not seem to have succeeded in having the education of girls taken as seriously as the education of boys within the Tehran Bahá'í community, at least if we may use the criteria of finances to judge this point. They did succeed in making the internal operation of the girls school largely independent of the male authority structures of the community and in fostering a deep concern in the women of the community for the education of girls. The American women brought with them an expertise that, allied with their honorary male status, enabled them to legitimize and actualize the wishes of the leading women of the Tehran Bahá'í community to an extent that would have hardly been possible without their presence. Many Iranian Bahá'í women shared in the development of secular education for the girls of their community, but the four Western Bahá'í women were a necessary leaven in the process.

The Western Bahá'í women themselves had an undoubted belief in the validity of the content and method of "advanced" Western education, but this was balanced by a concern that these advantages should be integrated into a program that also developed a committed sense of national indentity. The Western women may have had considerable doubts about the value of certain aspects of Iran's past and present, but they had none about the importance of its future and the need for women to play an active role in the making of that future.

The Western women were also concerned that the girls of the Bahá'í community be firmly grounded in their faith, as well as given a good secular education. There was already a graduated system of instructing and examining the boys of the community and, in 1914, twelve centers where girls would be taught a similar program were established.[27] In 1915, Moody described the examinations held for these girls:

> We are also examining in my home, all the advanced girls who have completed the first and second courses in their study of the Revelation. We take them in small groups by request of the Spiritual Assembly. They are given simple gifts, as a remembrance—a penholder; a ticket bearing their name and stamped by the Mahfil Dars Aklagh [the organizing committee]; once we added a printed telegram from Abdul-Baha; another time one of Mr. Remey's illuminated cards; again, a photographic copy of a holy tablet. Miss Kappes loans out a beautiful gold medal sent by Miss Holmes, which is worn by each graduate in turn during one session of the class. We serve sherbet and tea, the pupils chant prayers and poems from memory and the atmosphere is just what one desires, nearness to each other and to the Beloved.[28]

By 1923, there were sixteen centers with thirty-two teachers and assistants and a number of visiting inspectors who examined the girls as they passed from one grade to the next.[29] In the area of developing religious education for girls within the Tehran Bahá'í community, then, the Western women also served an important leavening function.

Although it is beyond the scope of this essay to go into it in detail, it should be mentioned that the Western women did not limit their educational efforts to girls, but were also concerned with the adult Bahá'í women of Tehran, even providing some of them with training and experience in coping with mixed gender situations. No doubt their activities with the adult women strengthened the support available for their activities with girls.

The second period of Western Bahá'í women's resident influence in Tehran began with the departure of Moody and Adelaide Sharpe from the United States in late 1928. Moody returned to take up her practice again, and Sharpe took over the girls school. They were later joined by Sharpe's mother, Clara Sharpe, who assisted with the school and kept house for her daughter. As before, Moody was the main channel through which Western funds came to the school, mainly through the Kappes Memorial Fund.

They found the school in considerable financial difficulty, largely they felt because of laxity in collecting school fees, and they started a vigorous collection program that recovered much of the delinquent amounts. The school also had a debt for construction work. Moody paid part of this from the Kappes Fund, leaving the remainder to be paid in installments by the school committee. They also felt that some of the problem with the school had arisen "from ignorant management by underpaid teachers who of course lacked the inspiration to do their best."[30] Indeed, six of the original teaching staff had left, and Adelaide Sharpe had to train older girls to take classes. Sharpe and her principal assistant were both appointed to the school committee, the first time that it had included women.

As part of the reorganisation, the school was expanded further by adding a kindergarten, the Kappes Fund providing the furnishings. More significantly, in respect to the curriculum, a rug weaving department was opened with the hope that "in time this will be of some financial aid, tho' at first an expense."[31] The establishing of this latter department seems to depart considerably from the ethos that embued the Kappes regime. Even the hint of possible future financial advantage takes it beyond the "handicraft" level of her curriculum. Also, when one considers how important an issue workshop rug weaving was to those concerned with the welfare of children in the Middle East, since it was the main area of industrial exploitation and abuse of children in the region, to create such a department in what was considered one of the most "advanced" girls schools in Iran suggests that a different view was being brought to bear.

Adelaide Sharpe does not seem to have developed a rapport with her staff either. Even if she did train much of her newer teaching staff, in 1933 she could still write:

> I have no real competent help in the school and so many little things that the teachers should do fall on my shoulders and I find that I am quite worn out at the end of school. There are 34 teachers and when each one shirks her responsibilities you can imagine how tired I am at times.[32]

Despite Sharpe's opinion of her staff, the school's reputation remained high and the number of girls rose to 400 by late 1929, and to 750 by 1933.

The relationship between Moody and the Sharpes suggests much about the latter's attitudes to their new environment. After her return to Tehran, Moody found that her age did not permit her to practice full time, although for a while she did keep a free clinic and see a few paying patients. For the last four years of her life she was increasingly bedridden, suffering a number of bouts of dysentery and pneumonia. From her return, she lodged with a Bahá'í family the husband of which was virtually her foster son. The Sharpes maintained their own house at the other side of the city. Clara Sharpe warned Platt that if she ever visited them she:

> . . . must expect to find every thing in a very primitive condition. We have no luxuries here. While I am writing this a woman is

> sweeping the floor with some broom straws tied together, they are about a foot long. You can imagine the dust she leaves behind her. The usual method of dusting is to blow the dust where it has settled with your breath. Breath costs nothing, or sometimes slap here and there with any thing that is convenient. Not speaking the language makes it a little difficult to teach them how to work but little by little something can be done. I have yet to see a kitchen that is clean or that has any conveniences. They have no one place to put any thing nor very few methods for doing their work. I read much about this country before coming here and I thought they were often too hard and unjust but I could have written worse things two weeks after being here. One has to be here awhile to be able to realize what Baha'u'llah said when he wrote that it was a dark country. They can be excused for many things because there is nothing to do with. The new king is trying little by little to arrange for finances to have things manufactured, get clean water to drink, and have things a little more convenient.[33]

While the Sharpes did evolve a style of housekeeping more to their liking, they do not seem to have adapted as well to living in Tehran as the earlier women. However severe her strictures on the population generally, Clock could also state:

> We live so much more comfortably than people may think we do, our house is very nice for a Persian one, we have very nice coffee with real cream in the a.m. and altho we have but one servant we are good to him and he is very faithful, of course we are not quite as clean as we want to be for this is a country with plenty of dust.[34]

The two groups of women had come from different Americas. The first group had grown up with unpaved streets, oil lamps, garbage and attendant livestock in the gutter, and water supplies of uncertain provenance. Particularly for the two older women, Clock and Moody, there can have been little in the physical conditions of life in Tehran that was that different from the experience of much of their life in the United States.

New York at the end of the last century was not so different, as far as its cleanliness and "conveniences" were concerned, from the Tehran they lived in.

For the Sharpes, however, there was a much greater change. They came from an America of municipal services and soap, even of washing machines and vacuum cleaners. Moody's preference for living in a "native" household, rather than with them, they found explicable only by presuming her senility:

> Dr Moody has given us much pleasure this summer by coming several times and spending two days with us. She, too, enjoyed it so much. We want to keep her with us all the time because she is becoming more feeble and forgetful than she realizes and does not get the care there that she should. Altho they have money they have no idea how to take care of old or sick people & the conditions I have had to put up with when I go out to help her when she is ill make me sick at heart. She has turned over every thing she has to them to keep for her so whatever she wants she has to ask for it, which often she will go with out rather than ask and if I take the most necessary things out for her to use when I go out again they are lost. So we only take what is needed for the moment. This causes me too much trouble as she is too far away. It is difficult to get a carriage when you need it and takes much time. She has always paid her board there and met all her expenses. While if she were with us we would be glad to take the best care of her just because we love and appreciate her with out any thought of remuneration. Recently she had dysentery for about two weeks which left her very week. I went out and did my best to get her to return with me but she became very indignant, told me she had rather stay there and to go home and mind my business. Altho she always appreciates so much when I do go out to do things for her or take her things she needs and does not get there. I had some one go to the National Spiritual Assembly and see if they could not make it better for her there. She found it out and was very indignant and told me so in no pleasant terms. This does not make me feel the least hard toward her for I know she is old and childish and I am keeping away from her for a week or so hoping she will forget

> all about it and perhaps we may get her to come to us yet. She said one time she might have to come to us but would not until she had to as she would not burden us. We assured her in every way possible that it would not be a burden but a joy to have her, that we needed her in the work and that her place was with us. But they cry out there and goodness only knows what else and because they do not know how to take care of her she has to suffer for it. Altho she pretends it is a joy.[35]

The struggle over where Moody should live continued for the remainder of her life. The Sharpes were really concerned for her, and they felt they were acting for her own good. They obviously held her in high regard: Adelaide always introduced her as the "mother of the school" when she visited there. However, they were incapable of seeing her wish to stay where she was as a rational choice. She simply had to be senile or undue influence had to be involved. Part of this influence they felt to be directed toward Moody's money and the Kappes Fund. The Sharpes accused the family she lived with of appropriating her own money and of tricking her into handing over some of the Kappes Fund.

Whatever may be the actual facts of the last months of Moody's life, during the preceding years her correspondence does not suggest any great deterioration of her faculties, indicates that she had very few personal funds, and that she continued to operate the Kappes Fund as usual. The Sharpes tried to stop money being sent direct to Moody for over two years before her death on the grounds of her incompetence. Their continued claims of her incapacity during the last few months of her life, when she was not able to write and present her own views, must be taken in the light of the very probable exaggeration of their earlier ones.

It is clear from her own letters that Moody was in no way pretending joy at her circumstances. She was exactly where she wished to be. Her health was looked after by Dr. Yúnis Khán Afrúkhtih, and her care cannot have been that bad, since it saw her through four years of frequent dysentery and pneumonia. Though she was often restricted to her bed, or the house, she was much loved by the Tehran Bahá'ís and was regularly visited when too ill to go out:

> The friends here come to me often and we have beautiful meetings, chanting by these young brothers is simply heavenly food. I do not get around among the friends but next Sunday there will be a meeting of the women here . . . and I shall go up stairs and enjoy it with them.[36]

Moody died on 23 October 1934, after a final illness of twelve days. Her funeral was a considerable affair:

> Some of the children of the school led the hearse while the teachers of the school followed with her Baha'i sisters and then last but by no means least came her Baha'i brothers.
>
> The Baha'i cemetery is not a cemetery in comparison to the Moslem's but is a garden. Ours here is called the Everlasting Rose Garden. So Dr. Moody was taken to the Everlasting Rose Garden where a most impressive ceremony was held. Jenabe Fadil read the burial prayers.[37]

> Her burial was majestic because hundreds of Bahais men & women and Tarbiat Girls' school students thronged with flowers in hand and she lies near Dr. Clock and Miss Lillian Kappes, because it was her wish to be buried near them.[38]

The Sharpes persisted in their view that Moody had been "childish" and had been taken advantage of. That she had simply become so acculturated to the local environment that she preferred to live as part of it was inconceivable to them. This is what sets them apart from the earlier group of women. The dispute over what part of the Kappes Fund had, or had not, been embezzled—with a cognate dispute over Moody's will—continued for several years. But the girls school as an interested party only survived Moody by a few weeks.

> The closing of the school was a great shock altho we had expected that it might happen. The Bab's Martyrdom in this country is kept by the Arabic Calendar which came this year on the 6th of December Thursday, Friday is Muhammadan holyday and no schools are opened. Saturday afternoon a policeman came with an order from the Board of Education to close the schools. They said Tarbiat had been closed for no reason Thursday and the license for Tarbiat school existed no longer. This order came after school had been dismised and there was no time to tell all the children, so A & her assistant went to school the next morning at 6.30 a.m. before the policeman could get there so they themselves would be sure of getting in and as the children came to enter the school they had to be turned back. This was very hard as many of the little ones did not understand and called to Adelaide to tell the policemen to let them in and many cried. Our porter of the school also stood at the door and explained to the children that the school was closed because we had kept the Holyday of the Bab's Martyrdom. This annoyed the policeman very much and he told told him not to explain to the children but he said they would have to tell their mothers why & kept on telling why in a very loud voice. . . .
>
> The Bahai children have not gone to other schools, a few had been going to other schools and one man took his out because Tarbiat was closed. The Muhammadan children of course went to other schools but they are not satisfied or happy. Tarbiat School was far ahead of the other persian schools, in their text books, character training and every thing else. All the schools say this. The educated Muhammadans are with the Bahais. One important Muhammadan said he knew it was a Bahai school when he sent his children there and said that was no reason for closing the school and he would tell the Board of Education so. We had many of the

best families in town sending their children and they are feeling very badly about it. There are nearly 1500 pupils in both schools & about 50 teachers.[39]

The Sharpes stayed on in Tehran after the school was closed to continue other work with the community's women. Adelaide Sharpe, herself, eventually became the first woman elected to the National Spiritual Assembly of the Bahá'ís of Iran.

The activities of the American Bahá'í women who were involved with the girls school in Tehran encompass twenty-four years, but the earlier of those years seem to have been fueled with a vision that was lacking in the later ones. The early group of women went to Tehran to teach, but also to learn. They came to teach the methods and content of "advanced" Western education, but they also expected to learn from the history, devotion and life of the community they came to. They came to join their sisters in belief in creating a new day. The later group was both literally and conceptually a rescue mission. To rescue the school from its mismanagement, and to rescue the ignorant East through Western enlightenment.

Moody retained the old vision and was incomprehensible to those with the new. The early women came from an American Bahá'í community that was only recently established. It felt its ignorance of the history and practice of its faith and in its meetings with the Eastern Bahá'í community was eager to receive as well as give. The later group came from an American Bahá'í community that was rapidly institutionalizing and developing a self-image as the model for other communities to follow. Its humility and openness were the less for that. The early group saw their relationship with their hosts, particularly the women, as symbiotic: the future was to be their mutual creation. The later women saw their role as teachers.

It will take a great deal of study to eventually determine what the effect of these women was on the position of Bahá'í women in Iran generally. That there was no sudden, or even relatively rapid, change from inherited Middle Eastern patterns of gender interaction is apparent. But undoubtedly, the presence of the early group made considerable difference to a number of Bahá'í women in Tehran. The possibilities of their lives were changed, and they had choices that did not previously exist. The impact of the later group was much less dramatic, their activities being largely a continuation of, rather than a departure from, established patterns.

The biggest hurdle to change, the attitudes of men in the Bahá'í community, was not cleared by either group. Much of the support they received seems to have been from men who already had exposure to Western ideas. Most others who were prepared to support the separate education of a few girls were unlikely to have had any associated commitment to a basic change in gender roles. The mothers who sought wives for their sons from Kappes probably expressed the mass view of the utility of girls education. As in much of the Third World today, an educated girl was seen as a better bargain in the marriage mart.

NOTES

This essay draws generally on a familiarity with the holdings of the National Bahá'í Archives, Wilmette, Illinois. The specific manuscript materials cited are from the Thornton Chase Papers and Orol Platt Papers. Of the periodicals cited, the *Star of the West* is too well known to need further comment, the *Magazine of the Children of the Kingdom* was published by Ella Robarts from 1919 to 1924, and is an insufficiently known source of Bahá'í children's activities of those years. All quotations are reproduced here as in the source.

The statistics on the involvement of American Protestant women in overseas missionary work at the beginning of this essay are from a 1910 survey of the field excerpted in Rosemary Radford Ruether and Rosemary Skinner Keller (eds.), *Women and Religion in America:*

The Nineteenth Century, San Francisco: Harper and Row, 1981. Despite the title of this book, the documents and essays in it also cover the early part of the twentieth century.

1. Moody to Russell, 27 December 1909. Chase Papers.
2. Ibid., 24–25 January 1910.
3. Ibid.
4. Ibid., 27 December 1909.
5. Ibid., 27 November 1909.
6. Ibid., 29 January 1910.
7. Ibid., 11 January 1910.
8. Ibid., 2 January 1910.
9. Ibid., 24 January 1910.
10. Clock to Platt, 15 August 1916. Platt Papers.
11. Ibid., 20 November 1916.
12. Ibid., 29 January 1918.
13. Ibid., 20 November 1916.
14. Ibid., 9 July 1919.
15. Kappes to Platt, 31 August 1920. Platt Papers.
16. Clock To Platt, 29 January 1918. Platt Papers.
17. Ibid., 15 August 1916.
18. Ibid.
19. Ibid., 20 November 1916.
20. Ibid.
21. Ibid., 22 June 1917.
22. Ibid.
23. Kappes. "Programme of Exercises." Platt Papers.
24. Clock to Platt, 22 June 1917. Platt Papers.
25. Ibid., 9 July 1919.
26. *Magazine of the Children of the Kingdom*, no. 4 (September 1923) pp. 82–83.
27. *Star of the West*, vol. 5, no. 4, p. 74.
28. Ibid., vol. 6, no. 7 (13 July 1915) p. 54.
29. Moody to Platt, 21 May 1923. Platt Papers.
30. Ibid., n.d. [1929].
31. Ibid., 22 June 1929.
32. A. Sharpe to Platt, 26 February 1933. Platt Papers.
33. C. Sharpe to Platt, 4 March 1931. Platt Papers.

34. Clock to Platt, 29 January 1918. Platt Papers.
35. C. Sharpe to Platt, August 1932. Platt Papers.
36. Moody to Platt, 1 January 1934. Platt Papers.
37. A. Sharpe to Platt, 29 October 1934. Platt Papers.
38. Roozbehyan to Platt, 5 November 1934. Platt Papers.
39. C. Sharpe to Platt, 16 January 1935. Platt Papers.

THE SHAHYAD MONUMENT
Tehran, c. 1976.

RELIGION AND FAMILY PLANNING IN CONTEMPORARY IRAN

by Mehri Samandari Jensen, Ed.D.

Because of the ever-increasing interdependence of the nations of the world in economic and political matters, contemporary growth of population in the Third World has become a major cause of concern.[1] In many developing countries, the introduction of modern medicine and standards of public health have led to a marked decline in mortality rates. For the most part, this decline has not been accompanied by a lowering of traditionally high birth rates. The increase in population which has resulted has often made goals for economic and social development difficult to obtain, and in some instances has led to political instability.

One response to this problem has been the promotion of family planning programs by government agencies. The success of these programs in various countries has varied considerably, however. While some have experienced a marked decline in birth rates, others have found no such success. A major factor to be considered by experts in attempting to account for this difference is the wider pattern of socio-economic development. Briefly, it is argued by some that, as was experienced in developed countries generations ago, the growth of prosperity will lead to a lower birth rate. Therefore, it is expected that as the modern urban and industrial sector expands, so the birth rate will fall and Third World countries will experience a demographic transition to a Western-style population structure.

Unfortunately, experience indicates that this goal is not so easily attained. Many developing countries remain severely impoverished; and even where significant urban and industrial expansion has occurred, much of the population remains rural, maintains traditional attitudes toward desired family size, or resists the adoption of family planning practices.

One key factor in the preservation or change of traditional attitudes is religion. The impact of religion on differential fertility in the Middle East has been a controversial subject among population experts for many decades.[2] Dudley Kirk, the Director of the Demographic Division of the Population Council, in a lengthy discussion and a statistical documentation of all Muslim nations in the world, stated that "empirically Islam has been a more effective barrier to the difussion of family planning than Catholicism." He furthermore concluded that, within the important limitation of the data, it may be said that the Muslim birth rate was almost universally high, that it showed no evidence of change over time, and that it was generally higher than that of neighboring people of other major religions.[3] Richard A. Fagley, however, has refuted this generalization and concluded that underdevelopment and not Islamic teaching was responsible for the high birth rate among Muslims.[4]

A survey of the literature on the Middle East indicates that a majority of the research has been done to compare only Christians and Muslims, and that invariably this research concluded that in general Muslims had a much higher birth rate than Christians. The literature indicates that, not only was Muslim fertility high in the Middle East, it was also high in countries where Muslims live as religious minorities.[5]

But, the research findings regarding the impact of Islam on

family planning seem contradictorary and confusing. On the one hand they imply that the internalized values, religious beliefs, and the inner being of the human guides his or her behavior—as in the case of Muslims, who have the highest birth rates where they were found. On the other hand, the studies also imply that the cultural milieu and the outer environment, not religious ideology, determine fertility behavior.

Religion by itself cannot be the only factor affecting Muslim fertility, of course. It would seem that there are two interdependent factors responsible for high birth rates among Muslims: specific Islamic ideology and other social and cultural elements. Some of these latter elements include: agricultural modes of production, the underdevelopment of many Muslim countries, the low status of women in family and public life, male dominance, the emphasis on virility symbolized by having many children through male progeny, and even the need for old age security achieved through offspring who are obliged to care for their aged parents.[6] Religious factors that are unique to Islam and that may contribute to the high birth rate include: the lack of a taboo on sex and the enjoyment of the flesh, the practice of polygamy and temporary marriage (*síghih*), a high level of fatalism reinforced by scriptures that makes planning unfavorable since it is God that creates sexuality and determines procreation or barreness, the universality of marriage among women, and the fact that asceticism is not highly valued in Islam as it is in Christianity.[7]

From a survey of the literature pertaining to fertility rates in the Middle East, then, it would seem that the birth rate among Muslims is always high, and generally higher than that of neighboring people of other religions. Generally speaking, this conclusion results from comparing Muslim and Christian birth rates, and assuming that all other variables are held constant except the religious difference.

It is likely, however, that cultural values related to family planning are derived not from the religion of the peoples but from their culture of national origin, since most of the Christians in the Middle East make up separate nationalities in the region. In Iran, for example, Armenians, who comprise the majority of Christians, consider themselves culturally and ethnically non-Persians.[8] Although they have been settled in Iran for many centuries, they identify with the West and with the country of their origin, Armenia. To a large extent they are an unassimilated population, and their views are European. Generally they are regarded as non-Persians. For many centuries, the Armenians have been known as and called "foreigners" by the Iranian public. Universally they speak Armenian as their first language and Persian (*fársí*), the official language of Iran, or other local dialects as their second language. They even speak Persian with a noticeable and distinct accent. Their names and often their lighter complexion and mannerisms set them immediately apart from Persians. Thus, because of these differences between Christians and Muslims in Iran, it is not clear whether religion on the one hand or general cultural outlook and Western ethnic identity on the other contributes most to the lower birthrate among Christians.

An objective of this study was to reexamine the relationship between the religion and the birthrate of the population in Iran by correcting for this contaminating factor found in the background culture of the Christians. Another objective was to propose that religious affiliation alone does not weigh as heavily in determining individual behavior as does the degree of religiosity: the feelings, beliefs, practices, and knowledge of their respective religions.

The Iranian Bahá'í community provides an ideal comparative group in this context. Iranian Bahá'ís are an indigenous population of the same nationality and culture as Iranian Muslims. (We here exclude a minority of Bahá'ís of Iranian Jewish and Zoroastrian backgrounds.) Therefore, the only important difference from their fellow countrymen is their religion. The value of the Bahá'í community as a comparative group also stems from the clear ideological differences that exist between Muslims and Bahá'ís, particularly with regard to social teachings. Iranian Muslims tend to subscribe to a religious ideology that stresses fatalism and male dominance, that is resistant to Western influence and to the adoption of birth control measures in particular. Iranian Bahá'ís claim a belief in sexual equality that, when implemented, would lead to more egalitarian relationships between husband and wife, and emphasize the desirability of female education—both factors that are likely to facilitate readier acceptance of family planning. Further, Bahá'ís stress positive social action rather than fatalism.

Procedures and Methodology. A two-step procedure was used to select samples of Bahá'ís and Muslims. First, a Bahá'í sampling area was selected from a population, and then within each unit the samples of subjects were drawn. The reason for this approach was that taking a random sample of a religious minority in Iran is difficult, if not impossible. There are no reliable maps available which indicated the location of farms or housing within the villages. A list of Bahá'ís and Bahá'í villages was virtually nonexistent in the government records. Although many such villages are known and functioning, in the census records they might be completely dropped or listed as "religious affiliation not mentioned."

Amani's survey of religious minorities in Iran, published in 1970, makes no mention of the Bahá'í Faith, although it is known to be the largest minority group in Iran.[9] Instead of listing the Bahá'ís, there is a column comprising the largest percentage under the title "religion, others" or "religious affiliation not mentioned." It seems improbable that, in a country where religion is the most distinct criteria for social differentiation, far more important than race or ethnicity, so many nonreligious populations could exist. In 1972, when this investigator visited the government census bureau in Tehran and interviewed the general director, she was told that often a census worker may leave a predominantly or exclusively Bahá'í village and report the population as zero. When confronted, the answer would be "they are not human beings," or "they are only Bahá'ís." There were no such problems with identifying Muslim villages and towns.

Given these difficulties, it was decided to select Bahá'í subjects and villages with the assistance of the Bahá'í offices of membership and records, and local Spiritual Assemblies (*máfil-i rawhání*) of the Bahá'ís in the localities under investigation. The Bahá'í institutions were well known for their efficient registration system of birth, death, and declaration of faith. (Any individual over the age of fifteen declares his/her belief in the Faith in order to become a full member of the Bahá'í community.) Even this approach had difficulties, however, as periodically the Bahá'í centers and administrative offices have been confiscated by Muslims and their records seized or destroyed. These outbreaks of persecution have happened all too often, with the most recent raids occurring during 1980–1981. Bahá'í membership lists have also been used by the Muslims for harassment, assaults, and lynchings. Such religious discrimination and persecution against the Bahá'ís of Iran has led to the segregation of Bahá'í villages and communities. Due to this persecution, a nonrandom sampling procedure was used in selecting the Bahá'ís to be interviewed for this study.

The locales chosen for the study were in the province of Mazandaran, in northern Iran: Mahfroozak, a Bahá'í village; Lormahalleh, a semiurban area; Babol (Bárfurúsh), a city with many Bahá'ís; and Daryakenar, a prestigious resort city where only recently nine Bahá'í households had settled.

These places were then matched with similar Muslim settlements by controlling for distance from major cities, degree of mechanization, transportation facilities, types of crops, irrigation, and land tenure. In some cases the Bahá'í areas mentioned above had sufficiently large Muslim groupings to be used also as the source of Muslim sampling. This was true for the areas of Lormahalleh and Daryakenar. Gelmahalleh, a Muslim district in the town of Babol, had a few Bahá'ís in it, and so they were also contacted. The other Muslim sites chosen were Areteh, a Muslim farming village; and Shohada, another district of the Muslim city of Babol.

There were 245 households contacted, but not all of them met the criteria of sampling characteristics. In the end, 218 couples were interviewed (436 individuals). These were all married, living with their spouses, professed their religion to be either Bahá'í or Muslim, and were acknowledged by others to be members of that group.

The following variables were then documented by interviews in order to compare Muslim and Bahá'í family planning: the dependent variables of knowledge, attitude, and practice of family planning; and the independent variables of socio-economic status, income, occupation, education, religion, and degree of religiosity. The independent variable of religion and degree of religiosity was measured by a scale devised by the investigator since there was no satisfactory scale available to measure degree of religiosity across the religions of Islam and Bahá'í. Although these religions are both monotheistic and basically teach the same moral and spiritual principles, their religious terminology and concepts (Day of Judgment, sin, etc.) are very different. Social teachings also differ markedly, as do practices in marriage, divorce, inheritance, and other matters of personal status.

These problems manifested themselves during the preliminary interview session or pretest. It was found that questions that were based on the social teachings of the Bahá'í Faith were misunderstood or even regarded as offensive to the Muslims. For example, when Muslims were asked questions based on the Bahá'í principle of worldmindedness (such as whether or not he

TABLE 1

Sampling Distribution: The Number of Subjects Selected by Residence and Religion

Site	Type of Site	Total Households	Bahá'í Couples	Muslim Couples	Total Couples Contacted	Data Used
Mahfroozak (Bahá'í)	Rural	62	60	2	62	50
Areteh (Muslim)	Rural	58	0	58	58	50
Lormahalleh (Bahá'í)	Semi-urban	89	74	15	26	25
Gelmahalleh (Muslim)	Semi-urban	90	2	88	27	24
Shohada (only Muslim)	Urban	78	0	78	28	26
Babol (only Bahá'í)	Urban	--	25	--	25	25
Daryakenar (Bahá'í/Muslim)	Sub-urban	48	9	39	19	18
Total Couples					245	218

loved mankind) some were offended because the question was misconstrued to mean that they might be accused of loving foreigners, Westerners, or Bahá'ís. Thus, in the actual interviews for each religious group, a different set of questions was used to measure the functionally equivalent items for all five dimensions of religiosity developed by Faulkner, King, and Glock: the experiential (religious feeling), the ideological (religious belief), the ritualistic (religious practice), the intellectual (religious knowledge), and the consequential (the impact of religion on the individual in everyday life).[10]

The first step in data collection for the author was to meet a gatekeeper, a person who was influential and well-known in the village. Then, in his company, the investigator visited people and asked some preliminary questions without pencils, paper, or tape recorders. This procedure not only relaxed those to be interviewed and loosened the tight boundaries between the researcher and the subjects, but at the same time gave the researcher an idea of what kind of questions to put in the interview format and how questions should be asked to insure the validity and reliability of the data. In addition, the pretest of the instrument for data collection was accomplished.

The interviews were conducted by trained male and female interviewers. These were selected from the reputable and prominent members of the community or from people who were working for them or were related to them. This enhanced trust in the investigator and in the motives of the research. A pair of male and female interviewers visited the household members simultaneously whenever possible. Each interviewed the subject of his/her own sex in a variety of circumstances, comfortable, conducive, and convenient for the subjects (e.g., working on the farm, sorting out crops at home, pulling cotton from the pod, or walking to the spring to fetch fresh water). The interview was always conducted in the local dialect.

Results and Discussions. When the data was all in and the information organized, the results provided support for the hypothesis that the difference of religion, whether Muslim or Bahá'í, did affect family size in Iran. There were also other interesting observations that could be made. Differences between the rural, semiurban, and urban populations help to refine the original hypothesis. With this in mind, each village will be discussed in turn and compared to the others. It must be emphasized, however, that this was a pilot survey. Further work is needed to substantiate the author's findings.

TABLE 2

Mean Number of Pregnancies, Children Desired, Ever Born and Lived, by Socio-Economic Status in Areteh (Muslim)

Socio-Economic Status	Women Contacted %	Women Contacted #	Mean Number of Children: Pregnancies	Desired	Born	Lived
I. Landholding						
Large owner/farmer	10	10	6.1	6.4	5.7	5.3
Medium & small	36	18	6.2	6.3	5.5	4.9
Landless	46	23	6.0	6.3	5.3	4.8
II. Ownership of durable goods						
High	30	15	6.0	6.1	5.6	5.3
Medium	34	17	5.9	6.1	5.8	5.2
Low	36	18	5.5	5.9	5.3	4.9
III. Husband's occupation						
Farmer	60	30	6.0	6.2	5.7	5.5
Farm and non-farm laborer	30	15	5.7	6.0	5.7	5.1
Store keeper, etc.	10	5	5.9	5.7	5.3	4.9
IV. Husband's education						
6th grade/read & write	20	10	6.0	6.0	5.9	5.3
Only read	30	15	5.9	6.2	5.8	5.2
Illiterate	50	25	5.7	5.9	5.5	4.9
V. Wife's education						
6th grade/read & write	10	5	5.3	5.5	5.2	5.0
Only read	20	10	5.7	6.0	4.8	4.9
Illiterate	70	35	5.8	6.2	5.3	4.8

Table 2 presents the data gathered for the village of Areteh, the Muslim farming village. It presents the mean number of pregnancies, children desired, children born, and children who lived, by socio-economic status. It shows that fertility was high among Areteh residents, especially farmers. It is also interesting to note that the mean number of pregnancies, children desired, children born, and children who lived, is lowest among the more educated wives.

Table 3 presents the data gathered for the Bahá'í farming village of Mahfroozak. In terms of its socio-economic status and composition, the sample is similar to that for Areteh, although there are significantly more large land owners and farmers (24% as compared with 10% of the samples). The major difference is in terms of education, however. Among the Bahá'ís of Mahfroozak, 50% of the husbands and 46% of the wives are fully literate (that is, can read *and* write) or have received an education up to at least sixth grade. By contrast, among the Muslims of Areteh, the figures are 20% and 10% respectively. It is of note that not only is the Bahá'í sample better educated, but the level of education of wives is similar to that of husbands, in marked contrast to the situation in Areteh.

The data suggests that the Bahá'ís were practicing their religious principle of the equality of men and women in universal education. Long before the literacy corps was established in Iran to combat the high illiteracy rate, local Spiritual Assemblies of Bahá'ís in many villages where there were no schools were offering adult education classes independent of the government. Women were especially encouraged to attend these classes. It is a belief among Bahá'ís that enlightened mothers enlighten their children. Therefore, in Mahfroozak, women received a better education, and this is most likely reflected in their attitude toward birth control.

Turning to the number of children desired, pregnancies, and live births, we can note consistently lower rates for the Bahá'í sample, even when the level of education and socio-economic status is held constant. This difference is particularly marked in the case of the more educated wives and husbands. Thus, for the fully literate groups, the mean number of pregnancices is 1.5 higher in the Muslim village for the educated husbands (6.0 as compared with 4.5) and 0.9 higher for the educated wives

TABLE 3

Mean Number of Pregnancies, Children Desired, Ever Born and Lived, by Socio-Economic Status in Mahfroozak (Bahá'í)

Socio-Economic Status	Women Contacted %	Women Contacted #	Mean Number of Children: Pregnancies	Desired	Born	Lived
I. Landholding						
Large owner/farmer	24	12	6.0	5.7	5.6	5.5
Medium & small	46	23	5.8	5.7	5.6	5.3
Landless	30	15	5.9	6.1	5.5	5.0
II. Ownership of durable goods						
High	30	15	5.7	6.9	5.6	5.5
Medium	40	20	5.6	5.2	5.5	5.3
Low	30	15	5.5	5.4	5.2	5.0
III. Husband's occupation						
Farmer	70	35	5.4	5.6	5.2	5.3
Farm and non-farm laborer	20	10	5.9	5.8	5.6	5.3
Store keeper, etc.	10	5	5.8	5.5	5.3	4.9
IV. Husband's education						
6th grade/read & write	50	25	4.5	4.4	4.3	4.2
Only read	30	15	5.1	5.3	4.9	5.0
Illiterate	20	10	5.2	5.8	5.0	4.9
V. Wife's education						
6th grade/read & write	46	23	4.4	4.3	4.3	4.2
Only read	36	18	5.1	5.0	5.0	4.8
Illiterate	18	9	5.2	5.8	5.3	4.7

(5.3 as compared with 4.4). For those who are illiterate, or can only read, the differences are 0.7 for both husbands and wives (each 5.8 as compared with 5.1). We can also note that in the Bahá'í village, the number of children desired by husbands and

TABLE 4

Mean Number of Children Ever Born by Socio-Economic Status in Semi-Urban Areas of Lormahalleh and Gelmahalleh

	Mean Number of Children			
Socio-Economic Status	% Women	Bahá'ís (N=25)	% Women	Muslims (N=24)
I. Landholding				
Large owner/farming	11	5.8	9	6.0
Medium & small owner	50	5.7	26	6.0
Sharecropping	9	5.6	15	5.9
Landless	30	5.3	50	5.6
II. Ownership of durable goods				
High	26	5.3	20	5.7
Medium	30	5.5	20	5.9
Low	44	5.7	55	6.0
III. Husband's occupation				
Professional/technical	15	2.9	2	3.5
Large business/management	5	3.1	0	4.3
Small business/management	20	3.2	3	4.7
Sales/clerical	30	3.2	5	4.9
Farmer	25	5.2	90	5.9
IV. Husband's education				
College/secondary	4	2.5	2	3.2
6th grade/read & write	87	3.0	35	3.5
Only read	8	3.9	3	4.2
Illiterate	2	4.0	60	5.3
V. Wife's education				
College/secondary	3	2.2	0	2.3
6th grade/read & write	85	2.9	16	3.5
Only read/no schooling	10	3.5	9	4.9
Illiterate	2	3.9	75	5.5

wives is similar, while in the Muslim village, literate wives desire fewer children than literate husbands.

Table 4 presents the total number of children ever born, by socio-economic status, in the semiurban area of Lormahalleh and Gelmahallea. The detail of this table shows that there is still a high percentage of people who are landowners or farm owners in these semiurban areas. They may live on the outskirts of the town and not on the the farm, but they are farming. Consequently, they may maintain some rural values and rural mentality, together with urban values. Results indicate that their birth rate was lower than rural people.

In this type of sampling area there were more professional and technical people, and more people engaged in business, management, and sales when compared to the rural areas. This is especially true among Bahá'ís. There were more wives in professional and technical positions, owners of small businesses, and members of the clerical occupational class, again, especially among the Bahá'ís. But, overall, the two samples were not of comparable populations, 90% of the Muslims being farmers while only 25% of the Bahá'ís were.

Compared with the villages, there were far more educated women in these semiurban samples. This was particularly true of the Bahá'í sample, in which some 87% had some schooling or were at least able to read and write. The women in the Muslim sample were very different—only 16% had received schooling or were able to read or write. Of the schooled group, the mean number of children born to the Bahá'ís was 2.9, while for the Muslims it was 3.5. For the unschooled group, the figures were 3.6 and 5.4 respectively.

Table 5 shows the mean number of children ever born, by socio-economic status, in the Muslim urban area of Shohada and the Bahá'í households in the urban area of Babol. In these areas, there were property owners who own land and villages but they did not do the farming themselves. However, the number of children among Muslims was still slightly higher than the Bahá'ís in these types of residences. But, when education of the husband was higher, the number of children was lower, especially if the wife's education was also higher.

In this category there was not much difference between the

Table 5

Mean Number of Children Ever Born by Socio-Economic Status, Religion, and Degree of Religiosity in Urban Area of Shohada (Muslim) and Babol (Bahá'í)

	Bahá'ís (N=26)		Muslims (N=28)	
	Mean # of Children Born	Degree of Religiosity	Mean # of Children Born	Degree of Religiosity
I. Property holding				
Large	3.2	29	4.1	12
Medium and small	3.5	26	4.3	15
None	4.2	12	4.9	29
II. Ownership of durable goods				
High	3.1	28	3.2	12
Medium	3.5	25	3.7	19
Low	3.9	14	4.8	27
III. Husband's occupation				
Professional/technical	2.5	30	3.1	6
Large business/management	2.6	30	3.1	5
Small business/management	2.8	27	3.3	11
Sales/clerical	3.0	19	3.8	20
Laborer/peddler	3.1	17	3.9	26
IV. Wife's occupation				
Professional/technical	2.3	29	2.9	5
Business management	2.3	29	3.4	6
Sales/clerical	2.4	20	3.5	11
Servant/laborer	--	--	3.9	25
V. Husband's education				
College/secondary	2.5	28	2.9	5
6th grade/read & write	2.9	21	3.1	6
Only read	3.2	19	4.1	11
Illiterate	3.5	10	4.3	28
VI. Wife's education				
College/secondary	2.1	29	2.3	5
6th grade/read & write	2.4	23	3.3	6
Only read	2.9	18	3.5	16
Illiterate	4.6	9	4.6	29

mean number of children among the two religious groups. Again we note that Table 5 shows the fertility rates for women of all ages. Still the desired number of children among the women who have higher education was much lower than that among those in the uneducated and illiterate population.

Figure 1 shows the degree of religiosity of Muslims and Bahá'ís by number of children ever born. It should be viewed together with the information presented in Table 5, which showed the number of children ever born by socio-economic status and degree of religiosity in the urban areas. The study of Figure 1 and Table 5 indicates that the higher the level of education of the Bahá'ís, the higher the degree of religiosity and the lower the number of children. On the contrary, among Muslims the higher the degree of religiosity, the lower was their level of education and the higher the number of children ever born. This might be due to the principles of the Bahá'í Faith that encourage education among all members, and that in turn keep the members in touch with progressive principles.

Table 6 shows the mean number of children ever born by

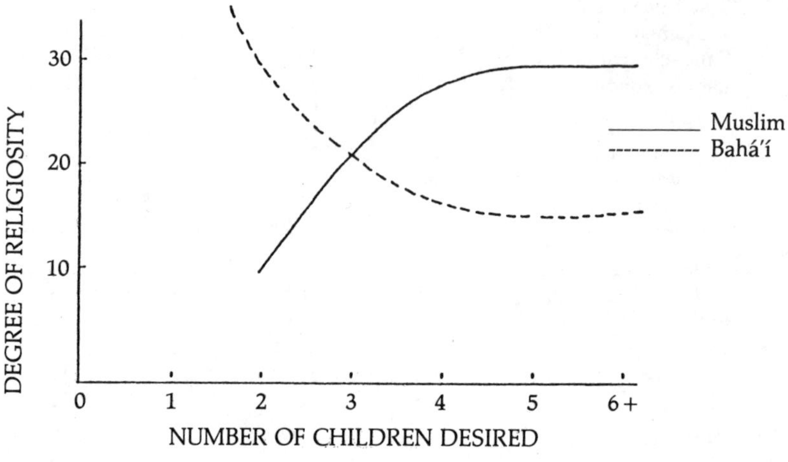

FIGURE 1. Degree of religiosity by number of children desired among Muslims in the urban area of Shohada District and Bahá'ís in the city of Babol.

TABLE 6

Mean Number of Children Ever Born by Socio-Economic Status, in Suburban Area of Daryakenar (Bahá'ís and Muslims)

Socio-Economic Status	Bahá'ís (N=9)		Muslims (N=9)	
	% of Women	Mean # of Children Born	% of Women	Mean # of Children Born
I. Property holding				
Large	95	2.5	97	2.6
Medium and small	5	2.7	3	2.9
None	--	--	--	--
II. Ownership of durable goods				
High	93	2.3	97	2.5
Medium	7	2.4	3	2.7
Low	--	--	--	--
III. Husband's occupation				
Professional/technical	59	2.5	83	2.6
Large business/management	37	2.5	17	2.7
Medium & Small manaagement	4	2.6	--	--
IV. Wife's occupation				
Professionaltechnical	37	2.3	15	2.4
Large business/management	13	2.4	2	2.6
None	50	2.6	83	3.1
V. Husband's education				
College/secondary	98	2.3	75	2.7
6th grade/read & write	2	2.5	25	2.9
Only read	--	--	--	--
Illiterate	--	--	--	--
VI. Wife's education				
College/secondary	95	2.1	10	2.2
6th grade/read & write	5	2.5	80	2.8
Only read	--	--	10	2.9
Illiterate	--	--	--	--

socio-economic status in the prestigious resort area of Daryakernar, an urban area with both Muslims and Bahá'ís. In this necessarily small sample, the number of children was very low among both groups. There was a high percentage of younger professionals using the residence in this area as a second home. The subjects were generally large property owners whose wealth was obtained through inheritance and family fortune. It is important to bear in mind that, among Muslims at least, the pattern of arranged marriages is still usually practiced. Marriage within the same socio-economic status group was common. Only recently, during the 1970s did professionally educated men who might not be wealthy marry women from wealthy families who might not necessarily be educated. Whether the same pattern held true among the Bahá'ís is uncertain. Certainly, arranged marriages were far less common and are officially discouraged.

The inverse relationship between fertility and socio-economic status noted above held true for this group. The number of children born was slightly lower among the Bahá'ís as compared to Muslims, but the difference was not significant. As the education of the wife increased, the number of children declined for Muslims and Bahá'ís—a pattern noted in the other localities as well. However, there were more Bahá'í women who were educated and engaged in professional fields and in small business in all areas.

Looking at other combinations of this data, Table 7 presents the mean number of children ever born by socio-economic status, residence, religion, and use of birth control devices for only those women between the ages of fifteen and twenty-four in Areteh and Mahfroozak. It can be seen that the percentage of women who use birth control is much higher among Bahá'ís than among Muslims and the mean number of desired children is much lower among the Bahá'ís. But when the level of education is high, there is much less difference between Bahá'ís and

Table 7

Mean Number of Children Lived and Desired by Socio-Economic Status, Religion, and Use of Birth Control Devices Among Women 15–24 in Mahfroozak and Areteh

	Bahá'ís using Birth Control (N = 100)		Muslims using Birth Control (N = 100)	
	Mean # of Children		Mean # of Children	
Socio-Economic Status	Lived	Desired	Lived	Desired
I. Land and durable goods				
High	2.9	2.0	3.3	3.2
Medium	3.1	2.5	3.5	4.0
Low	3.2	3.1	4.1	4.1
II. Husband's occupation				
Professional/technical	--	2.0	--	3.0
Large business/management	--	2.1	--	3.1
Small business/management	2.9	2.2	3.1	3.2
Sales/clerical	2.9	2.2	3.2	3.3
Farmer	3.0	3.2	4.4	4.1
Laborer	3.0	3.1	4.3	4.0
III. Wife's occupation				
Professional/technical	--	2.0	--	3.2
Large business/management	--	2.0	--	3.2
Small business/management	2.9	2.2	3.1	3.5
Sales/clerical	2.9	2.3	3.3	3.7
Farmer	3.2	3.0	4.9	4.8
Laborer	3.3	3.0	4.5	4.9
IV. Husband's education				
College/secondary	--	2.0	--	2.3
6th grade/read & write	2.3	2.0	--	2.2
Only read	2.4	3.0	3.5	3.3
Illiterate	3.3	3.5	4.2	4.0
V. Wife's education				
College/secondary	--	1.9	--	2.0
6th grade/read & write	2.9	2.1	--	3.2
Only read	3.1	2.3	4.2	4.1
Illiterate	3.2	3.9	4.8	5.2

Muslims in regard to the use of birth control, desired number of children, or the actual number of children.

One finding of the study which should provoke further research is the effect of differences in the degree of religiosity. The data for the urban areas of Shohada (Muslim) and Babol (Bahá'í) suggests very divergent relationships between the number of children desired and the degree of religiosity among the two groups. Thus, for the Bahá'ís, the higher the degree of religiosity, the lower was the number of children desired. For the Muslims, the number of children desired increased with the level of religiosity. These patterns are shown graphically in Figure 1, and are revealed in more detail in Table 5. This table also demonstrates a second pair of relationships between religiosity and socio-economic status and education. Briefly, among the Bahá'ís the higher levels of religiosity were found among those of higher social status and level of education; while among the Muslims the relationship was reversed, with higher levels of religiosity associated with lower social status and levels of education.

These patterns are further supported by the data presented in Table 8, which shows the relationship between the level of the wife's education and the degree of religiosity for the urban, semiurban and rural samples. In both the urban and semiurban samples, the two divergent relationships are strongly expressed. They can be discerned, however, even in the rural samples. The overall patterns are shown graphically in Figure 2, which relates the degree of religiosity to the level of education.

Finally, the age variable must be considered. There is only a small difference between the birth rate among Bahá'ís and Muslims in the rural areas, especially among the older generation. This could easily have been the result of the lack of knowledge and availability of birth control devices. However, among the younger age group of women aged fifteen to twenty-four, the younger Bahá'ís did use birth control more often than Muslims

Table 8

Degree of Religiosity of Bahá'ís and Muslims Residing in Urban, Semi-Urban and Rural Areas by Education of the Wives

	Degree of Religiosity[a]					
	Urban		Semi-Urban		Rural	
Wife's Education	Bahá'ís (N=34)	Muslims (N=37)	Bahá'ís (N=26)	Muslims (N=27)	Bahá'ís (N=50)	Muslims (N=50)
College or secondary	29	9	28	12	25	--
6th grade/read and write	26	13	25	12	23	25
Only read	20	24	19	23	19	26
Illiterate	--	27	--	28	18	29

[a]Degree of Religiosity scores are composites of the scale of religiosity:

30 - 21 = high
20 - 11 = medium
10 - 1 = low

and their desired number of children was closer to the number of living children they had. In semiurban and urban areas where the level of education among Muslim and Bahá'í women was close to being the same, the difference between the number of living children was minimal.

Conclusions. The research indicates that one factor which appears to clearly differentiate the Bahá'ís from their non-Bahá'í compatriots in Iran is the higher levels of education found in the community as a whole. There may be little difference among those of higher socio-economic status, but among those of lower status—and particularly among women—the Bahá'ís are better educated. This has resulted, not just from the Bahá'í belief in the importance of education, but from the practical steps that the Iranian Bahá'ís have taken over the years to implement that principle.

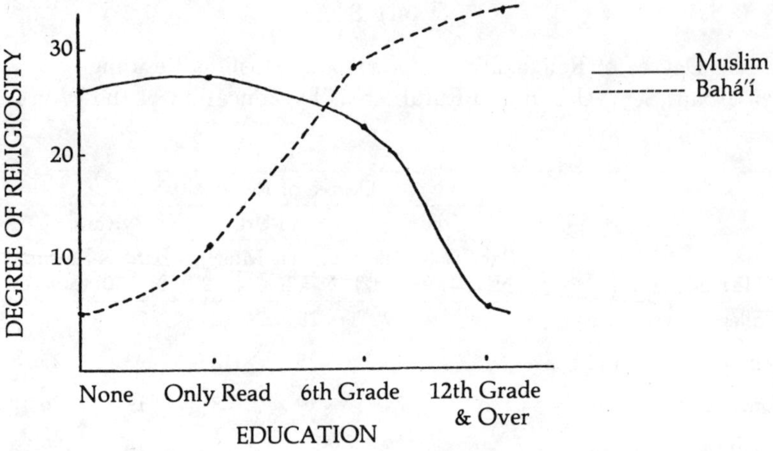

FIGURE 2. Degree of religiosity of the Bahá'ís and Muslims by level of education.

Education, and particularly the education of women, appears to be a crucial factor in determining differences in birth rate. We may reasonably suppose that the Bahá'ís' strong support for female education is a major reason for the lower birth rate among the Bahá'í community, especially in the lower socio-economic groups.

A second factor, and more difficult to determine, is the effect of Bahá'í beliefs in the equality of the sexes and in the need for consultation between husband and wife as equals. It is not reasonable to suppose that all Bahá'í couples automatically implement such principles, but we may suppose that these beliefs have some impact on the community as a whole. Indirect evidence for this impact may be provided by the fact that Bahá'í husbands and wives generally desired similar numbers of children, while among Muslims the husbands generally desired more than the wives.

Most interestingly, the findings of this study indicated that the higher the level of education among the Bahá'ís, the higher their degree of religiosity and the lower their mean number of children. This was not true in the Muslim sample where higher levels of education were associated with low levels of religiosity, and high levels of religiosity were associated with high levels of fertility. We may reasonalbly assume that among the Bahá'ís, modern education and progressive social principles mutually reinforce one another. One consequence of this is a lower level of fertility, especially among the more religious and educated. By contrast, among the Muslims, modern education and high levels of religiosity are in tension with each other.

In conclusion, the findings of this investigation were consistent with the hypothesis of the study. They indicate that the conceptual framework upon which this study was based is at least a partial explanation of why Muslims have a higher birth rate than neighboring people and countrymen who have similar national, racial, and ethnic characteristics. It was concluded that the religious principles of Islam and the Bahá'í Faith are in fact very different and that these differnces help to explain the differences in fertility patterns.

The results of this study are not definitive. Further and more extensive research is called for to determine whether the results obtained in this study are typical of demographic patterns in Iran as a whole. Again, the ideological impact of the Islamic Revolution and the new Islamic government on family planning behavior needs to be investigated. More generally, the whole question of the relationship between religion and ideology and demographic behavior requires closer and more careful examination.

NOTES

This paper is based on an extract from the author's doctoral dissertation, "The Impact of Religion, Socio-Economic Status, and Degree of Religiosity on Family Planning among Moslems and Baha'is in Iran:

A Pilot Survey Research," submitted for the degree of Ed.D., University of Northern Colorado, 1981. The author wishes to offer her thanks to Mr. Joseph Weixelman for his help in preparing this article for publication from the text of her dissertation.

1. See generally, United Nations, Department of Social Affairs, Population Division, "The Determinants and Consequences of Population Trends" *Population Studies* 17 (January 1953) pp. 17–25 and Paydarfar, A. A., *Demographic Consequences of Modernization: A Population Analysis of Iran and Comparison with Selected Nations* (Washington, D.C.: American Institute for Research, 1967).

2. M. Moezi, "Marital Characteristics in Iran" in *Scientific Study of Populations*. Papers presented at the Sydney Conference, Australia, Summer 1970.

3. See H. Rizk, "Social Psychological Factors Affecting Fertility in the United Arab Republics" *Marriage and Family Planning* 25 (February 1963) pp. 69–73; D. Kirk, "The Factor Affecting Moslem Natality" in Bernard Berelson (ed.), *Family Planning and Population Program* (Chicago: University of Chicago Press, 1966).

4. R. H. Fagley, Doctrines and Attitudes in Regard to Fertility" in O. Schieffelin (ed.), *Moslems' Attitude Towards Family Planning* (New York: Population Council, 1967). See also F. O. Okedji, "Social-Legal Consideration and Family Planning Programs in Africa" *International Journal of Sociology of Family* 5 (Spring 1975) pp. 66–84, who supports Fagley's conclusions.

5. Rizk, "Social Psychological Factors"; Kirk, "The Factors"; C. Wendle and G. Sabaugh, "Social Status and Family Size of Iranian Industrial Employees" *Milbank Memorial Fund Quarterly* (1962–63) pp. 436–43; M. Hartman and H. Hartman, *The Effect of Change in Social Environment on Women's Roles* (Ramat-Aviv, Israel: Tel-Aviv University, 1978).

6. Fagley, "Doctrines and Attitudes"; Okedji, "Socio-Legal Considerations"; Moezi, "Marital Characteristics."

7. Moezi, "Marital Characteristics"; M. Amini, *Demographic Survey of Religious Minorities in Iran* (Tehran: University of Tehran, 1970 (in Persian).

8. Amani, *Demographic Survey*; J. A. Arberry, *Religions in the*

Middle East: Three Religions in Concord and Conflict (2 vols.) (London: Cambridge University Press, 1969); R. James, "Armenians in Persia" *Contemporary Review* 169–170 (April 1946) pp. 245–47.

9. Amani, *Demographic Survey*. The absence is especially remarkable since the Bahá'í minority was both economically and intellectually significant in Iran before the Revolution.

10. J. E. Faulkner and G. F. DeJong, "Religiosity in 5-D: An Emperical Analysis" *Social Force* 45 (1966) pp. 154–246; M. King, "Measuring the Religious Variable: Nine Proposed Dimensions" *Journal for the Scientific Study of Religion* 6–7 (Fall 1967) pp. 173–90; C. Y. Glock, *Religion and Society in Tension* (Chicago: Rand & McNally, 1965.

Index